SAMS
Teach Yourself

Beginning
Databases

Ron Plew
Ryan Stephens

SAMS 201 West 103rd St., Indianapolis,

Sams Teach Yourself Beginning Databases in 24 Hours

Copyright © 2003 by Sams Publishing

International Standard Book Number: 0-672-32492-X

Library of Congress Catalog Card Number: 2002112344

Printed in the United States of America

First Printing: April 2003

06   05   04   03   4   3   2   1

Trademarks

All terms mentioned in this book that are known to be trademarks or service marks have been appropriately capitalized. Sams Publishing cannot attest to the accuracy of this information. Use of a term in this book should not be regarded as affecting the validity of any trademark or service mark.

Warning and Disclaimer

Every effort has been made to make this book as complete and as accurate as possible, but no warranty or fitness is implied. The information provided is on an "as is" basis. The authors and the publisher shall have neither liability nor responsibility to any person or entity with respect to any loss or damages arising from the information contained in this book.

Bulk Sales

Sams Publishing offers excellent discounts on this book when ordered in quantity for bulk purchases or special sales. For more information, please contact:

U.S. Corporate and Government Sales
1-800-382-3419
corpsales@pearsontechgroup.com

For sales outside of the U.S., please contact:

International Sales
+1-317-581-3793
international@pearsontechgroup.com

ASSOCIATE PUBLISHER
Michael Stephens

ACQUISITIONS EDITOR
Carol Ackerman

DEVELOPMENT EDITOR
Kevin Howard

MANAGING EDITOR
Charlotte Clapp

PROJECT EDITOR
Matthew Purcell

COPY EDITOR
Barbara Hacha

INDEXER
Mandie Frank

PROOFREADER
Leslie Joseph

TECHNICAL EDITOR
Hal Fulton
Benoy Jose
Christopher McGee

TEAM COORDINATOR
Cindy Teeters

MULTIMEDIA DEVELOPER
Dan Scherf

INTERIOR DESIGNER
Gary Adair

COVER DESIGNER
Alan Clements

PAGE LAYOUT
Julie Parks

GRAPHICS
Tammy Graham
Laura Robbins

Contents at a Glance

Contents

About the Authors

RYAN STEPHENS is president and CEO of Perpetual Technologies, Inc., an information technology consulting and training firm in Indianapolis, Indiana. He has specialized in database technology and SQL for over 13 years, working as an Oracle programmer/analyst, Oracle database administrator, consultant, IT manager, and adjunct professor at Indiana University-Purdue University in Indianapolis, where he has taught SQL, PL/SQL, UNIX, Oracle Oracle DBA, Oracle Development, and database design courses. Ryan resides in Indianapolis with his wife, Tina, and their children, Daniel, Autumn, and Baby Stephens.

RONALD R. PLEW is vice president and CIO for Perpetual Technologies, Inc., in Indianapolis, Indiana. Ron has served as an adjunct professor at Indiana University-Purdue University in Indianapolis, where he has taught SQL and various database courses. He holds a Bachelor of Science degree in Business Management/Administration from Indiana Institute of Technology, Fort Wayne, Indiana. Ron also serves in the Indiana Army National Guard, where he is the programmer/analyst for the 433rd Personnel Detachment. Ron's hobbies include golf, chess, and collecting Indianapolis 500 racing memorabilia. He shares ownership of Plew's Indy 500 Museum with his brothers, Mark and Dennis; his sister, Arleen; and mother, Betty. Ron lives in Indianapolis with his wife Linda. Ron and Linda have four children, ten grandchildren, and one great grandchild.

Contributing Authors

CHRISTOPHER ZEIS is the technical manager/CTO and Oracle database administrator for Perpetual Technologies, Inc. He is an Oracle Certified Professional and an expert consultant in database technology and administration. Chris also serves in the Indiana Army National Guard as an Oracle database administrator.

JOHN NEWPORT received a Ph.D. in theoretical physics from Purdue University. Following graduate school, he worked 11 years as an avionics software consultant for the U.S. Navy. He is the founder of Newport Systems Incorporated, a consulting group specializing in software requirements and design. Dr. Newport is a member of the Institute of Electrical and Electronics Engineers. He is also a commercial pilot with instrument and multi-engine ratings. His wife, Nancy, is manager of an online database system.

RIZWAN KHAN received his B.S. in Public Affairs from Indiana University Purdue University at Indianapolis. He is an Oracle Certified Professional 8i and Microsoft Certified Professional. He has administered Oracle databases on NT and various flavors of Unix operating systems. His experience includes designing, developing, and administering databases for the Indianapolis Police Department. Currently, he is an Oracle Database Administrator for Perpetual Technologies working at the Department of Defense in Indianapolis, Indiana.

MATT HURST has worked for the Indiana Army National Guard in various administrative areas and for the past seven years as the personnel programmer. Along with the programming duties Matt has accomplished for the guard, he also instructs the guard's users in SQL. Matt has also played a major role in teaching SQL and SQL*Plus for Perpetual Technologies as well as contributing to the revision of the *Sams Teach Yourself SQL in 21 Days* book. He would like to give his undying thanks to Koko and Bop for their inspiration and patience with their dad.

CRIS CALHOUN is an Oracle and Microsoft SQL Server database administrator contracted to the federal government by Perpetual Technologies, Inc. He is certified in Oracle8, Oracle8i and has held two SQL Server certifications in the past. His work experience includes database administration and development for a major airline, a state government, and the federal government.

DAVID J. RODRIGUEZ is a certified Oracle Database Administrator. He currently works for Perpetual Technologies, Inc., for the Department of Defense. Previously, he worked as a DBA in the insurance, communication, and financial industries, focusing on database tuning, query tuning, and backup and recovery. David holds a degree in Electrical Engineering from Wright State University, Dayton, Ohio, and a degree in Electronics Technology from the University of Puerto Rico, Bayamón. He is a licensed professional engineer for the State of Indiana. When he is not a DBA, he is interested in statistics, signal processing, baseball card collecting, and dancing.

GARY BRASSARD has been involved in the design, development, and use of databases for over 20 years as an IT professional. His experience covers a wide variety of industries including insurance, manufacturing, distribution, fulfillment, and IT consulting. He has also held positions at two state colleges in Indiana teaching programming and database courses. Mr. Brassard holds a technology degree from Purdue University and a business degree from Indiana University. Married for over 20 years, he and his wife, Tammy, have five children.

ROBERT A. SWEARINGEN is currently an independent consultant specializing in the design and development of applications based on relational database systems. Robert also assists Perpetual Technologies, Inc., in the areas of IT training and software development. With more than 15 years in the industry, his work has covered diverse disciplines such as cloud chemistry, capital facilities, insurance, agricultural chemistry, and the control of robot-based systems. His clients have included universities, HMOs, insurance providers, and chemical companies. Robert holds a Master's degree in Physics from the University of Michigan and Bachelor's degrees in Physics, Math, and Education from the California University of Pennsylvania.

ROBERT F. GARRETT is the Director of Software Development at Perpetual Technologies in Indianapolis, Indiana. Bob holds a Bachelor of Science degree in Computer Science and Mathematics from Purdue University and is a Sun Certified Java Programmer. Bob has six years of experience as a programmer including integral participation in the development of financial systems, document management systems, and software designed for mobile phones and handheld computing devices. Bob enjoys outdoor activities, motorcycling, automotive repair, and has his eye on a private pilot's license. Bob lives in Indianapolis with his wife Rebecca and cocker spaniel Molly.

Dedication

This book is dedicated to my family: my wife, Linda; my mother, Betty;
my children, Leslie, Nancy, Angela, Wendy; my grandchildren, Andy, Ryan, Holly,
Morgan, Schyler, Heather, Gavin, Regan, Caleigh, and Cameron;
my great-grandchild, Chloe; my brothers, Mark and Dennis;
my sister Arleen; and my sons-in-law, Jason and Dallas.
Thanks for being patient with me during this busy time. Love all of you.

—Poppy

This book is dedicated to my children: Daniel, Autumn,
and Baby Stephens (arriving shortly), and to their beautiful mother, Tina.

—Ryan

Acknowledgments

Thanks to all the people in our lives who have been patient during our work on this project; mostly to our wives, Tina and Linda. Special thanks to all our contributing authors. Thanks also to the editorial staff at Sams Publishing for all of their hard work to make this book an excellent work for those wanting to learn databases. It has been a pleasure to work with each of you.

—Ryan and Ron

We Want to Hear from You!

As the reader of this book, *you* are our most important critic and commentator. We value your opinion and want to know what we're doing right, what we could do better, what areas you'd like to see us publish in, and any other words of wisdom you're willing to pass our way.

As an associate publisher for Sams, I welcome your comments. You can email or write me directly to let me know what you did or didn't like about this book—as well as what we can do to make our books better.

Please note that I cannot help you with technical problems related to the *topic* of this book. We do have a User Services group, however, where I will forward specific technical questions related to the book.

When you write, please be sure to include this book's title and author as well as your name, email address, and phone number. I will carefully review your comments and share them with the author and editors who worked on the book.

E-mail: feedback@samspublishing.com
Mail: Michael Stephens
         Sams Publishing
         201 West 103rd Street
         Indianapolis, IN 46290 USA

For more information about this book or another Sams title, visit our Web site at www.samspublishing.com. Type the ISBN (excluding hyphens) or the title of a book in the Search field to find the page you're looking for.

Introduction

Welcome to the world of databases! Databases are part of our everyday lives. The world cannot function without them. Every year, we become more and more reliant on databases. Databases are used to manage information that individuals and organizations use to operate. There are many users of databases, from those who use the Internet to order products to those who design and manage the databases themselves.

This book, *Teach Yourself Databases in 24 Hours*, is designed to introduce database concepts, issues, and terminology to the beginning database user. This book will provide a broad view of databases and is arranged in such a manner that the reader is introduced to a variety of database-related information. This book is suitable for an audience ranging from the nontechnical individual who desires to understand terminology to the individual considering a future database-related career.

Who Should Read This Book?

This book was written for any individual—young, old, short, or tall—who has an interest in learning the basic fundamentals of databases. Maybe you are in school or recently graduated and need or want to learn about databases. Maybe you have decided to change your career path and explore the world of information technology (the logical starting point is databases). Maybe external forces such as your employer or the market have forced you to look more closely at the security of your career and you are looking to expand your horizon and possibly search for a new career or job. Maybe your employer has downsized and you have just been told that you are now the "database guy" or "computer guy" (or gal) and you need to get your feet wet. Who knows, maybe you are just curious and are desperate for reading material to keep you company while you curl up at night near your crackling fire.

Regardless of your situation, if you want to learn about modern database technology and you don't know much about databases, this book is for you. This book has been created by a group of database experts who interact daily with databases to survive—and who were once in your shoes.

How This Book Is Organized

This book initially addresses fundamental questions: Why are databases necessary? Who uses databases? What different types of databases are in use today? The answers to these questions, provided in Hours 1–4, are a foundation for the existence and utility of database systems commonly used today.

After the fundamental questions are addressed, the focus of the book switches to a light technical discussion of database architecture. In Hours 5–10, the reader is introduced to concepts involving the different database storage environments and architectures.

Database design, implementation, and management are important and complex topics. Hours 11–13 provide a look into these areas. The individual interested in a database administration career may find the material presented during these hours to be particularly relevant.

The future database developer might enjoy the material presented in Hours 14–18 (and 19–22). During these hours, methods of accessing databases are examined. Some of the material during a few of these hours may tend toward the technical side. If you are not interested in database development or database application development, you may decide to skim over these hours. I encourage you not to skip the hours completely, because they will provide you with some idea of what goes on behind the scenes to make a database application functional.

The final hours of this book discuss the trends and direction in which database technology seems to be heading and career paths available in database technology.

What's on the Web Site?

We have included supplemental material on our Web site, www.perptech.com/sams.html. This site has information related to all the books we have written for Sams Publishing. On the Web site, you will find general information about databases, links to other database-related sites and vendors, links to open-source database products, sample scripts and database designs, technical notes, technical scripts, sample databases, a SQL quick reference, and other ingredients to maximize your learning experience.

Good luck with databases! We hope you enjoy this book.

PART I

Database Fundamentals

Hour

HOUR 1

What Is a Database?

Welcome to the world of databases! Databases are all around us. We all use databases—many times unknowingly. Most organizations use databases and most careers involve interacting with some form of database. Many types of databases exist, but all forms, types, and implementations revolve around the same core principals discussed in this book. During this first hour of your journey into databases, the scope is narrow, but absolutely necessary. During this hour you will learn what data is, what a database is, and why databases are useful. These are very basic concepts, but they provide a good place to begin.

NEW TERM *Database* is an object or mechanism that is used to store information or data.

- What is data?
- What is a database?
- What is a database management system?
- Why are databases so popular?

What Is Data?

Before understanding databases, you must first understand data. Data is a collection of information. This information could be used as a basis for reasoning, discussion, calculation, processing, or other activity.

NEW TERM   *Data* is a collection of one or more pieces of information

Data is usually gathered through the means of a device. This device could be as simple as a pencil scratching against a dinner napkin, as laborious as a data entry clerk tapping buttons on a keyboard, or as complicated as an unmanned probe hurtling millions of miles through the abyss of space, beaming a stream of ones and zeros back to our tiny, fragile planet.

When taken alone or out of context, data can be very boring indeed, but when used appropriately, data eventually provides a foundation for knowledge.

Very common examples of data include (but are definitely not limited to) the following:

- Names of people
- Names of places
- Names of things
- Descriptions of people, places, and things
- Dates and time
- Numbers
- Calculated values
- Salary information
- Quantities
- Locations
- Contact information
- Personal information
- Business information
- Documents
- Images
- Video
- Audio

- Product specifications
- Inventory information
- Product order information
- Bank account information

These are just a few broad examples. Let's take a simple example with which we are all familiar: the checkbook register. Following is an example of data in your checkbook register:

- Check number
- Date the check was written
- Who the check is written to
- Remarks/description
- Debit amount
- Deposit amount
- Balance

Related to your checkbook register is your checking account. Following is an example of data that your bank maintains for your checking account:

- Your name
- Your social security number
- Your account number
- Other personal information
- Your current balance
- History of checks cleared
- History of bounced checks
- Deposit history
- Automatic debits
- Automatic deposits

What Is a Database?

A database is a mechanism that is used to store information, or data. Information is something that we all use daily for a variety of reasons. With a database, users should be able to store data in an organized manner. After the data is stored, it should be easy to retrieve information. Criteria can be used to retrieve information. The way the data is stored in the database determines how easy it is to search for information based on multiple criteria.

Think about the size of the collection of data humans currently possess. We have mapped our DNA structure, sent countless beeping tin cans into space and under waters, and collectively spent millions of hours performing research. This data collection must be huge—so huge, in fact, that we might become lost within its bounds. We are swimming in an ocean of data that grows larger at increasing rates. How then do we locate a subset or piece of data from this enormous collection? This data needs to be organized and a system established so that information can be retrieved at will. Otherwise, what use is this enormous collection?

The system that organizes the data should hypothetically meet certain standards and offer certain features. For example, the data organization system must be one that protects the integrity of the data. If a data item is stored as the value 15.999, it should be reported as exactly that, not some other value. The system must ensure security of certain data. For example, the whole world doesn't need to know the effective horizontal and lateral thrust provided by a certain type of jet mechanism installed on a government-developed flying saucer. This is sensitive data.

The solution we have developed to store this data is the database. Databases store collections of related data. These collections can be of nearly any size, but databases often hold terabytes of data for companies, educational institutions, and research laboratories. Figure 1.1 provides a simple illustration of a database.

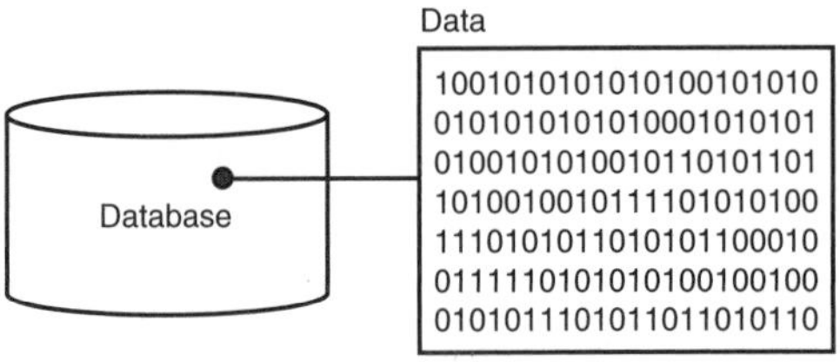

FIGURE 1.1

Understanding a basic database.

Note that a database is simply a collection of data. The phone book is an example of a database (one that does not change after it is printed). When this database is on a computer, some type of data management system is needed to control the data and ensure data integrity, security, and reliability, among other things.

Everyone uses databases regularly; some databases are manual and others are automated. Some simplistic examples of databases with which we are all familiar include

- Personal address books
- Telephone books
- Card catalogs at libraries
- Online bookstores
- Personal finance software
- Road maps

More sophisticated examples of databases include

- Human resource systems
- Pay disbursement systems
- Bank systems
- Insurance claim management systems
- Product inventory and order management systems
- Medical treatment and patient history systems
- Product manufacturing management systems

Standard Features of a Modern Database

As previously mentioned, some databases are simple and others are complex. However, all databases contain standard features that exist as expected ingredients. Some of these common features are the following:

- *Data storage needs are met*—The database must have the capability to store all the required data. If you fill up your Rolodex, you may have to buy new cards for it to store new names.
- *Data is readily available to the end user*—The data must be readily available to the user. If it is not, the database does not serve its obvious purpose.
- *Data is protected through database security*—If the database is not protected, an unauthorized person can damage the data, whether intentionally or not.
- *Data is manageable*—The database must have the capability of relatively easy data management, including methods for updating data, adding new data, deleting data, and using the data in any other required fashion.
- *Data accuracy level is high*—The data should be accurate. If data becomes heavily inaccurate, it is useless.
- *Database performs well*—You should be able use the database with a reasonable amount of effort and be able to get results in a reasonable amount of time.

- *Data redundancy is low*—The same data should be stored as few times as possible, preferably once. For example, if you store someone's name twice in your Rolodex, you have to update both locations if their phone number changes.

- *Data must be easy to retrieve*—One of the primary concerns when using a database is the capability to retrieve data. Data should be easy to find so that it can be used for its intended purpose.

What Is a Database Management System?

A database management system (DBMS) is the system that provides the logic necessary to ensure and reinforce necessary standards on the data.

DBMSs must meet basic standards such as those listed earlier: data integrity, data security, and data reliability.

DBMSs provide a means of accessing the data stored inside the database. These systems manage important issues such as concurrent access (multiple accesses at one time) of the data, efficient access of the data, data backup, and data recovery.

Without DBMSs, the data would be really disorganized. This is not to say that data in some databases is not disorganized! There are plenty of examples of heinous organization out there. DBMSs provide a good means of organizing the data within. Using the system properly is the responsibility of database designers and administrators.

NEW TERM   *Database Management System (DBMS)* is a system of rules that are part of the database software and dictates logically how the data is stored, treated, and accessed

Figure 1.2 demonstrates the topics covered to this point. The DBMS contains an assortment of modules that control the data and access to the data. This management system also contains a database. The database contains data.

FIGURE **1.2**

DBMS components.

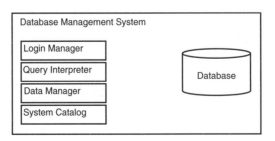

DBMSs vary in features and functionality. The remainder of this book will discuss aspects of different types of DBMSs from several points of view.

Why Are Databases So Popular?

DBMSs have revolutionized the way we store and access data. When a commercially proven DBMS is installed and configured properly, it is no longer necessary to maintain paper files (however, paper backups would be critical in recovering from the unlikely case of absolute loss). Thus, the file cabinets used extensively not so long ago, in a galaxy not so far away, tend to sit dormant today.

Imagine a file cabinet or two chock full of resumes. Not so long ago when human resources employees wanted to choose a candidate with a certain skill, they had to search by hand through all these files and manually scan each resume for the skill. Keep in mind that resumes are formatted differently, and different people use different words to convey the same meaning. This search process might have taken hours. With database technology, these resumes can be stored in a computer. This search can be performed in seconds or less, a dramatic increase in productivity.

Computerizing enterprise data storage has allowed automation of many tasks. Now that data is stored in a manner that is accessible by the machine, the machine can be used directly to input and process that data. Human intervention can be all but eliminated from many tasks.

This is reflected in processes such as

- Online ordering
- Statistical analysis and tracking
- Online package tracking (a human scans the package)
- Online payment processing
- Online auction (eBay) bidding processing

DBMSs provide protection and efficient access to the data stored within databases. This protection comes in the form of reliability, integrity, robustness, and security. Data is commonly the most important asset of a business or institution. Protecting that asset is therefore also important. Thus, database management systems have quickly become very popular.

Summary

In this hour you were introduced to a few basic terms and concepts. The concept of data was described with the concept of a database. Databases were created to store data (which has the tendency to collect and collect). Database management systems were created to manage databases and to protect and ensure the utility of the data stored within these databases.

Workshop

The following workshop is composed of quiz questions and practical exercises. The quiz questions are designed to test your overall understanding of the current material. The practical exercises are intended to afford you the opportunity to apply the concepts discussed during the current hour. Please take time to complete this workshop before continuing. You can refer to the answers at the end of the hour.

Quiz

1. What does DBMS stand for?
2. What is stored in a database?
3. List three or more examples of simplistic everyday databases that we all use.
4. List three or more standard and expected features of a database.

Exercises

1. To get an idea of the amount of data some institutions hold, visit the following Web site:

    Mars Global Surveyor Web site: http://www.msss.com/.

    Each of the images you encounter on this Web site is stored within a database.

2. What type of data do you think might be stored in a pharmacy's database? Why is it useful for this information to be stored within a database?

3. Browse eBay, the popular online auction Web site: http://www.ebay.com.

    Perform a search for DVD, and note how many results are returned.

    Perform a search for CD, and note the number of results returned.

    Your search might fail because it returns too many items. The point of this exercise is to demonstrate the vast size of the database in use at eBay. Millions of items are listed for sale at any one time.

Answers to Quiz

1. Database management system.

2. Data.

3. Examples of simplistic everyday databases that we all use:

    Personal address books

    Telephone books

    Card catalogs at libraries

    Online bookstores

    Personal finance software

    Road maps

4. Standard and expected features of a database:

    Database is protected.

    Database is easy to manage.

    Database stores accurate data.

    Data is easy to retrieve.

HOUR 2

History and Evolution of Database Environments

In the early days of computing, computers were as large as rooms and less powerful than many handheld calculators of today. These days, most people have computers in their homes; these computers are many times smaller and orders of magnitude faster than those early machines. Technology has evolved at an amazing pace and is still evolving today.

Data storage technology has progressed from small, simple flat files of yesterday to large, complex relational data management systems in use today by millions of users.

As the types of computer processing evolve, a database should be able to exist in several computer environments for ease of access and affordability. There is no need to use an expensive computer system if the application will not need high speed and large storage capacity.

As time goes on, the need for information keeps growing. However, all this development started at one point. This hour describes the early database systems and their evolution to what is mainly in use today. Also, it presents an overview of computer environments in which a database can operate.

During this hour, you will learn about modern database environments.

The highlights of this hour include

- Exploration of modern database environments
- Understanding about the evolution of database environments

Exploration of Modern Database Environments

Databases can be used in many types of computer environments. Many types of database environments are currently available. You will learn about these different environments during this hour. Let's begin with the basics and define the term *database environment*.

What Is a Database Environment?

A database environment is the collection of surroundings in which the database resides. The database environment includes any applications or query processes that are used to operate on the data. Certain applications might allow users to access the data from within the database environment; others might allow users to access the data from outside the database environment. An example of such an application is a Web-based data query application. A Web-based application allows a user to access the database from thousands of miles across the planet, or possibly into space.

Users of a database environment perform a multitude of different functions. The requirements vary as different users search for, modify, or create new data.

Users of a database environment might be physically or logically restrained from accessing all or parts of the data.

A database environment is the collection of the hardware and software (operating system) on which the database resides. This hardware includes any network equipment needed by users to access the database. The database environment can be a deciding factor when determining what database model to use for a situation and how this database will be developed, deployed, and managed.

This hour discusses three database environments. These three environments make up the majority of databases in use today. Figure 2.1 illustrates a basic database environment.

A ***database environment*** is the combination of hardware, networking, and software that the database resides on.

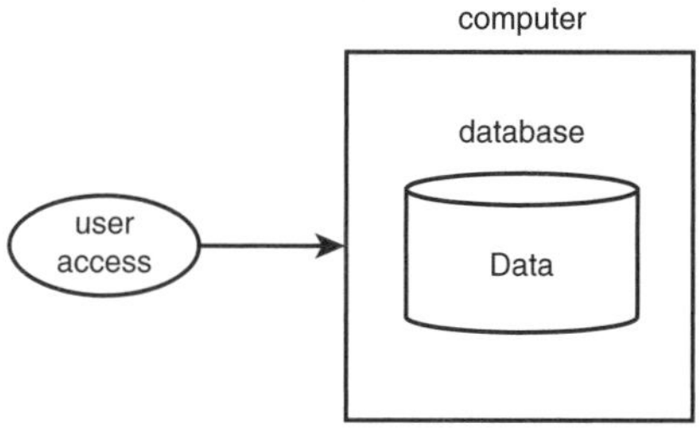

FIGURE 2.1

Understanding the database environment.

computer

database

user access → Data

The environments are

- The client/server environment
- The multitier environment
- The Web environment

> Database environments involve mainly hardware, operating system platforms, and network usage.

Exploration of the "Legacy" Mainframe Environment

A mainframe is basically a very large computer. It derived its name from the way the computer was built. All the units of the main computer—memory, communication, storage, processing, and so on—were built in a frame, hence its name. Their main purpose is to run applications for large businesses and government. Mainframes are characterized not only by their large physical size and high cost ($100,000s), but also by their massive internal memory, high-capacity external storage, and hardware redundancy, which make them very reliable. Mainframes can run continuously for years without interruption. Figure 2.2 shows a simple mainframe environment.

Users can access a mainframe through a "dumb" terminal. It is called dumb because without a mainframe connection, the terminal is useless. The terminal has no processing capabilities of its own.

Mainframes are not only still in use, but also new and improved models are being produced by companies such as IBM and Hitachi. In fact, it is estimated that about 60% of corporate America uses mainframes today. Some mainframes have been configured to run multiple operating systems, providing the environment for a virtual machine.

Therefore, it reduces costs and administrative expenses of purchasing and maintaining hundreds of personal computers.

FIGURE 2.2

Understanding the mainframe environment.

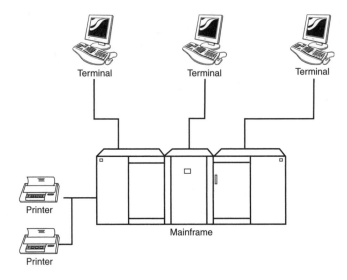

NEW TERM   A *mainframe* computer is one that is very large in size and in terms of its storage capacity. They are built to allow for numerous concurrent users and can be configured to run several different operating systems at the same time.

Understanding the Client/Server Environment

The client/server architecture is different from the mainframe. Here a client computer, not a dumb terminal, connects to a server computer over a network. The physical difference between a mainframe and a server is becoming smaller and smaller. Mainframes are becoming more affordable and servers are becoming more powerful. The difference between a regular client computer and a server is that the server is a computer running "server software." The terminals have client processes and the servers have server processes.

It is perhaps important to note that the client machine typically has a wide range of software installed on it as well. Software that allows the client to communicate with the server database as well as perform various sundry business tasks. Some examples of these might be File Transfer Protocol software that allows the client to move files from the database to the client, word processing, and spreadsheet to name a few.

NEW TERM The *Client/Server* environment utilizes "smart" computers that have software installed on them that allows tasks to be performed either locally or through the network. The database resides on a specified machine on the network and the clients connect to the database through the network.

The client/server environment is one in which a central, sometimes dedicated, machine, called the server, provides functionality for multiple machines, called clients. In the database client/server environment, the database exists on the server and is called the *database server*. Every user who uses the database does so over the network via a client.

The client is a separate machine. This requires applications on the client machine to access the database server through the network. Information is passed between the client and server using some type of database connectivity interface, such as open database connectivity (ODBC) or other vendor-specific database connectivity software. Figure 2.3 illustrates a very basic client/server database environment.

FIGURE 2.3

Understanding the basic client/server environment.

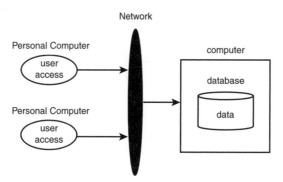

When a user needs to process a transaction, the client process at the terminal requests service from the server process that fulfills the client request. For example, for users to connect to a database, the client first needs to have "client software" installed in their PCs. The user will run the software to connect to the database, but in reality, what takes place is that a process at the terminal or client will request a server process to connect the terminal to the database.

After the server process fills the request, the database takes over and the client is connected to the database. The server process has done its job. If the server process that provides connectivity to the database stops, the connection between database and client will still remain. However, new connections will not take place until this server process starts again.

The advantages of the client/server architecture over mainframe architecture are the following:

- *Scalability*—The number of users can be increased into the thousands (horizontal scalability). Increased number of servers can be accommodated in the network (vertical scalability).
- *Efficient use of computing resources*—Processor-intensive tasks can be placed in servers with more computing power, freeing slower processors to work in applications that can work with less processing resources.
- *New technology can be incorporated into the system*—Mobile databases are now possible with the advent of wireless networks. Terminals such as personal digital assistants (PDAs) can now be used not only to access and administer databases remotely, but also to download information that has been gathered at the end of the day.

The main problem with the client/server environment is that the client software is installed on many machines. This can prove to be a hassle when a new version of the application is developed or when the current version is updated. The new version of the application must be installed on each client machine; the process can be tedious and time consuming. This time consumption translates into extra costs of maintenance in the long run.

It may be true that additional costs arise from maintaining a separate application on each client's computer, but there are also many benefits. The main benefit is distributed processing. Each client has a unique set of resources (CPU, memory, disk storage, and so on). These client resources can perform part of the application processing. This removes some of the load from the server, and it allows the server to service more requests and respond more quickly.

Because client machines can process data on their own and run additional applications, users can be more productive. For example, a client machine can be connected to the database server while simultaneously working with a word processing document, checking email, scanning the system for viruses, and the like. Figure 2.4 shows a more detailed illustration of a client/server architecture.

The client/server architecture not only has the characteristics of the mainframe architecture, but it incorporates the flexibility to change and grow at the same speed of business requirements.

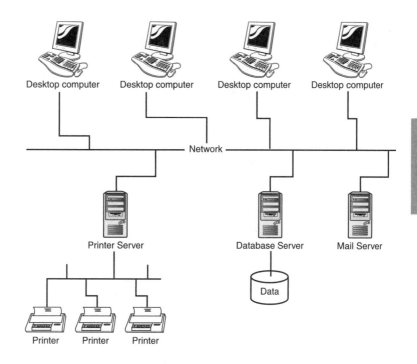

FIGURE 2.4

A more detailed look into the client/server architecture.

2

Understanding the Multitier Environment

In a client-server environment, connectivity to the server can be in one of two ways: two-tier and n-tier architecture.

- *Two-tier architecture*—Connects the client directly to the server. In reality, the client is the "client tier" and the server is the "server tier." Normally, the "tier" is omitted. This is the same way a terminal is connected to the mainframe. The two-tier architecture is suitable for small organizations.

- *N-tier architecture*—This arrangement introduces another computer between the client and the server. Although n-tier suggests that multiple computers can be between the client and the server—and sometimes that is the case—the most common arrangement is only one computer in the middle, making it a three-tier architecture. The three-tier network model is also appropriately known as mid-tier architecture. A third computer avoids overwhelming the servers with a high number of users. Figure 2.5 shows a diagram of a three-tier architecture.

NEW TERM   *Two-tier* environment is such that each client machine directly accesses the server machine.

In an **n-tier** or **multi-tier** environment a third computer acts as an intermediary between the client and the server.

FIGURE 2.5
Understanding the multiple tier database architecture.

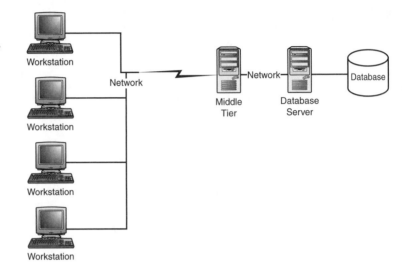

A three-tier model can do the following:

- Provide translation services between the client in a client/server architecture to an old legacy system in a mainframe.
- Control the number of users connecting to the server and balance the load.
- Host applications that will connect to the server database.
- Control the number of simultaneous requests placed on the server.

The multitier environment is an environment in which functionality of the database application is broken up into different portions, called *tiers*. Because of its complexity, this environment type is usually found in database-oriented business applications.

The three layers (multitier environments often consist of three tiers) are logically interconnected and share information. We can demonstrate the complexity of the three-tiered environment by explaining the three-tiered model as a double-layered client/server environment. The first client/server interaction occurs between the first layer (application layer) and the middle layer (logic layer). The second client/server interaction occurs between the second layer (logic layer) and the third layer (database layer).

In the three-layer architecture, the overall logic of the application is broken down into separate, useful components. The first layer presents an interface to the user, usually a graphical interface. The data collected in this first layer is passed through simple error-checking routines and passed down to the second layer. The second layer contains the bulk of the application logic and all the database connectivity. Inside the second layer, the data is filtered through business logic routines, packaged into communication, and passed down to the third layer. The third layer, the database layer, is where the raw SQL transaction is processed. Any data that is generated in the third layer is passed back up to the second layer, filtered, and passed back up to the first layer.

In multitier architectures, data is mapped within the middle tier. Most middle-tier designs separate object-relational mapping into two major processes within the middle tier:

- Handling database connections and performing database transactions using database language such as SQL
- Translating database requests into object-oriented method calls (specific queries can be called from specific method calls)

Middle-tier logic translates the results of SQL statements into business objects and sends these objects up to the first tier. The client application, or first tier, never has details about the database schema that sits behind this whole system. This type of architecture is more flexible and maintainable. Changes made to the functionality of the graphical user interface, for example, do not necessarily require changes to be made to the business logic. More importantly, changes made to the database layer might require corresponding changes to be made to the middle layer, but not to the application layer.

The three-layer, multitiered environment has hardware requirements in addition to those of the previous client/server environment. A graphical interface application is installed on client computers; an application server stores and serves the middle layer applications; and the database server is the third layer.

Some benefits of this architecture are increased data security, reusable business/application logic, increased flexibility and control, and minimized administration. Data security is increased because the end user cannot directly access the data in the database or information about the database. The database implementation, location, and architecture are all completely hidden from the end user.

Understanding the Web Environment

The Internet, also known as the World Wide Web, is defined as a network of networks linking computers to other computers around the world. Your computer connects to Web site content, whether it is text, pictures, or a database through the Internet with the use of a browser. No additional software is required from your side. However, several components make this happen. See Figure 2.6 for an overview of the Web environment.

FIGURE 2.6

Diagram of the components for a database Web connection.

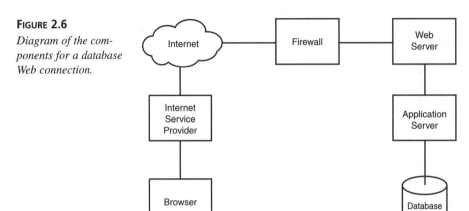

The following components are necessary:

- *Internet browser*—A program residing in your computer that enables you to access the Internet and receive documents, images, and sounds from Internet sites.
- *Internet Service Provider (ISP)*—If you are not directly connected to the Internet, a service provided by a company (America Online, Juno, Earthlink, and so on) connects you to the Internet, usually for a fee, although some ISPs are free. The ISP is connected to the Internet and enables your browser to send out your request to connect to the site you requested.
- *Firewall*—A combination of computer programs installed where your computers communicate with the Internet. It looks at the incoming and outgoing data and, based on established policy tables, decides whether to allow the connection to progress or to block it.
- *Web server*—Specific software that enables serving Web pages and data to the Internet.
- *Application server*—Software that translates information from a database, for example, into meaningful information to be displayed by the Web server. It also isolates the database from the user so that the user does not need to learn SQL or any specific database commands.

Databases connected to the Internet work as follows: The browser accesses the Internet through your ISP. Through the Internet, the desired Web site is reached. The Web server returns a Web page of the site you are accessing. This page has a place for you to write a search request parameter. Here you can specify a name, a city, a street, and so on that will return information related to your input.

The request is sent to the Web server and is passed to the application server. The application server formulates a query from the request and sends it to the database. The application server sends the results of the query to the Web server, which will put it into a Web page format that you see in your browser. One Web site that has searchable databases is www.searchsystems.net. At the time of this writing, this Web site had more than 8,700 public record databases, and most of them can be accessed free of charge.

The Internet environment is a special case of the multitier environment. As with the multitier environment, a central server provides applications to many unique clients over the network. This central server is part of the first tier, the application layer, and is called the Web server. This Web server can communicate to a middle layer application/business logic server, which can communicate to the third layer, or database server.

In the Internet environment, many organizations are using an n-tier architecture. The n-tier architecture is a concept similar to that found in the three-tier environment. In the three-tier environment, there is a client layer, an application layer, and a server or database layer. An n-tier environment has any number of tiers. The number of tiers in the environment is the number required to complete the desired transaction or request.

The Internet computing environment is unique because information is transferred along a public network and access to the data is allowed from long distances. In an internal client/server environment, a user might be restricted to local systems within the corporate intranet. In many cases, client machines can still access databases outside of the corporate intranet, but additional customized software might be involved.

Internet computing gets power and usefulness from the transparency of the application to the end user. In the Internet computing environment, an application has to be installed on only one server, the Web server. A user with an Internet connection and a supported Web browser installed can connect to the URL of the Web server. The application accesses the Web server as designed and then returns the requested information to the client. These results are displayed on the user's PC by the Web browser. End-user application setup and maintenance is very simple in the Internet environment because very little installation, configuration, or maintenance is required on the client. The installation, configuration, and maintenance occur on the Web server instead. This reduces the risk of inconsistent configurations and incompatible versions of software between client and server machines. When changes are made to the application, changes are made in one central location, the Web server.

The Internet environment introduces the database to a host of security risks that are not as prevalent when the database is restricted to local access. Additional hardware and software is needed to ensure the security of the data within the database. Hardware such as firewalls and software such as intrusion detection systems and database security mechanisms must be in place to secure the data. Certain enterprises, such as financial institutions, are required by law to have certain security measures in place.

Summary

This hour presented modern database environments and architectures and the strengths and weaknesses of each. The three environments in this hour were client/server, multitier, and Web. This hour also presented an overview of three database environments. Keep in mind that these database environments are computer specializations in their own right and that there is much more to be said than what was discussed in this section. However, a brief introduction of each covered the basics to provide you with a general understanding.

Q&A

Q Most of the environments discussed in this hour use a basic client/server interaction. Is there an environment where this is not the case and the database is accessed directly?

A Yes and no. If the user (most often the system administrator) physically sits at the database server and logs in, and then uses that database with some command-line tool provided by the database vendor, you might say that the administrator is directly accessing the database. However, depending on the tool in use, this may not be the case; it is possible for client and server to share a machine.

Q Is the Web database environment the only environment with security risks?

A No. The multitier and client/server architectures, which are typically used from under one roof, are at risk by internal employees. People who use the database every day know the database well and could use that knowledge maliciously, often without raising the suspicion of administrators or managers. Security measures such as roles and privileges should exist to protect the data from the inside.

Workshop

The following workshop is composed of quiz questions and practical exercises. The quiz questions are designed to test your overall understanding of the current material. The practical exercises are intended to afford you the opportunity to apply the concepts discussed during the current hour, as well as build on the knowledge acquired in previous hours of study. Please take time to complete this workshop before continuing.

Quiz

1. When does it make sense to implement three-tier architecture?

2. What is the job of a Web server?

3. Does connecting to a database in a mainframe environment require any type of special software on your machine?

4. Is database or network security a particular issue in a client/server environment?

5. What is the client/server environment?

6. How does the multitier environment use client/server architecture?

Exercises

1. Draw a simple sketch of the following Web environment: Access to the Amazon.com bookstore from your home computer.

2. Draw a simple sketch of how a home client/server environment might look.

Answers to Quiz

1. The three-tier architecture is appropriate when a high load of database activity needs to be spread across multiple computers to improve performance and security.

2. A Web server is a database that handles communication between an end user (Web browser) and a database that contains data that must be accessible to Web users.

3. Mainframe environments do not require any software on the local or users machine because they connect directly with the database via a dumb terminal. Client/Server environments do require some sort of database connectivity interface, such as ODBC. However, ODBC only allows for a connection to the database. There still needs to be some sort of software that allows the client to actually communicate with the database. This software might be an application designed to communicate with a database in a client/server environment. There also exists terminal emulation software that allows the client to communicate with the database.

4. Security is always an issue regardless of the environment. Care must be taken that the proper permissions are granted and maintained, that firewall software is installed and maintained.

5. The client/server environment uses a single, central server to provide services for multiple clients dispersed over a network. In the database world, the database exists on the server, and the clients access the server to use the database.

6. The multitier environment uses the client/server model between each tier. The client/server model effectively brings the tiers together. The first tier (user-interface layer) acts as a client to the second tier (application layer). The second tier acts as a client to the third tier (database layer). Additional tiers in an n-tier environment are similarly connected.

HOUR 3

Relating to Modern Databases

You have spent the last two hours getting a good introduction to the concept of "database." Hour 1, "What Is a Database?" reviewed some of the basics, such as why we have databases, ways in which databases are used, and how the large volumes of data are used and refined to help those in business make informed decisions. In Hour 2, "History and Evolution of Database Environments," you learned some of the different ways in which the handling of data has evolved from a data management perspective and the hardware architectures typically used to handle databases. Now that the foundation has been covered and you have a clearer concept of what a database is, it's time to look at some reality-based systems that use databases. In this hour, you will look at a few common examples of database usage and take a closer look at the way data is managed and stored within these databases.

The first example studies the process of purchasing from a popular Web retailer. Another takes a look at a practice that has had some share of controversy—file content sharing. Other examples may not appear to be as technology intensive as the first two, but as you take a closer look at getting a prescription filled and using an ATM (automated teller machine), you will see that databases play an integral part in those systems as well.

By the end of this hour, you should have a clearer understanding of where databases are used in normal daily activities and transactions, from shopping to banking to retail purchases, whether in a conventional bricks-and-mortar store location or on the Net.

Using the Internet

The proliferation of home-based computing, along with Internet access from work locations, has fueled an exponential growth of World Wide Web (WWW) sites and users. As this growth occurs, the number of retailers offering their goods and services via the Internet has skyrocketed. The types of companies with Internet presence represent a wide variety of domestic and international business entities. Familiar brick-and-mortar retailers, although well established and usually well financed, have not necessarily dominated the Internet retail landscape. Some of the most frequently purchased items on the Net include books, videos, and CDs. Amazon.com, a well-known company dominating this market sector, is the subject of the first example. The Internet is becoming a thriving environment for modern databases.

The intent of this hour is to identify common real-world databases to which we all can relate. In subsequent hours, we will discuss in more detail the elements that comprise databases such as those discussed in this hour.

Making a Book Purchase

Our first example involves a common real-world database that many of us have used; Amazon.com. If you have never visited the Amazon.com Web site, you can reach it by entering http://www.amazon.com into the location bar of your browser and clicking Go. Figure 3.1 shows an example of the Amazon.com home page.

Because the number of items in the Amazon.com database is so large, broad product categories are presented on the left side of the Web page. Choosing a product category helps to narrow the number of items within the database that will eventually be viewed. For this example, select the Books category. Then you are presented with another list of products, all book categories. Figure 3.2 shows how you can drill down into the Books category.

FIGURE 3.1

Amazon.com home page.

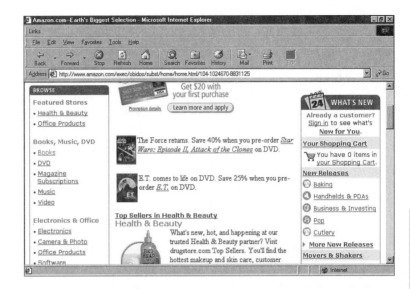

FIGURE 3.2

Limiting your interest to books.

As you survey the content on the second page, you can begin to get a feel for the extensive database that must be in use behind the scenes at Amazon.com.

The right side of the page shows the bestsellers based on an hourly recomputation. To calculate this bestseller list, a sales history database (probably tracking sales transactions by customer number and by ISBN) must be searched. The top 10 selling ISBN numbers are returned. These top-selling ISBN numbers are then used to retrieve the book titles, authors, and other book information that is presented on the Web page in tabular format.

The left side of the page has a column of book categories. This implies that the database of books available is still too large to simply scroll through all the selections. The Web site enables you to further limit your search of the book database by category of books. In this example, when you pick the Computer and Internet category, a subsequent page is displayed, enabling you to continue to "drill down." After you have narrowed the selection of books from the database to a small electronic "shelf" area, you can browse the shelf for the book of your choice.

As an alternative, the entire database of books can be searched from the home page. Indexing of the database allows the user to quickly identify books of interest by author, by title, or by topic.

The database also has editor reviews, customer reviews, inventory availability data, and pricing information for each book.

If you find the book you want and decide to make the purchase, a customer database record is retrieved to find the customer name, address, city, state, zip, and phone number. Most often, when making an online purchase, your email address is also requested so that order confirmation and shipping advice information can be conveyed to you electronically. If the information is not found in the database, a series of screens will be presented for you to provide the needed data to populate your customer record.

Now that Amazon.com can identify you as the customer, and you have selected the books you want to buy, it's time to take your electronic shopping cart to the checkout line. This process fills some database table(s) with sales information. Beginning with your customer number, Amazon.com needs to determine your shipping address. If you are a repeat customer, your previously used shipping address is retrieved from the database and displayed for you. If this isn't the address to which the order is to be shipped, new Ship To address information must be entered and tracked in the database specifically related to this order. Hour 2 discussed the concept of a relational model database. Your trip to Amazon.com builds relational database entries about you and your order. Figure 3.3 shows the page where this data is stored in the database.

After Amazon.com knows where the order is going to be shipped, the method of payment must be specified. The ordering system asks you to indicate which credit card you will be using. After indicating card choice, the credit card number and expiration date is entered along with the exact cardholder name. The credit card information you provide is then verified by using another database to ensure the card's validity. Figure 3.4 illustrates the payment process.

FIGURE 3.3

Shipping data for your order.

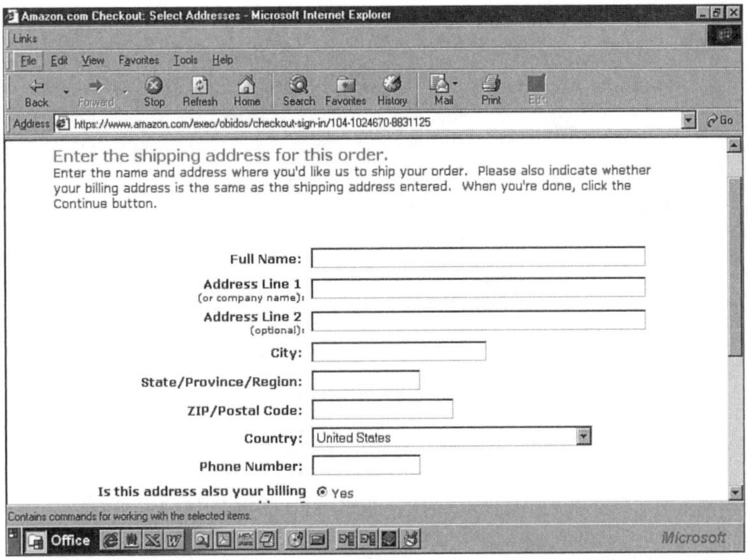

FIGURE 3.4

Paying for your order.

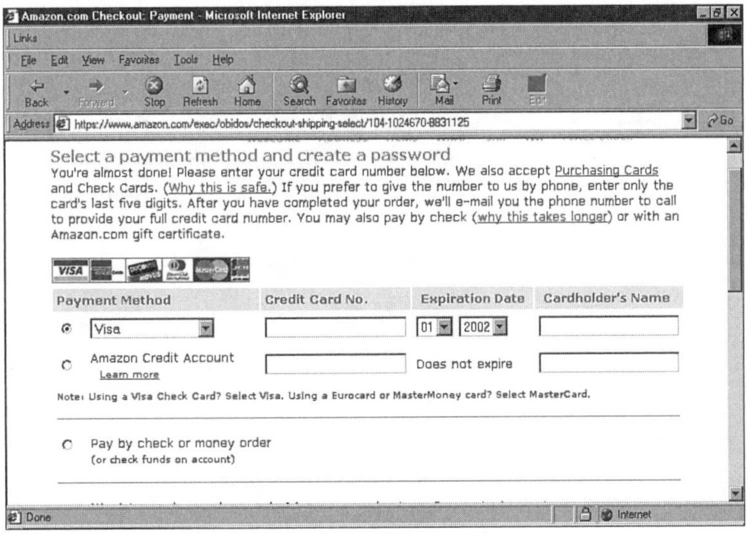

After the credit card information is provided and verified, the Amazon.com system submits your credit card information along with your order's total value to a credit card servicing authority. The credit card company validates your card number against its database, checks the credit limit and available credit amount, and determines whether the sale can be approved. After the credit card company records your purchase details into its database, the sale authorization number is returned to Amazon.com where it is recorded into your sales transaction record. Now Amazon.com has recorded several data items into your customer record: billing data, shipping data, book ISBN and quantities, credit card data, and purchase authorization number.

The sale transaction data is then used in several ways behind the scenes. Minimally, the sale transaction has to be used to update the inventory on the books and items that have been shipped. This triggers activity for the purchasing group, which must reference the supplier database for minimum order quantity, shipping costs, and book costs to determine an economic order quantity and place an order for inventory replenishment. This purchase order database is used to check inventory receipts at the time the books are received into their warehouse from the publisher or distributor.

Finally, the sale transaction will be used periodically in a forecasting model database to determine buying trends, seasonality factors, and beta factors. These factors are all determined by evaluating the sales transaction database over a long period of time. The purchasing and inventory control groups within a company will use these predictive forecasting quantities to adjust inventory levels and inventory dollar investments to optimize a minimization of inventory dollars and maximization of customer serviceability.

The database at Amazon.com also displays other book titles in which you may have an interest. The database has association rules, like identifiable trends, where users interested in book A have demonstrated an interest in books B and C and also have shown an interest in books from author D. This data, more complex in nature than simply a list of books in the database, is derived by evaluating large volumes of historical data by user, by author, or by title. Figure 3.5 shows the results of the historical data for trends.

FIGURE 3.5

Suggested buying trends.

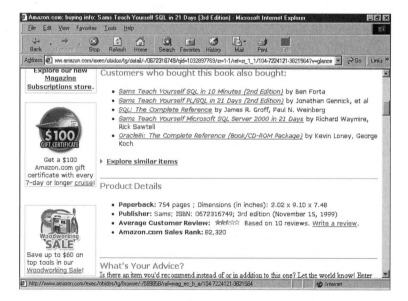

Downloading Information from the Internet

A wide variety of file content sites on the Net enable you to download anything from white papers and articles of interest, screensavers, software packages, games, movies, and music. The most publicized site may be Napster.com, with all the legal battles and court injunctions, but the site you will look at is called Kazaa.com. Kazaa.com provides free software to search its databases and to download files. If you have not visited the site, enter www.kazaa.com into your browser and click Go. Figure 3.6 shows an example of the Kazaa.com home page.

FIGURE 3.6

Kazaa.com home page.

3

The navigational aids on this site are similar to those at Amazon.com. The database of available music is too large for a user to browse through the available titles, so the site enables you to begin your search within a category, such as Top 40, Jazz, Country, or Rock/Pop. These categories are essentially subsets of all song titles in the database. The database can also be segmented using other qualifiers, such as by artist or by album.

When a particular file is identified to download, another database is searched to determine which connected users have your file available for download. You will typically have a chance to view the sources of your file, connection speeds, and file size. After the source is picked, a peer-to-peer transfer from the source PC to your PC occurs. Figure 3.7 shows all the peers identified for your file download.

If you are after a particular type of file, you can narrow your search of the database to include only one type. Kazaa.com supports searches for audio, video, images, documents, and software.

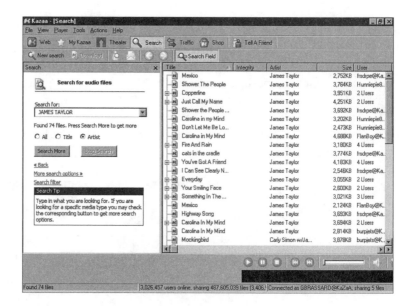

FIGURE 3.7
Sources for your file.

Many times, you can find other files from the database that have something in common with a file you have already downloaded. For instance, you can find files from the same artist or author (audio, image, documents), from the same album (audio), and from the same publisher (video, software) .

Everyday Transactions

Most of us use databases daily and may not realize it. The following sections describe a few everyday situations in which people access and utilize data from a database. By understanding real-world, daily activities, you will gain a better understanding of database usage and will be able to better apply these concepts to understand the corporate world.

A couple of everyday transactions with which everyone is familiar are

- Getting a prescription filled
- Using a bank machine

Getting a Prescription Filled

The next example walks you through a process everyone does at some point—having a prescription filled.

As you are standing in your local pharmacy waiting for your prescription, you may not think that this transaction is database intensive. But, if you were to take a closer look, hundreds of gigabytes of data, maybe terabytes, are involved in this routine transaction.

When you evaluate a transaction like this one, it is helpful to look at one layer of the transaction at a time, peeling away successive layers, just like peeling an onion. Figure 3.8 shows the "layers" of this transaction that you will review.

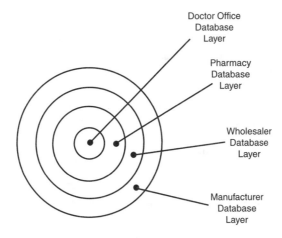

FIGURE 3.8

Transaction layers for a prescription purchase.

Doctor Office Database Layer

Pharmacy Database Layer

Wholesaler Database Layer

Manufacturer Database Layer

The Doctor's Office Databases

You can start by looking back to the beginning of this transaction—at the doctor's office. A database must be kept of each patient, including data elements such as name, address, phone number, insurance carrier, closest relative, medical history, and family history. Billing records, payment receipts, appointment schedules, and insurance filing information make up other databases that are used often.

The Pharmacy Databases

The actual pharmacy has database information that it maintains on a broad range of subjects. The most obvious one is you—the customer. Every pharmacy will have, minimally, a database of customer name and address information, customer date of birth, prescribing physician and phone number, insurance carrier, and past prescription history of each customer.

The insurance company, HMO, or PPO provides each pharmacy with another database that must be used extensively. This database is called the formulary database. It contains an approved list of brand drugs, approved generic substitutions, dosages, and National Drug Code (NDC) information. Your insurance prescription card more than likely has a specific formulary that the pharmacy must reference to ensure that the drug used to fill your prescription, or an allowable substitution, will be covered by your insurance. This type of database may also be used by the physician's office to ensure that the drug they want to prescribe can be filled, without any substitution or dosage change, when you get to the pharmacy.

Another database that is used prior to filling the prescription is the drug interaction database. The prescribed drug may have serious interaction issues if used in conjunction with medications currently in use. The database identifies potential interaction problems, provides a detailed explanation of the interaction consequence, and possibly suggests alternatives.

After the formulary and interaction databases have been utilized, the prescription is ready to fill. The pharmacy inventory database is checked to determine whether the NDC being requested is in stock and at what shelf location it can be found. The inventory database must track expiration dates of each drug to prevent outdated medication from being dispensed. After the prescription is filled, the available on-hand inventory for your medication must be reduced by the quantity or volume of your prescription.

If the medication is not available in stock, the pharmacy must search through its wholesaler database to determine the best source for the drug. The wholesaler database identifies each of the wholesalers from whom the needed drug can be acquired, the cost from the wholesaler, and possibly the inventory availability at the wholesaler.

The final database to be reviewed at the pharmacy is the order database. This database contains all the outstanding orders that have been placed with all the wholesalers. They may represent simple inventory replenishment orders or special orders for drugs not normally stocked. If the orders are for narcotic items, or Schedule 2 drugs, special order and tracking requirements must be met to satisfy the requirements of the Drug Enforcement Administration (DEA). Figure 3.9 shows the database entities involved at the pharmacy layer.

FIGURE 3.9

Pharmacy layer databases.

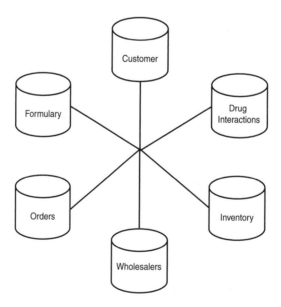

The Wholesaler's Database

As you continue to peel away layers in the transaction, you see that the next layer represents the drug wholesaler. The pharmaceutical supply chain in the United States is typically serviced by a wholesaler that operates between the manufacturer and the retail or hospital pharmacy.

The wholesaler layer begins with an extensive customer database. Name, address, billing address, and accounts receivable information are maintained. A customer who represents a large chain, such as K-Mart, may have Ship To destinations all over the country. Each of the Ship To locations must be maintained separately for order tracking and for sales analysis purposes.

A separate database that identifies every drug and strength is used by the wholesaler to ensure that the customer's intent on which drug they want to purchase from the wholesaler is clear and, in turn, to make sure the drug the wholesaler purchases from the manufacturer is explicitly identified. This database, by NDC number, changes frequently with new manufacturers, generic suppliers, dosage changes, and the constant introduction of new drugs. The management of this type of database has spawned new businesses in the pharmaceutical industry because of its complexity and volatility. Many wholesalers purchase this database with quarterly updates to ensure that they have an up-to-date NDC database.

Most national and regional wholesalers have multiple distribution centers, or DCs, located throughout the country or throughout the geographical area they serve. Each of these DCs has an inventory database that is a focal point of their operations. The inventory database must identify each item that the DC stocks, and for each item, many inventory management attributes are tracked. Something as simple as the picking location can include a forward picking location, a backup picking location, a bulk location, a backup bulk location, packaging quantities, packaging dimensions, packaging weights, expiration dates, and lot-tracking information along with inventory quantities at each location. With thousands of items at a DC, you can begin to see the complexity and size of the inventory database required for each DC within a wholesaler's operation.

The wholesaler's database will always include, among other items, a shipping and invoicing database and an accounts receivable database. Figure 3.10 shows the database entities involved at the wholesaler layer.

The Manufacturer's Database

A manufacturer has many databases that are very similar to those of the wholesalers. The supply-chain relationship between pharmacy and wholesaler is very similar to the relationship between wholesaler and manufacturer. There are a few additional databases, though, that are unique to the manufacturing process.

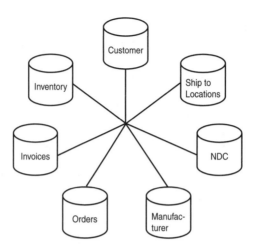

FIGURE 3.10

FIGURE 3.10

Wholesaler layer databases.

The first unique database you will look at in this layer of the transaction is the product database. The product must contain a list of raw materials, or recipe ingredients, that make up the product. Careful attention must also be given to the manufacturing process. The FDA (Food and Drug Administration) expects every manufacturer to stringently adhere to the recommended process to produce the drug. The database has extensive instructions and quality control data for each step within the routing or operational steps in the manufacturing process.

The other database that is unique to the manufacturer in this transaction is one that tracks the capacity of each manufacturing process. Whether it is a material movement operation, a mixing operation, an application of heat, or a packaging operation, each operation has a finite limitation in terms of hours available and capacity. A complex database is required to look at all the scheduled shop orders, retrieving the lot size of each order, multiplying the shop order quantity by the routing quantity, and then determining the work center or material-handling equipment necessary to complete the operation. Each of these extended routing operations are aggregated by work center and compared to the finite limitations noted earlier. The required due dates of the shop orders are used as a starting point, and the entire process is backward scheduled to determine when the shop order would need to begin to meet the required completion date. When you factor in scheduled and unscheduled maintenance, breakdowns, and required setups and quality inspections, the database necessary to adequately evaluate capacity requirements and material requirements planning is significant. Figure 3.11 shows the database entities involved at the manufacturer layer.

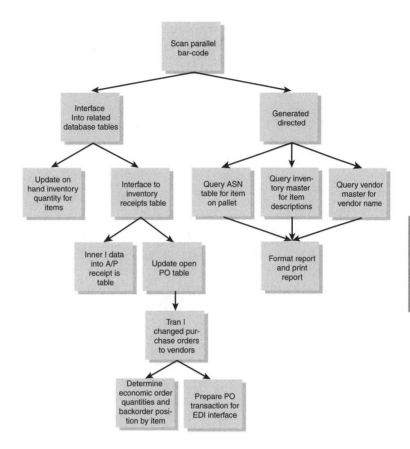

FIGURE 3.11

Manufacturer layer databases.

Using Your Bank Machine

The next example involves a transaction that takes only a few minutes to complete—you are going to look at the databases that are used when you visit a bank and use the ATM.

Don't let the quickness of the transaction fool you—the databases are busy whenever you walk up to use the ATM! You will look at the account database and the financial transaction database in a cash withdrawal example.

When you insert your ATM card into the bank machine, the first thing that must be completed is to identify the account number of the user. The user may be using a local bank or may be using another bank that is part of a participating network. The bank must search its account databases and try to find a match within their system. If this fails, the account number can be searched against a database that represents participating banks.

After an account record is identified, the user is prompted for a PIN, or personal identification number. The PIN is verified against a database entry. The transaction, for obvious reasons, is canceled if the user does not supply a matching PIN.

After the PIN verification is completed, the account details are retrieved from the database regarding the types of accounts that you have—checking, savings, or both. The ATM prompts you for the type of transaction you are interested in completing. Typical transactions are deposits, withdrawals, transfer savings to checking, and check account balances. For this transaction, you are going to withdraw cash from your checking account.

Now it's time for you to indicate how much cash you need. A couple of databases must be accessed at this point. The first is easy—determine how much money you currently have in your account. The second is more involved because most ATM systems limit your withdrawal amounts in a 24-hour period. The system issues a SQL select statement against the database to add the transaction amounts of all withdrawal transactions for your account within the most recent 24 hours. If the daily limit minus the returned summed amount is greater than your transaction amount, you get the cash. If not, you will be limited as to how much can be withdrawn, or you may not qualify to receive any cash.

Beyond the portion of the transaction that you see, a couple more databases are being used. The transaction must be recorded, with account number, account type (savings or checking), date, time of day, type of transaction, and amount. This is used to post the transaction to your account and compute your current balance. This is the database of transactions that you see on your statement at the end of your banking period. The transaction is also used to post to the general ledger database for the bank. If any ATM charges apply, these annoying charges are recorded in the transaction database described previously.

The final database is composed of ACH (Automated Clearinghouse) transactions that are forwarded to the Federal Reserve System so that banks can clear transactions across the country. Each of these transactions are logged to a transaction database for reconciliation purposes in the event of a failure within banking computer systems.

Nontechnology Databases

You commonly use a number of database-related sources of information in the course of your daily life that you might not readily recognize as databases.

The most common of these is the phone book. It is nothing more than a printed version of a customer and business database that contains names, addresses, and phone numbers. The printed version is organized by last name for easier retrieval of records from the database.

The second example is an item you have used since you were in grade school—the dictionary. Each "database" entry in the dictionary contains a number of pertinent items. Besides the correct spelling, it contains pronunciation guides, syllable indications, parts of speech category (noun, verb, and so on), and examples of the word used as different parts of speech.

Summary

You have spent this hour taking a look at a number of transactions that utilize databases in a variety of ways.

The Internet examples of purchasing a book from Amazon.com and downloading a file from Kazaa.com were, by the very nature of the transaction, database intensive. In fact, since the Internet is *only* a digital interaction, it must be database intensive. When you compare the Net to walking into a brick-and-mortar store where you are surrounded by a three-dimensional store with aisles, shelves, and products that you can see, touch, try on, and listen to, the Net has to have a more extensive relational database for its products just to compete! The amount of data that it can lead you to and present to you is a key determinant in the online store's success in completing the sales interaction.

The everyday brick-and-mortar transactions you reviewed—getting a prescription filled and using an ATM—were also database intensive. You evaluated each transaction, much like peeling an onion, one layer at a time. Each successive layer had some similar database requirements and some that were unique to their layer within the supply chain.

Finally, you looked at a few examples of activities that you've done for years without even realizing that a database was being used—using a phone book and looking something up in the dictionary.

Hopefully, now that you've finished your look around at some common "transactions," you have a better appreciation for how extensively you use databases.

Workshop

The following workshop is composed of quiz questions and practical exercises. The quiz questions are designed to test your overall understanding of the current material. The practical exercises are intended to afford you the opportunity to apply the concepts discussed during the current hour, as well as build on the knowledge acquired in previous hours of study. Please take time to complete this workshop before continuing. You can refer to the answers at the end of the hour.

Quiz

1. Databases are used only in transactions you complete on the PC and on the Internet. (True or False)

2. A simple transaction such as getting a prescription filled probably requires, when you consider several layers of the transaction, how much data storage?

    a. 5,000 bytes

    b. 50,000 bytes

    c. 5 megabytes

    d. 500 megabytes

3. Every transaction will have a unique set of database requirements. (True or False)

4. A database is best used to support which type of data? Choose all that apply.

    a. Static current data

    b. Dynamic current data

    c. Static historical data

    d. Dynamic historical data

5. When particular records or rows from the database are needed, what is used to retrieve them?

    a. ATM

    b. NDC

    c. SQL

    d. ACH

Exercises

1. Find five databases you can search on the Internet.

2. You will probably visit a retailer, such as Wal-Mart, K-Mart or a grocery store, within the next few days. Identify two or three databases that are in use when you go through the checkout.

Answers to Quiz

1. False. Databases are used in almost every transaction that you conduct. Everything from buying milk at the grocery, to checking out a book at the library, to getting your car serviced requires the use of many different databases at several layers of the transaction.

2. d. When you take into consideration all the different layers within the supply chain, the answer is probably much greater than 500 megabytes.

3. False. Many of the examples had a customer database with name, address, city, state, and zip. There are many similarities in the database requirements in the examples presented in this hour and in most transactions that you conduct daily.

4. a, b, and c. A database can support current data, both static in nature, such as customer name and address, and dynamic in nature, such as inventory on hand values that may change from minute to minute. A database, usually referred to as a data warehouse, is a good example of static historical data. Dynamic historical data cannot exist; dynamic and historical would be, by definition, mutually exclusive events.

5. c. ATM stands for automated teller machine. NDC stands for National Drug Code. ACH stands for Automated Clearinghouse. Answer c, SQL, stands for Structured Query Language, which is the standard for retrieving data from a relational database.

Answers to Exercises

1. If you start your browser at Yahoo and do a search on "databases" you get 7,691 hits! Film, software, the U.S. Patent Office, medical, and movies are five that appear on the first page.

2. The one that is most obvious is when the cashier scans your item. A database is used, by UPC (Universal Product Code), that uniquely identifies every item. The record is retrieved to determine the current retail price.

   A second database is in use that captures the UPC and quantities of every sale and is used as a point-of-sale inventory replenishment system. This database is used to automatically generate orders to the retailer's distribution center to refill the shelves.

   A third database may be in use if you are going to pay with check or credit card. Your checking account must be checked against a master database to ensure that you do not have any checks outstanding that have been returned for NSF (non-sufficient funds). It will also check against a database that adds the dollar amount of checks you have written within any 24-hour period. Limitations are established that require a manager's approval, as a "stop loss" measure in the event someone is trying to pass bogus checks.

Hour 4

Relating to Modern Databases Users

You have spent the last hour going through several examples of how databases are used in your everyday activities. Simple things that you may not have previously given much thought to in terms of their database usage have taken on a different look.

You looked at everyday transactions such as using an ATM, going to Wal-Mart, or getting a prescription filled; they are, in actuality, transactions that require complex databases and computer systems.

You also looked at Internet transactions, such as purchasing a book at Amazon.com and downloading music at Kazaa.com, that require even more databases to complete. Without the bricks and mortar of stores that you can physically travel to, the Internet retail store must rely more heavily on the use of databases to help you find the product you want. After the product is found, it usually takes more exhaustive use of databases in the forms of pictures, descriptions, customer testimonials, and so on to help convince you, the buyer, to go ahead and put the product in your electronic shopping cart.

In this hour, you will look at many of the different roles that come into play to bring those databases we use into existence. Keep in mind that every IT department is different and that many of the roles we will look at could be the responsibility of one person.

You will also look at some "users" of the database besides the end customer.

NEW TERM   *User* is the person, organization or process that utilizes the database in order to conduct some sort of business.

Techies—From Idea Inception to Implementation and Management

Every database application begins as someone's idea for a new way to build a business—and it really doesn't vary much from banking to real estate to grocery stores to an Internet retailer.

Someone within an organization identifies some new product to market, a service to offer, a way for business partners to form alliances, or simply to improve the efficiency of a current business process that will add to the bottom line of their company. This new idea is sponsored and discussed at different organizational levels until it is given a formal stamp of approval to become a project. After the approval for the project is secured, the necessary time and money can be budgeted and the necessary personnel assigned to bring the new idea to fruition. Figure 4.1 diagrams the organization chart of the IT team that will develop a new database.

NEW TERM   *Techie* is slang for Technical person in the IT (Information Technology) field. For the purposes of our discussion, it is the people who transform the abstract business rules of the project into reality inside the computer

The first role that you are going to look at in more detail in the process of bringing a database into existence is that of the business analyst.

Business Analyst

The business analyst has a unique role within the discussion of the use of databases. This is really the only role you will be looking at, until you get to the actual users of the database that may not necessarily be a true "techie"! The business analyst must have an excellent understanding of the business and of the processes that are involved in the completion of a transaction or the offering of a service, but this person may not have a technical background. Often, however, someone who has a technical background and has experience in structured systems analysis and design fills this role.

Figure 4.1

IT organization chart.

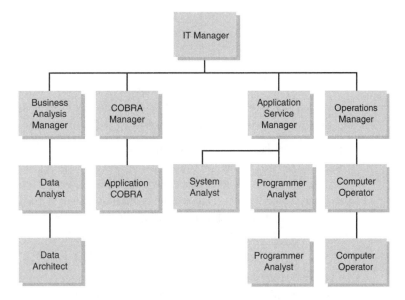

 A ***Business Analyst*** is someone within the given organization who possesses an in-depth knowledge of the business and has the communication skills required to convey that information to those developing the database.

The work that is completed by the business analyst is sometimes overlooked and under-valued. The success of the project and any hope of maximizing the impact on an organization by completing the project are determined by the quality of the work completed by the business analyst. Each of the remaining roles you are going to look at in the development of the database is predicated on the work completed in the previous step. With the business analyst going first, if the project gets off to a good start, it has a good chance of success. If it's wrong in this phase, the project may get completed, but the opportunities to really impact the business may be diminished.

The business analyst will work with the project sponsor to understand the project objectives. The complexity of the organization, and all the different departments or functions within an organization, often create a challenge for the business analyst to clearly identify the objectives and to limit the scope of a project to workable boundaries. Objectives should be clear, quantifiable, measurable, and feasible.

After all objectives are completed, the analyst will review the current process or products and identify what needs to be added, removed, or changed within the organization to effect the desired outcome. Depending on the nature of the project, the business analyst may complete a Business Process Reengineering (BPR) study. The BPR may lead to completely redesigned workflow processes to improve the efficiency of the operation before database technology is applied to meet the project objectives.

Data Analyst

When the project review is completed, the business analyst begins the next phase of the database development work with the data analyst. The data analyst has the job of trying to determine all the data elements that will be required to achieve the project objectives.

The role of the data analyst is not to try to develop a logical or physical model of the database. That will be the job of the next person in the progression toward having a database to implement. The goal of the data analyst is to identify all the needed data elements and their attributes. Data elements are things such as customer name, customer address, and telephone numbers. Their attributes could be 25 characters, 30 characters, and 10 digits, respectively.

The data analyst will begin by having a "walk through" of the workflow or processes that the business analyst developed. At each step of the process, quite a few data elements usually are needed to complete the step, and most projects involve several steps. Let's take a look back at one of the examples in the previous hour and see how complicated and detailed this job can become.

 The *Data Analyst* takes the information from the Business Analyst and determines the required data elements and their attributes.

In both the prescription example and the Amazon.com example, a warehouse full of inventory had to be managed at one layer of the transaction. Figure 4.2 shows an overview of the inventory receipts workflow prior to the new database project.

The project called for a database to be built that would log all the inventory receipts and that would be able to automatically interface with the purchasing system. The goal of the project is to reduce internal operating expenses at the company. In the current system, the purchasing department receives daily a copy of the bill of lading and packing slips from the receiving dock and matches the receipts to an open purchase orders database. The business analyst completed a BPR study and suggested that much more significant operating efficiencies can be gained by automating several other interfaces and implementing EDI and bar-coding systems at the same time. Figure 4.3 shows the proposed workflow for the new system.

The data analyst will work through each of the steps in Figure 4.3, noting each of the data elements that will be needed to complete every step of the new workflow.

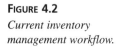

FIGURE 4.2

*Current inventory
management workflow.*

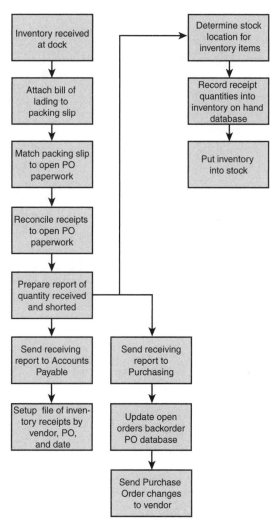

Data Architect

Now that all the data elements and attributes have been identified, it's time for someone
to get all that data organized. As the name implies, that's the job of the data architect.

The data architect's job is critical to the success of the performance of the database. The
objective the data architect has is to develop a logical model of the new database. A
poorly designed logical model will lead to a poorly designed physical model in the next
step, and once the physical model is put into production, structural flaws that are the cause
of performance problems can be very difficult, time-consuming, and costly to correct.

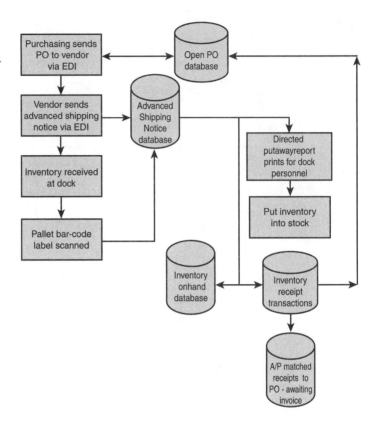

FIGURE 4.3

Proposed inventory management workflow.

NEW TERM   The *Data Architect* takes the data elements and puts them into a logical model of how the database is to be, utilizing concepts of normalization.

At a risk of oversimplification, to put some form to the logical model of the new database, the data architect completes the work by organizing the related data elements into tables. A table, such as the item master table in our inventory example, would contain data elements such as the item number, item description, quantity on hand, quantity on order, vendor number, inventory location, UPC number, and last cycle count date. The table would also have the attributes listed for each data element, which consists of the data type and its length. Examples of common data types are character, numeric, and date data. The length of a data element can vary from one character to several thousand characters.

The data architect also works through a process of data normalization that helps reduce, if not eliminate, redundant data. Hour 7, "Using Tables and Keys for Fundamental Data Storage," will give you much more detail regarding tables and the normalization process.

Database Administrator

NEW TERM While working in conjunction with the System Administrator, the ***Database Administrator*** physically creates the database in the computer.

Now that the database has been modeled logically, it's time for the database to start to take shape physically. That's where the database administrator begins his or her work.

The database administrator usually begins by working in close contact with a system administrator to ensure that adequate resources are available to support the new database project. Those resources could include new disk units, disk controllers, server memory, routers, hubs, and modems. The database administrator must develop estimates of the additional load the new database project will place on the system resources based on the logical model developed in the previous phase and based on the anticipated business activity levels supplied by the business analyst. When those two aspects are factored together, the database administrator can provide the system administrator with a reasonable estimate of resource requirements.

The system administrator will identify for the database administrator where, physically, the database needs to reside on the server and will also upgrade the system as needed to provide an acceptable performance level for the new database. Now the database administrator gets busy.

The logical model needs to be converted to physical tables and indexes. The database administrator develops scripts to create the database, tables, indexes, clusters, and sequences. After this preliminary work is completed, the data that already exists, maybe from a variety of sources, needs to be populated into the new database.

Before the database ever goes into a production state, the database administrator develops scripts to back up the data files, control files, and log files that will be used for database recovery—as soon as a database recovery is needed, and that day *always* comes around eventually! The database administrator and system administrator should work together to develop the backup and recovery strategy for the database at this juncture in the process and begin to follow those guidelines from the first day the database is in existence.

Finally, the database administrator also sets access privileges to the database for whoever will be the application database administrator and for the development staff of analysts and programmers.

4

Systems Analyst

You have a database that is in a production environment and already populated with data. Now all you need is a way for your users—internal and external customers—to access the database. That's where the systems analyst role begins.

The systems analyst works with the workflow diagram that was presented in Figure 4.3 and with the business analyst to gain a full understanding of the project requirements. The project sponsor, along with management representatives from each of the functional areas of the business who will be involved in the new project, should also meet extensively with the systems analyst during this phase.

The objective that the systems analyst has is to develop individual program specifications that will be used by the programming staff in the next phase. After the systems analyst knows the inputs and outputs of each step in the workflow, all that is left is to review what needs to transpire between the two.

 Systems Analyst is the person who develops individual program specifications that will be later used by the programmer to develop specific applications

The systems analyst will develop a set of system functions that must be accomplished for every step in the workflow diagram. Each of those system functions goes through a process known as functional decomposition until the systems analyst gets down to a specific function or small group of functions that will become one program within the new system. Figure 4.4 shows an example of the results of the functional decomposition process that a systems analyst would go through to develop the program specification for the new database project.

Along with each program specification that the programmer analyst will use, the systems analyst develops a detailed list of the input tables and fields used, along with the required outputs that the program is expected to produce.

Programmer Analyst

You are getting pretty close to having a database available for use. The programmer analyst works closely, first with the systems analyst and then with one user or with a group of users to fully understand the function of the program. A logical place for the programmer to start is at the ending—that is, by discussing what output the program will need to produce.

The output of the program may include one or more of the following forms: a generated report, a screen inquiry, or a database file that will be used to interface with another computer system.

FIGURE 4.4

*Functional decomposi-
tion diagram.*

Scan parallel
bar code

Interface
Into related
database tables

Generated
directed

Update on
hand inventory
quantity for
items

Interface to
inventory
receipts table

Query ASN
table for item
on pallet

Query inven-
tory master
for item
descriptions

Query vendor
master for
vendor name

Inner I data
into A/P
receipt is
table

Update open
PO table

Format report
and print
report

Tran I
changed pur-
chase orders
to vendors

Determine
economic order
quantities and
backorder
position by item

Prepare PO
transaction for
EDI interface

NEW TERM   ***Programmer Analyst*** creates inquiry screens, forms, report data files based upon
the requirements of the users and the database.

Let's take the simplest requirement first—the report. Usually, with this requirement, the
programmer is dealing with a database that already contains the data that will be used to
generate the report. The program may be as simple as providing a listing of the item
master file from the inventory system. On the other hand, the report request may be for
an inventory analysis report that shows inventory turns, economic order quantities, and
suggested inventory reorder points. The processing requirements for this report will
require the programmer to use several existing transactional database tables to determine
sales levels over a given period of time, vendor lead times, order quantities, production
orders in the queue, and material requirements for those orders. Additionally, the programmer will have to be supplied factors to use in some of the computations, such as
inventory carrying costs and internal purchase order costs. The exact computations to be

completed will have to be determined by several user groups within the company—inventory analysts, operation management, and cost accounting—and reviewed with the programmer.

The next type of program is similar to the report, except the output is to the screen, which is referred to as being online. The same type of variations in complexity can exist in a screen inquiry in terms of developing the data elements to provide to the user. But, in addition to the content, the programmer must also be concerned with the flow of the program and whether or not "drill down" capabilities must be provided. If the inventory analysis report described in the preceding paragraph was produced for the screen, the programmer may be required to display the sales transactions that were used in the computations, the vendor receipts, the source of the loads on the production floor which are generating the material requirements—or all these options.

The final output type, a database file to be used to interface to another computer system, may be the easiest to produce for the programmer. It usually involves fewer computations and typically is more of a reformatting or summarization process.

Applications Database Administrator

You have already learned about the database administrator in a previous section of this hour, but here is another specialty within the IT department.

An applications database administrator will be responsible for the day-to-day support issues surrounding the database system going into production. Several pre-implementation and post-implementation issues must be dealt with by the applications database administrator.

 Applications Database Administrator ensures the security of the data and the database. They also 'tune' the database to make sure that it performs well.

The easiest, but maybe the most tedious, is the issue of security. The applications database administrator must work with the management team that will be responsible for the database and identify all the database users. Each user must be created on the system and then database privileges, frequently at the level of table and function, must be determined. For example, many of the users will need to be able to view the inventory master file, but the capability to add or delete specific records might be limited to a few individuals working in a supervisory capacity.

The applications database administrator will also be involved in "tuning" the database. After the database is implemented, specific use of the databases, or specific times of days, may cause unacceptable response times. The applications database administrator must try to isolate the cause or causes of this problem and "tweak" the system to improve the performance. This work may lead the applications database administrator back to the system administrator to evaluate whether additional system resources are needed.

Operations

The discussion of the users of the database would be incomplete without mentioning the operations group within the IT department. This is the group that monitors the use of the systems, makes sure users can sign on to the system, and usually handles the media for offline backups.

Backups are usually kept onsite for some period of time, but for disaster recovery purposes, a backup should be rotated to an offsite storage area.

 The *Operations* staff monitors the systems in terms of security and connectivity. They also perform back-up/recovery tasks.

Internal Database Users

Now that you have a database in a production environment that is being used by external customers, as in the examples in the previous hour, there is still one more group that will regularly work with the database. Probably the most intensive use of the database will be by the management and users within the company that owns the database.

You can bet that internal to Amazon.com, the databases that they have are mission critical to their success and those databases are used throughout the day, every day, to evaluate sales transactions, sales promotions, new items, shipping and fulfillment, inventory accuracy, new customers, and billing.

You will often hear users comment that they must "query the database" to find some piece of information they need. This refers to using some SQL interface into the database to extract data based on specific criteria. If this extract will be needed regularly, a report or inquiry program will be developed and made available to the user, but many times the data is needed on an ad hoc basis. Figure 4.5 illustrates some issues that may surface in our inventory database example and the queries of the database that could be used to assist management in making decisions.

4

FIGURE 4.5

Database query examples.

Inventory Issue		Database Query	
1.0	Cycle count discrepancy needs resolved	1.1	Inventory locations for a specific item with on hand quantities and total quantity
		1.2	Inventory receipts for a specific item since last cycle court date
		1.3	Inventory adjustments for a specific item since last cycle court date
		1.4	Shipments for specific item since last cycle court date
2.0	Need to determine number of months coverage current inventory provides for a specific group of items	2.1	Shipments by month with average shipment quantity for each item
		2.2	Sum of on hand for all inventory locations for each item
		2.3	Sum of on order quantities from Open PO file for each item
3.0	Need to adjust seasonal flowrack items to improve picker effiency for upcoming quarter	3.1	Count of the number of inventory locations available in the flowrack area
		3.2	Sum of the shipment history by item for same quarter last year in descending order
4.0	Determine warehouse metrics for previous month	4.1	Sum of all payroll hours for all warehouse personnel for previous month
		4.2	Count of number of orders picked for previous month
		4.3	Count of number of line items picked for previous month
		4.4	Count of number of items cycle counted for previous month
		4.5	Compute inventory accuracy by evaluating sum of inventory adjusts due to cycle counts and the sum of inventory on hand at cycle count

Summary

The uses of databases in our daily lives have grown at an astronomical rate during the past decade. We encounter their use in all kinds of daily transactions from the simple withdrawal of cash at an ATM, to ordering a new book from Amazon.com, to making a purchase at our local grocery store. But you might not have thought through the process of how those databases were developed and all the different roles that people have to fill to bring those databases into existence.

Every IT organization has the potential to look quite a bit different from the next one, but all the development steps covered in this hour have to be completed. A number of factors control the makeup of an IT organization, but the main factor is simple—money! The size of the IT shop will be a function of the size of the budget the IT management has at its disposal. Another factor is whether the business will use packaged software, custom applications, or some combination. If a company strictly uses packaged software, the need for specialization within the IT group will be diminished.

Every database begins as a result of a brainstorming session in which a new service, offering, or business structure is identified that has the potential to have a positive impact on the company's bottom line.

A database project will pass through many phases on the way to being implemented. The business analyst, data analyst, data architect, database administrator, systems analyst, programmer analyst, and operations team are all critical, behind-the-scenes resources that are responsible for making a database available in a production environment.

Although each of us uses databases throughout our daily transactions, the most extensive use of those databases is by internal customers. The management personnel who have daily operational responsibilities for their businesses are constantly using the databases to analyze, play "what if" scenarios, research issues, and reconfigure products and services in a constant attempt to improve their business.

Workshop

The following workshop is composed of quiz questions and practical exercises. The quiz questions are designed to test your overall understanding of the current material. The practical exercises are intended to afford you the opportunity to apply the concepts discussed during the current hour, as well as build on the knowledge acquired in previous hours of study. Please take time to complete this workshop before continuing. You may refer to the answers at the end this hour.

Quiz

1. The development of a database involves which resource(s)?

    a. Software

    b. Server memory

    c. Disk

    d. Personnel

    e. All of the above

2. The development of a database is a streamlined and simple process. (True or False)

3. When resolving issues with the database, which issue is most difficult to correct?

    a. Available disk area is too small

    b. Insufficient server memory

    c. Database design

    d. Network design

4. The most extensive use of a company's database is by which group?

    a. Database administrators

    b. Internal users

    c. Programmers

    d. External users

5. Place the following personnel in the correct sequence according to their logical involvement in the development of a database.

    a. Database administrators

    b. Application database administrator

     c. Programmer analyst

     d. Operations

     e. Data architect

     f. Systems analyst

     g. Data analyst

     h. Business analyst

Exercises

1. You have just been named CIO of a startup fulfillment company that will provide distribution services for a number of national manufacturers. You will have to develop custom software for your warehouse management system, but you will buy packaged software for all your financial applications.

   You need to keep your staff to a minimum because of cash-flow concerns as a startup company. Consultants are available for all positions on a short-term basis.

   Create an organization chart that will be suitable for your new IT department.

2. For the company described in exercise 1, identify four groups of users who would consistently execute queries against the new database.

Answers to Quiz

1. e. Regardless of the size of your company or the size of your IT shop, new database applications will impact all the resources listed. Depending on the database application itself, though, the impact on those resources can vary significantly from application to application.

2. False. Although every database development project goes through logically the same steps as outlined in this hour, the process can take many twists and turns. Rarely is it streamlined and simple.

   When the process necessitates that a BPR be completed, for example, the complexity of a project can be increased drastically.

3. c. The redesign of a database is always a more complex task than buying more memory or disk space.

   A redesign would require the involvement of almost all the database personnel who were discussed in this hour, because the work of each step is predicated on the successful completion of the previous phase. If you have to go back to the data architect phase, you can see how much work would go into getting a redesigned database back into a production environment.

4. b. The internal users of a database will undoubtedly place the most significant load on any production database. Although most databases have external users, it will be the internal users who will analyze the data the most extensively and for periods of time that are more comprehensive.

If the database is not experiencing production problems, the database administrators and programmers will place very modest loads on the database.

5. h, g, e, a, f, c, b, d. The development of any database will follow the logical sequence of the roles covered in this hour. However, in smaller shops, one person could fill many or all of the roles outlined. Regardless of the number of personnel involved, each of the steps that make up the structured analysis and design approach to the development of the database will need to be completed.

Answers to Exercises

1. There is no right or wrong answer to this exercise. To help minimize cash-flow demands during the startup phase of the new company, your organization chart should not include too many permanent employees.

A number of consultants could be used for phases of the development project where the demand for those specific skills would decrease significantly after their phase of the project is completed. The residual need for their skill could be filled by one of the remaining permanent employees.

2. The first example of users of the new database would be external clients—those manufacturers for whom the startup will be providing fulfillment services.

A second example would be the customers of the clients—those companies or individuals to whom the product will be shipped. They may be checking the status of their order or simply checking the availability of inventory.

A third example is the receiving department warehouse workers. As inventory is received, if a stock location that the system should be using is too full for the new inventory, the warehouse personnel may have to query the database for an inventory location that would be suitable for the new shipment.

A final example is the billing department. If a question is raised regarding the client's invoice for services, the billing department may have to query the database to determine the number of warehouse locations used, the number of line items picked, the number of orders shipped, and the number of inventory receipts processed during the previous month.

4

PART II

Database Architecture and Storage

Hour

HOUR 5

Understanding Modern Database Architectures and Environments

A database architecture refers to a chosen method to organize data in a manner that is most suitable for an organization. There are many database architectures to choose from. As with database environments, database architectures have evolved over the years to accommodate changing business needs. Additionally, new methods concepts have been developed as technology has increased through research and a better understanding of data itself. During this hour, we will discuss the following concepts:

- Evolution of legacy database architectures
- Evolution of modern database architectures, leading to more detailed discussions in later hours of the popular relational and object-oriented databases.

NEW TERM *Database Architecture* refers to a chosen method to organize data in a manner that is most suitable for an organization.

Exploration of "Legacy" Database Architectures

The term *database* started with the advent of computers and the electronic processing of data. A database is a place to store and retrieve information, no matter how little or how much data is stored. Before computers were invented, a database, or data bank, as it was known then, could very well be a list or a record book of things you had to sell and the price of each item. A database is defined as an organized collection of data values. We still do lists and record books, but because computers have the capability to store and process a great amount of information, the term database has been more closely associated with complex systems that have the following characteristics:

- Databases give users the capability to query and modify the data with a language developed for that purpose. The Structured Query Language, or SQL, which is the standard language for querying modern relational databases, is covered in Hour 15, "Understanding the Standard Database Language: SQL."

- The database should safeguard the information it possesses. The number one rule of a database is to protect the data. No unauthorized person should be able to see and/or alter the database records.

- Databases provide various options to keep from losing data and should have the capability to restore data to a specified point of time in case of a computer malfunction, a human error, or a natural disaster.

- Databases handle the concurrent access of a number of users who will benefit from sharing the information contained—that is, without allowing the actions from one user to affect those of another user and accidentally corrupt the data.

- In the case of more complex business models, the database should provide a way to remotely access the data. An example is using the Internet to make a purchase or find information. Thousands of people connect at the same time to the same databases to buy books or car parts, to do research, and to find just about anything. Another example of concurrent users occurs with the processing of a credit card, which can take place at the location where we buy our goods or where we retrieve money from a bank machine.

First, we begin with a background of the evolution of so-called "legacy" database environments in chronological order, starting with the flat-file database system. Then we will explore hierarchical and network databases as they evolved after the flat-file databases.

Understanding the Basics of the Flat-File Database

The first method used to organize data electronically was in the form of flat files. In the 1950s, it was normal for computer programs to manage and store their own data and flat files. These "*flat files*" looked very similar to the way a filing system is organized. A filing system contains a collection of documents in folders organized alphabetically, by date, subject, and so on. The information inside the folders is not indexed in a way that enables you to find the desired document almost immediately. You have to look for it in sequential order until you find what you are looking for.

Flat-file storage is a simple means of storing a small amount of application data. The programmer decides on a format and stores the application data using this standard.

NEW TERM   *Flat-file Database* is a text, character delimited data file that can be scanned in sequential order to locate data.

The file consists of a collection of strings and might be advanced or organized enough to contain a simple table. The typical flat file is split with a delimiting character and is stored as ASCII text. If the data is simple enough, this delimiting character could be a semicolon or colon. More complex strings are delimited using tabs, line feeds, or a carefully chosen combination of characters.

When the application needs certain data, the flat file is searched and parsed until the data is encountered. Searching file data is inefficient. If the collection of data is expected to grow with application usage, the data should not be stored in a flat file. Rather, the data should be stored in a DBMS.

Flat files are well suited for storing small lists and data values (such as application preferences), but can quickly get complicated when used to replicate more complex data structures. Flat-file data storage is acceptable for small amounts of data not expected to change in format or storage capacity. Figure 5.1 illustrates a simple flat-file database architecture.

5

FIGURE 5.1
*Understanding basic
flat-file database
architecture.*

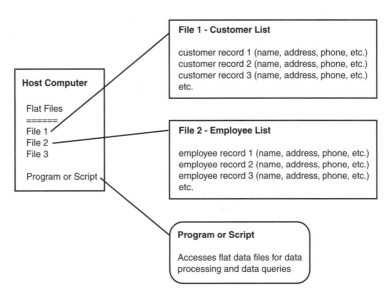

File 1 - Customer List

customer record 1 (name, address, phone, etc.)
customer record 2 (name, address, phone, etc.)
customer record 3 (name, address, phone, etc.)
etc.

Host Computer

Flat Files
======
File 1
File 2
File 3

Program or Script

File 2 - Employee List

employee record 1 (name, address, phone, etc.)
employee record 2 (name, address, phone, etc.)
employee record 3 (name, address, phone, etc.)
etc.

Program or Script

Accesses flat data files for data
processing and data queries

In a flat file, the data is accessed using computer programs that read and write into the files. Figure 5.2 shows what a flat file looks like with data.

FIGURE 5.2

*Sample flat file
with data.*

LAST	FIRST	CREDIT CARD	ITEM NO.
Chandler	Becky	1243364488	65332
Chandler	Becky	1243364488	87321
Chandler	Becky	1243364488	23132
Mount	Gene	4343243433	97989
Becker	John	3402934433	08090
Becker	John	3402934433	74938

Flat files have several problems when used to store data. A problem with using flat files to store data is data corruption. If an application crashes while the file is open, it is unknown whether the file is intact. If the application was writing when the crash occurred, the data will most likely not be intact. Another problem is lack of concurrency. Multiple applications cannot open the same data file at the same time.

Since no query language existed that would access the data, no search capability was available. A business could write a daily file that kept records of its daily sales. This file would contain the name, form of payment, and item that was sold. If a customer bought one item or more, the customer's name and related information would be included on the file as many times as items bought, every time an order was placed.

You could do a search by looking through the files in order of dates, but after that the search would be sequential. Also, the recording of the same information for every order creates unnecessarily large files and a longer data search. In addition, because flat files cannot link to each other, the same person with the same information can appear in other flat files at different dates. Questions such as, "How many repeat customers did the store have in a year?" would take a very long time to answer because every file would have to be examined individually and sequentially.

Understanding Hierarchical Databases

Information systems evolved from file storage to a database system with the hierarchical database model. It was first introduced in the late 1960s and its name was derived from the way it stored data. This database stored data in structures called records, which were the equivalent of the table rows in the relational database model. These records were arranged in an upside-down tree architecture. The first record, also known as root, had one or more child records. These child records had their own child records, but all records except for the root had only one parent, which did not have a parent, forming a "hierarchy"; hence its name. Figure 5.3 shows an example of a hierarchical database.

FIGURE 5.3

Hierarchical database model.

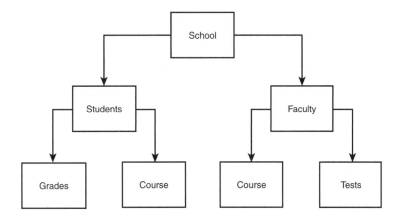

Hierarchical databases introduced the first relationships among data records. They were capable of one-to-many relationships. This type of relationship eliminated the redundancy characteristic of flat files. This way, the customer appeared only one time, instead of one time per item purchased. The table in Figure 5.2 could be divided into two tables, as shown in Figure 5.4.

NEW TERM	***Hierarchical Database*** contains a base or root level of records with subsequent related records.

FIGURE 5.4

Reducing flat-file redundancy.

LAST	FIRST	CREDIT CARD
Chandler	Becky	1243364488
Mount	Gene	4343243433
Becker	John	3402934433

ITEM NO.
65332 87321 23132
97989
08090 74938

Here, Table A is the parent of Table B; therefore, Table B is the child of Table A. For every entry in Table B, there is one entry in Table A. An additional column, in this case the customer_id, could be used to relate Table A to Table B.

Compared to modern databases, the hierarchical database model has its limitations. One of them is that it can contain only one tree per database. In Figure 5.3, the hierarchical tree shows that "one student can take one or more classes" and "one faculty member can teach one or more classes". Because it is not possible to have more than one parent table, the records for the school classes had to be repeated. Also, if a change in a class took

5

place, both class records had to be updated. Therefore, *data redundancy* still was a big issue.

Navigation through the hierarchical database records was another limitation. To access any record, the user needed to start at the root of the tree and navigate down from parent to child to reach the desired record. Therefore, users needed to be familiar with the way data was stored.

The hierarchical database imposes a strict relationship between parent and child. Child records cannot exist without a parent record. Although this is fine for enforcing removal of the child records if the parent record was to be deleted, at times it is desirable that child records exist without parent records. For example when a new class is organized, and neither a student has registered nor a faculty member has been selected to teach it, it is not possible to add it to the database.

Another situation that had to be dealt with in the hierarchical database was that there was no definitive method available for the allocation of space for records. As a result one could easily run out of space or have wasted space very quickly.

Nevertheless, this database was very popular with those who used it, because it reduced the time to access information as compared to a filing system or a flat file.

Understanding the Network Database

Like the hierarchical database, the network database gets its name from the way data is structured. Here, records are linked to each other forming a network of links. This database model was introduced in 1971 when an improvement to the limitations of the hierarchical model was sought. Figure 5.5 shows a diagram of a network database.

 Network Database combines individual hierarchical databases into a larger one.

The network model is similar to the hierarchical model. However, the following important differences improve functionality over the hierarchical database:

- Network databases can have more than one tree. All prior hierarchical databases can now be combined into one. Each tree is combined into the schema, or a set of related tables in a database.
- Network databases have support for many-to-many relationships. Because records in hierarchical databases could have only one-to-many relationships, relationships such as customer and movies, for example, could not be established. A customer can rent more than one movie and more than one customer can rent a movie. This simply means that many copies of the same movie are available. With the hierarchical model, only one copy of a movie can exist in the store for the model to work.

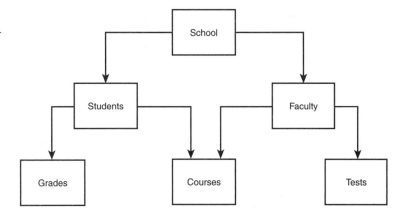

FIGURE 5.5
Understanding the network database model.

- Navigation on the network model can start in any record, in contrast to the hierarchical model, which needed the user to start at the tree root. Still, familiarity with the record architecture is needed to retrieve the desired information.

Although the network model was a great improvement over the hierarchical model, maintenance and implementation were difficult. Also, changes in the database required changes in the application using that database. Because the application already had a programmed starting point for navigation, any changes in the database structure would mean that the preset navigation rules of the application would yield the wrong results. A new database architecture was needed that could be used by non-technical staff who did not need to be familiar with the organization of the records.

Exploration of Modern Architectures

In this portion of the hour, the most common database architecture in use today—the relational database model—is introduced and described. In addition to this very common model, two emerging technologies, object-oriented database architecture and the object-relational architecture, are introduced. We will also discuss the concept of multimedia and distributed databases.

The content in this hour is intended to provide a brief overview of modern database architectures as they apply to the adaptation of these methods over the years. Subsequent hours will discuss the most common modern architectures (relational and object-oriented) in greater detail. The vast majority of this book applies to the relational database architecture.

Overview of Relational Database Architecture

The relational database is the most widely used database model in the market today.

The theory for relational databases was born from a research paper written by mathematician Edward Frank Codd from the IBM Research Laboratory in 1970. The motivation for his investigations was to protect users from having to familiarize themselves with the structure of the database, as was the case with the previous two database models. Another reason to look at relational databases was to form a basis for treating redundancy, or data repetition, and over dependence on physical implementation. Changes in the database meant changes in the application.

His research was based on two branches of mathematics: set theory and predicate logic. The relational database derived its name from "set relations," a component of set theory.

Dr. Codd's paper proposed the storage of data in relations or tables rather than records to promote *data independence*. This means that data could be changed without affecting application programs, which is one of the problems of the network databases. Figure 5.6 shows a simple illustration of a relational schema.

 A ***Relational Database*** is a database that stores data in a series of objects known as tables. These tables are a specialized set of the overall enterprise or business that the database is designed to represent, and they contain data that corresponds to other *sets* or tables within the database.

FIGURE 5.6

Simple example of a relational database model.

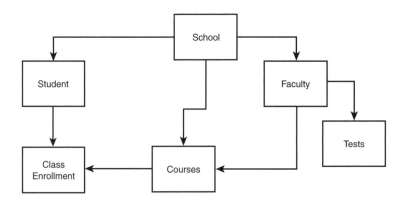

Tables in a relational database are made of columns and rows. Columns are also referred to as fields and they contain data based on a specific field. Rows are also referred to as records and they contain each individual entry that exists in a table.

Through data independence, the physical location of the records or rows in a table is unimportant. Users do not need to become familiar with the database structure. However, a means of isolating a specific row on the table is necessary. This is achieved by having a field or column on each row with a unique value, different from all other rows in that table. The column used for this purpose is known as the *primary key*. The primary key enables the user to retrieve just one row from among the others in the table.

Numbers are used mostly in this column because they are unique and because there are infinite numbers of them, but not always. Examples of primary keys used in our daily life are order numbers to identify a store purchase and license plate numbers to identify our cars on the road. The local pizza restaurant uses our telephone number to relate it to our address. The government, medical databases, and financial institutions love to use our social security number. This number is not only unique; it also identifies the same person in any database where it is used. Consequently, it is very important to protect our personal "primary key" because it represents us.

Through the introduction of SQL with relational databases, it is now possible to retrieve information in ways not possible before. Previously, all records were made available at once, but with SQL, you can retrieve one row or all the rows of the table that complies with a given condition. The next few paragraphs show how relationships work in a relational database using the standard database language of SQL (SQL is covered in more detail starting in Hour 15, "Understanding the Standard Database Language: SQL"). For example, study the data in the three tables that follow:

TABLE 2.1 STUDENTS Table

STUDENT_ID	FIRST_NAME	LAST_NAME	DEGREE	ADMITTED
1	JANE	SMITH	ENGINEERING	22-MAY-00
2	ROGER	LIVINGSTONE	NURSING	12-SEP-98
3	JOSE	SANTIAGO	BIOLOGY	23-JUN-99
4	MARTHA	KIRICH	ENGINEERING	12-JUN-94
7	JEAN	DOYLE	PHARMACY	04-APR-85
8	LYNN	DENNIS	LAW	15-MAY-85
9	NAOMI	BAKER	BUSINESS	10-JUN-85
10	ELIZABETH	WARD	DENTISTRY	22-FEB-85
11	BERNARDINE	PETERS	EDUCATION	31-MAR-88
12	GEORGE	SHAW	JOURNALISM	02-APR-99
13	LUIS	DUNCAN	LAW	31-MAY-99
14	JOHN	LOUIS	DENTISTRY	01-JUN-96
15	IVAN	RODRIGUEZ	PHYSICS	02-APR-01

continues

5

TABLE 2.1 continued

STUDENT_ID	FIRST_NAME	LAST_NAME	DEGREE	ADMITTED
16	CHRIS	ALBERTS	LIBRARY SCIENCE	06-APR-00
17	RAYMOND	PORTER	MEDICINE	15-APR-01
18	RICHARD	LEWIS	LAW	16-APR-02
19	JASON	MARTIN	BUSINESS	28-SEP-00

TABLE 2.2 LAW_101 Table

STUDENT_ID	SECTION	HOURS	L	G
8	101-1	1:00pm	N	B
13	101-1	1:00pm	N	A
18	101-2	7:00pm	N	B
9	102-2	7:00pm	N	B
19	102-2	7:00pm	N	A

TABLE 2.3 BUS_101 Table

STUDENT_ID	SECTION	HOURS	L	G
4	B101-1	3:00pm	N	C
9	B101-1	3:00pm	N	A
1	B101-1	3:00pm	N	A
14	B101-2	5:00pm	N	A

The following SQL query will list all those students in the law school:

```
Select * from students where degree = 'LAW';
```

STUDENT_ID	FIRST_NAME	LAST_NAME	DEGREE	ADMITTED
8	LYNN	DENNIS	LAW	15-MAY-85
13	LUIS	DUNCAN	LAW	31-MAY-99
18	RICHARD	LEWIS	LAW	16-APR-02

The * in the select statement means "all fields." Relational databases also introduce the concept of joins, in which data from more than one table can be selected to retrieve related information. For example, if you want to list those students taking course BUS_101, the following query will return that information:

New Term *Join* is the process by which, in a relational database, data is selected from two or more tables.

```
select first_name, last_name and degree
from students, bus_101
where bus_101.student_id = students.student_id;
```

FIRST_NAME	LAST_NAME	DEGREE
JANE	SMITH	ENGINEERING
MARTHA	KIRICH	ENGINEERING
NAOMI	BAKER	BUSINESS
JOHN	LOUIS	DENTISTRY

A more complex query joining three tables will provide those students who are taking both BUS_101 and LAW_101.

```
select first_name, last_name, degree
from students, law_101, bus_101
where law_101.student_id = students.student_id
 and
law_101.student_id = bus_101.student_id;
```

FIRST_NAME	LAST_NAME	DEGREE
NAOMI	BAKER	BUSINESS

These queries demonstrate how the primary key, in this case the student_id, facilitates the search for records. Hour 6, "Understanding Relational Database Architecture," covers relational databases in more detail.

A relational database consists of many relations in the form of two-dimensional tables. The rows and columns of these relational tables contain related tuples. The logical aspect is created of relational databases by organizing data into tables. Figure 5.7 illustrates a simple relational database architecture.

New Term *Tuple* refers to rows of data in a table within a relational database.

There are various restrictions on the data that can be stored in a relational database. These are called constraints. The constraints are domain constraints, key constraints,

5

entity integrity constraints, and referential integrity constraints. These constraints ensure that there are no ambiguous tuples in the database.

FIGURE 5.7

A look at a more detailed relational database architecture with data.

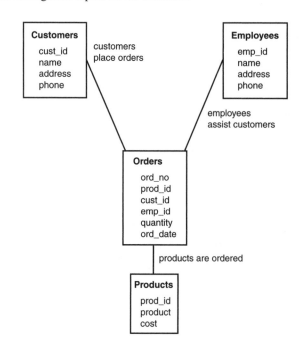

There are two types of relational databases, each of which is associated with particular uses. A particular relational database type is used based on the required uses of the data. These two types are the Online Transactional Processing database and the Online Analytical Processing database.

A transactional, or Online Transactional Processing (OLTP), database is a relational database that is used to process information data on a regular basis. A good example of a transactional database is one for class scheduling and student registrations. Take as an example a university that offers several hundred classes; each class has at least one professor, and between 10 and 300 students.

Students register and drop classes as needed. Classes are constantly added, removed, modified, and scheduled. The collection of data that powers this system is dynamic and requires a great deal of input from the end user. Imagine the paperwork involved and the staff required in this situation without the use of this OLTP database.

NEW TERM *OLTP or Online Transactional Processing Database* processes transactions over the Internet or network.

An Online Analytical Processing (OLAP) database is one whose main purpose is to supply end users with data in response to queries that are submitted. Typically, the only transactional activity that occurs in an OLAP database concerns bulk data loads. OLAP data is used to make intelligent business decisions based on summarized data, company performance data, and trends. The two main types of OLAP databases are Decision Support Systems (DSS) and data warehouses. Both types of databases are normally fed from one or more OLTP databases. A data warehouse differs from a DSS in that a data warehouse contains massive volumes of data collected from all parts of an organization; hence, the name *warehouse*. Data warehouses must be specially designed to accommodate the large amounts of data storage required and enable acceptable performance during data retrievals.

New Term   The *OLAP or Online Analytical Processing Database* processes queries for information over the Internet or network.

Object-Oriented Database Architecture

An object-oriented database is a database system that is designed to work with an object-oriented programming language to store data. Object-oriented database management systems are discussed in detail in Hour 10, "Welcome to Object-Oriented Databases," but here we will give a preview of the concepts and environment of an object-oriented database.

This type of database was introduced in the mid 1990s as the Internet era emerged. Object-oriented databases (OODB) were conceived because, although relational databases have improved many aspects of data management, the relational database faces limitations on the data types it can handle. With the advent of the Internet, ways to store objects such as voice, pictures, video, and text documents were sought. The relational database data types were seen as too rigid and limited because they could manipulate only numbers, dates, and characters.

New Term   *OODB or Object Oriented Database* stores data in an object form and thus, provides for greater options in how the data may be later used.

One thing to note about object-oriented databases is that they are also referred to by the term *object databases*. The terms *object-oriented database* and *object database* mean the same thing in this text. An object database system is defined by a minimum of these two requirements: the system should meet the qualifications of a DBMS, and the system should be an object-oriented system.

The qualifications of a DBMS include data storage with persistence, secondary storage management, concurrency, recovery, and an ad hoc query facility. To be an object-oriented system, the DBMS should be able to store data in object form from the object-oriented languages in use today. It is important that the object database system have the capability to support complex objects, object identity, data encapsulation, abstract data types or classes, class inheritance, method/function overriding combined with dynamic binding, and extensibility. This is a long list of industry buzzwords! If you are interested, you might pick up a textbook and discover the meaning of those buzzwords that you do not understand.

When the DBMS supports this long list of terms, it qualifies as an object database management system (ODBMS). An ODBMS serves to make database objects look like programming language objects for one or more object-oriented programming languages. An ODBMS essentially extends the language by supporting persistent data, concurrency control, data recovery, and associative queries.

Object-oriented databases are designed to blend with object-oriented programming languages such Java, C++, and Smalltalk. Any application written in Java, C++, or Smalltalk might, for example, use an object database.

Two reasons that a company might decide to use object databases are less code (decreased development time) and increased code efficiency. Both of these reasons stem from the same principle—store data like it is used.

The first benefit, less code (decreased development time), exists because when using Java or C++, the programmer will not need to map the internal program data to a database using a sublanguage such as SQL. Instead, the programmer writes data storage code in the programming language. The immediate result is less code (sometimes dramatically less code). Figure 5.8 illustrates a simple object-oriented database architecture.

FIGURE 5.8

Understanding object-oriented database architecture.

Person
name
address
phone
(person attributes are inherited by customers and employees)

Customers
credit card #
credit card type
credit card expiration

Employees
salary
dependents
withholding
emergency contact

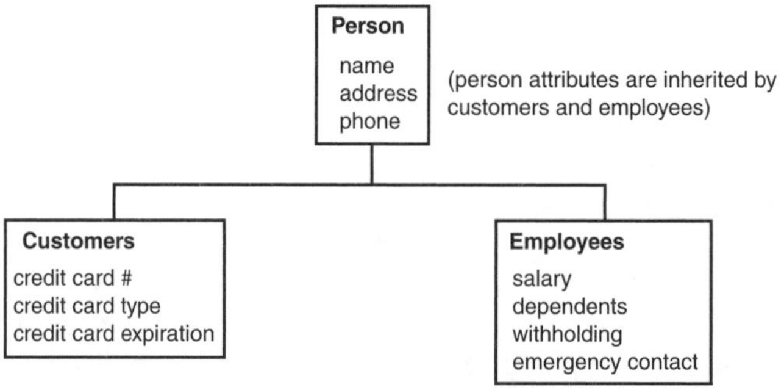

An ODBMS offers performance increases that have been reported in the range of 10 to 1,000 times faster than a standard relational database management system (when used with an object-oriented programming language). These sometimes remarkable performance results are possible because the data is read off the disk in the native format for Java or C++; no translation necessary.

Some of the disadvantages of OODBs are risks when migrating a relational database to an OODB. Given their differences, it is risky to convert one model to another and expect flawless functionality.

OODBs are not guaranteed to run in as many platforms as relational databases do. Even when OODBs are developed in Java, which makes them very portable, complex Java code might have a problem in certain environments that may be difficult to migrate into. In addition, companies that support OODBs do not have the high budgets that some relational database companies have. Relational database companies can absorb the costs associated of supporting their products in many platforms.

Each OODB tends to have its own proprietary code. The same occurs with relational databases. However, it is more difficult to find people with the specific skills to work in a given OODB than it is to find people to work in the relational databases of Oracle or Microsoft SQL Server, for example.

OODBs are commonly used in computer-aided design (CAD). This can be a simpler alternative to manipulating objects that relational databases manipulate in a more complex fashion, but relational databases also are incorporating more of those attributes that OODBs have, as you will see in the next topic.

> Use an ODBMS when you have a business need for high performance on complex data. But, what does that mean exactly? Briefly, when you meet a business need, you either make or save some money. High performance, in the context of an ODBMS, means that you literally could see a performance improvement of between 10 to 1,000 times compared to an RDBMS.

Object-Relational Database Architecture

As its name implies, an object-relational database incorporates object-oriented features on top of its basic relational functionality. Oracle8, released in June 1997, was the first database to incorporate object-oriented characteristics in its relational database. It extended the set of data types beyond the number, dates, and characters to the point that you can create your own data types.

You can create, for example, the data type called employee. This simple data type can contain name, employee id, date of hire, and department. It appears as one column in the table, but it contains four data points. This is an example of *encapsulation*, forcing the concept of the attributes of an employee. In essence, every time an employee is entered into a table, you can specify that all four attributes are needed. Also, one variable of this data type in a procedure can be used to pass information, but in reality, four (or more if you want) points of information are actually passed along.

NEW TERM   *Encapsulation* is the combination of two or more column attributes being combined into a single data type.

Oracle also incorporated the use of large objects. It allows the storage of more than one character and binary-based documents per table row, up to four gigabytes. For larger documents such as movies, a table can have a pointer to an object in the form of a file outside the database. Although it is operating system specific, there is no set limit to the size of these types of objects.

NEW TERM   *Object-Relational Database* combines the attributes of OODB with the capabilities of a relational database.

Extended relational and object relational are synonyms for database management products that integrate components of relational and object databases. There is no official definition at this time of an object relational database management system (ORDBMS), but object relational database management systems use features from relational and object database management systems.

The objective of an ORDBMS is to provide object data storage in a relational type of environment. ORDBMSs use a hybrid type of data model that incorporates object support into a RDBMS.

In a traditional RDBMS, simple data is stored in tables. This data could be integers, strings, real numbers, and so on. In the case of ORDBMS, the data stored within the tables can be objects. Transactions are performed on these objects using an extended form of SQL called SQL3 that is currently under development.

The results of queries to an ORDBMS are tuples (rows). The relational model has to be modified to allow this functionality with objects and to maintain seamless data integrations with object-oriented programming languages.

If a DBMS claims object-relational capabilities, this DBMS might demonstrate the following properties: user-defined data types, object support (abstract data types), and inheritance support. Figure 5.9 illustrates a simple object relational database architecture.

Law enforcement is one example of where the object characteristics of relational databases are used. The Federal Bureau of Investigation uses this type of database for the storage and analysis of fingerprints. This information is associated with photographic images of known criminals, linking a fingerprint to one person out of thousands in a matter of seconds. You will learn about other applications for the storage and retrieval of sound, video, or a combination of the two in the section "Understanding Multimedia Databases."

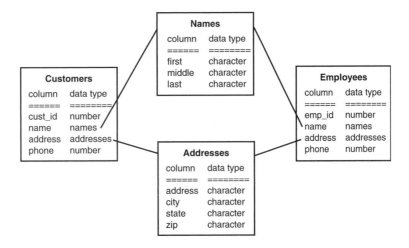

FIGURE 5.9

Understanding object relational database architecture.

Understanding Multimedia Databases

Multimedia databases are very similar to object–relational databases. However, they have different requirements to manipulate large objects such as movies, music, text, and video, and at the same time hide from the user the logistics involved to make this happen.

Multimedia databases have three principal requirements:

- *Volume of data*—A compressed video frame typically occupies 10KB. At the standard rate of video display of 30 frames per second, approximately 300KB per second are retrieved. This is much greater than any typical query.

- *Continuity*—The video or audio should flow uninterrupted.

- *Synchronization*—More than one stream of data may be retrieved from the database. This can be in the form of stereo sound, video and audio, and/or closed caption, which includes text, audio, and video data that is retrieved simultaneously and coordinated with each other.

Multimedia databases require considerable hardware support in terms of memory capacity, storage capacity, speed, and high network transfer rate. There is still work to be done in the reduction of image and audio files. Although compression formats such as MPEG and JPEG have reduced the size of these files, the trade-off is that data quality is affected.

If a high-quality format is used, network transfer time is increased, which limits the number of concurrent users who can share the contents at a given time.

5

Applications for multimedia databases can be found in television networks to manage advertisements. Also, medical information systems have endless possibilities in the areas of imaging display, medical distance learning, and storage of three-dimensional medical image records.

Understanding Distributed Databases

A topic of active research, a *distributed database* is a set of databases with common characteristics distributed over a network and stored on two or more computers. The idea of dividing a database and spreading it over a network brings the possible benefit of working in parallel to process queries faster. To the user, this type of system would look like one database, when in reality, more than one is being accessed. Distributed databases have not been fully implemented because researchers face technical issues such as the following:

New Term **Distributed Databases** are a set of databases with common characteristics and are distributed over a network and are also stored on two or more computers.

- *Distributed Query Processing*—Although some ideas have been presented on this subject, no set strategy exists to execute each query over the network in the most cost-effective way. The query must be divided across the network to retrieve information, and its results must be pieced together in an organized manner.

- *Distributed Concurrency Control*—One of the most studied problems in distributed databases, concurrency control looks to preserve consistency of not only one, but many databases. In other words, if you need to gather certain points of information within the database to calculate an answer, you cannot allow changes in any of those elements before you arrive at your result. Otherwise, your result would be wrong and inconsistent with the data you used to do your calculation. One of the solutions is to lock those points of information you need before committing your transaction, and then release the locks when done. However, this takes us to the next problem.

- *Distributed Deadlock Management*—Suppose transaction A needs to retrieve certain information from database 1 and another point of information from database 2 to do a calculation. Transaction B needs the same information as transaction A from both databases. Transaction A locked the information transaction B needs in database 1 to finish its transaction, and transaction B locked the information transaction A needs in database 2. Both transactions are waiting for the other one to release its locks on the information they need. But this will not happen until each one has collected all information resources and committed its results. This is called a deadlock. The problem is how to prevent, detect, and recover from such dead-locks that span over a network.

If the problems that distributed databases face are solved, they promise advantages such as

- *Improved query performance*—Because queries are divided for parallel processing, performance is expected to greatly improve.

- *Improved reliability*—Distributed databases can also have duplicate information, called replication, which is the copying and maintenance of data on multiple servers. If one database goes down, the other one can be used while the first one is under recovery.

- *Improved expandability*—It is easier to accommodate the increasing size of a data-base in a distributed environment. In other words, if a database is growing too fast, other databases can be used to share the load.

Summary

This hour covered, in brief and without much detail, the history of databases since their inception. You learned about characteristics of each database model and how they improved on the previous architecture. The three architectures in this hour were the rela-tional database model, the object database model, and object relational database model. This hour also covered flat-file storage. The benefits and weaknesses of flat files were mentioned so that the reader could compare databases and flat files.

5

Q&A

Q Why is it inefficient to search through a flat file for data?

A In a flat file the records are written as a list. If the file is huge and the computer is searching for an item that happens to be near the top of the list, the search is over fairly fast. However, if the computer is searching for an item near the bottom of the list, every single item in front of the one sought is examined. Depending on the length of the file, looking at every item to see if it's the one you're after can be an incredibly slow process.

Workshop

The following workshop is composed of quiz questions and practical exercises. The quiz questions are designed to test your overall understanding of the current material. The practical exercises are intended to afford you the opportunity to apply the concepts discussed during the current hour, as well as build on the knowledge acquired in previous hours of study. Please take time to complete this workshop before continuing. You can refer to the answers at the end of the hour.

Quiz

1. What is the relational database model?

2. What is the object database model? What is a benefit of this model? What is a drawback of this model?

3. What was one of the problems with previous database models that the relational database solved?

4. What is the importance of the introduction of the primary key? Give an example of a primary key in your daily life.

5. What are drawbacks to storing data in a flat file?

6. What was the motivation behind the development of the object-oriented database?

Exercises

1. Study the following simple flat-file database. In the subsequent exercises, you are asked questions about the data in this flat-file database. The purpose is to exercise your basic knowledge of databases using a simple example. The concepts applied in these exercises apply to all modern databases. The colon is used in this flat-file database to delimit fields.

```
ID:LAST:FIRST:ORDER_ID:PRODUCT_NAME:COST:QUANTITY:TOTAL
1:SMITH:MARK:1:DICTIONARY:19.99:1:19.99
2:JONES:SAM:2:ENCYCLOPEDIA:99.99:1:99.99
1:SMITH:MARK:3:DICTIONARY:19.99:3:59.97
3:WILLIAMS:MARY:4:THESAURUS:14.99:2:29.98
PRODUCT_NAME:COST
DICTIONARY:19.99
ENCYCLOPEDIA:99.99
THESAURUS:14.99
```

2. Who has placed the most orders?

3. List products from least to most expensive.

4. What customer has spent the most?

5. Which product has been ordered the most?

Answers to Quiz

1. The relational database model is the model in which data is stored in two-dimensional tables. The data inside these tables is interconnected via relationships.

2. The object database model is the model in which data is stored inside a database in the form of an object. Data can be stored in object form directly from an object-oriented program. This object-oriented model sometimes enables quicker development and improved programming efficiency.

3. The relational database provided a method for reducing data redundancy through the way relationships are handled.

4. The primary key is a way to designate unique data in a relational database. The primary key is used to establish relationships between data and reduce data redundancy. An example of a primary key is a customer number. A unique customer number could be assigned to each customer in the database to ensure that each customer's data need be stored in only one place.

5. When data is stored in a flat file, there is the risk of data corruption, the issue of nonconcurrent access, and the issue of inefficient searching.

6. One of the main limitations of the relational database that is solved in the object-oriented model is the limited data types that can be handled by a relational database. The object-oriented database provides greater flexibility to the developer in defining data types for certain types of data; particularly large objects such as images, sound, and video.

Answers to Exercises

1. No answer.

2. Mark Jones has placed two orders.

3. Encyclopedia is $99.99.

   Dictionary is $19.99.

   Thesaurus is $14.99.

4. Sam Jones has spent the most, which totals $99.99.

5. Four dictionaries have been ordered.

5

HOUR 6

Understanding Relational Database Architecture

As stated in Hour 5, "Understanding Modern Database Architectures and Environments," all relational databases are built on the basis of a formal mathematical theory. This theory and several related principles first articulated by Dr. E. F. Codd, a mathematician working for IBM, provide an architecture that has revolutionized the everyday tools used for the storage and retrieval of data.

In this hour you will learn

- Why the relational database was needed
- Basic relational database theory
- The basic elements of a relational database
- How to understand the relationships between data
- How to communicate with a relational database

The success of the relational data model and the strategic acceptance of a standard language (SQL) give a high degree of portability both to applications and to knowledge. It also provides database practitioners the opportunity to grow in a field that reaches out beyond the concerns of particular vendors.

In this hour, you will learn about the concepts behind the relational database. You will learn how and why the relational database was developed, and you will see the way that formal ideas find their expression in the concrete objects of tables, keys, and indexes.

Why Was the Relational Database Needed?

It is safe to say that the relational database is the most widespread type of database implemented today. The popularity of the relational database lies within its capability to store data in an effective manner that minimizes the overhead to manage data and maximizes the way data can be used to solve many of today's problems related to data storage. The requirement for a database with features such as the relational database can be described by first identifying the problems posed by pre-relational databases and then by identifying how relational database theory provided solutions to these problems.

Problems with Pre-relational Databases

Although some pre-relational database systems were highly successful, they suffered from a number of shortcomings:

- Logical design of data was constrained by the physical requirements of data storage and access. Databases were designed to reflect the structure of the storage devices rather than the systems that were being represented.

- Retrieval and update had to be handled by applications that navigated the data on a record-by-record basis. Applying an update as a single operation to a set of data was not possible.

- Data integrity was the responsibility of the applications that manipulated the data. Consequently, the integrity of the database could not be guaranteed beyond the level of the integrity of every application accessing the data.

As a result, inserting, updating, deleting, and retrieving data was a complex programming task, and databases and any program accessing the data had the potential of harming its integrity.

How the Relational Database Provided Solutions

In a relational database management system (RDBMS), a designer can develop a data model based on the natural relationships among the entities under consideration and communicate that design to the RDBMS using an ANSI standard language (SQL). As part of the data model and the resulting SQL, the designer can define appropriate data types for all stored values, relationships between the entities, and column and table-level integrity constraints. The RDBMS takes on the responsibility for enforcing these data types, relationships, and constraints across all users and applications accessing the data.

The RDBMS also provides a means to query and manipulate data in the aggregate—that is, in sets rather than individual records. The language for communicating data manipulations is SQL.

Relational databases allow users and applications to specify what is to be done to the data and to communicate this using a consistent language. The low-level details of data manipulation are left to the RDBMS.

Understanding How Relational Databases Solve Today's Data Storage Needs

Before learning about the nuts and bolts of a relational database, it is important to understand a little about the history of relational databases and how relational databases solve today's data storage needs. Almost every book that covers relational database theory discusses to some degree the concepts introduced by Dr. E. F. Codd that make the relational database what it is today—this book does the same. These basic relational concepts by Dr. Codd were covered briefly in Hour 5.

Relational databases have become popular for a number of reasons. Primarily, the relational model, based on sound mathematical principles, has proven itself in highly diverse data applications. Many successful relational database applications have been created to solve problems in inventory, finance, engineering, science, banking, process control, and Internet commerce, to name just a few.

Second, the relational database management systems that have been made available commercially have successfully met the requirement of allowing applications to be independent of the implementations of the database management system. Also, by moving the concerns of integrity and security out of the application and into the database management system, these systems have proven to be very robust.

6

NEW TERM   *SQL* or Structured Query Language is the industry standard for communicating with a relational database.

Furthermore, the widespread acceptance of the relational model and the corresponding adoption of a standard language (SQL) have allowed practitioners in the industry to develop common practices and share experiences that apply to systems across numerous vendors and platforms. As a result, the database community has a shared level of maturity that stands out within the computer industry.

Basic Elements of a Relational Database

In this section, you will learn about the basic elements of a relational database. The basic RDB elements are

- Tables
- Keys
- Indexes

Tables are the data storage units in a relational database. Most tables have keys, which relate tables to one another and allow for optimal data storage with minimized data redundancy. Indexes are used to search for data and are similar to indexes found in the back of books. The following sections explain these concepts.

Tables

To understand the role of tables in a relational database, it is helpful to understand a little about the underlying mathematical concepts and how these concepts are represented. This section describes the mathematical concept of a *relation* and then shows how a table can be an effective representation.

Relation: A Mathematical Concept

In mathematics, a *set* is any defined collection. For example, you can think of the employees of a company as a *set*. It is easy to think of other sets, such as the set of phone numbers connecting to the same company.

Sets are often given a name; in some cases the name may be as simple as a letter. For convenience, the two sets mentioned previously might be named E (for employees) and P for phone numbers.

Sets can be combined in a number of ways. One of the simplest ways to combine sets is to form a *Cartesian product*. You can form a Cartesian product using sets E and P by listing all the combinations of employees (from set E) and phone numbers (from set P). The resulting list will look like a number of pairs of the form (employee, phone number).

The number of pairs that can be formed—that is, the number of members of the Cartesian product—is simply the number of employees times the number of phone numbers. Therefore, it is not surprising that the Cartesian product is often represented symbolically using the notation E×P.

When a Cartesian product is created, not all the combinations are useful. Usually, it is a subset of the set of combinations that has meaning. For example, the company phone directory is a meaningful subset of all possible combinations of employees and phone numbers for a company.

In mathematics, the term *relation* refers to a subset of a Cartesian product of two or more sets. A *relational database* gets its name by the fact that it is built on the concept of a *relation*.

 New Term A ***Cartesian Product*** is all possible combinations of two or more sets combined together.

Binary and n-ary Relations

The relation between employees and phone numbers is an instance of a *binary* relation because each member of the product contains exactly two values.

You can easily imagine relations involving more than two values. For example, the employee's office number may be included in the product. The set of triples (employee, phone number, office number) is a relation including elements from three sets. This is an example of a *ternary* relation.

The concept can be extended to *quaternary* and beyond to *n-ary* relations.

Representing a Relation as a Table

If you have looked at a company directory, perhaps on paper or in a computerized spreadsheet, you have seen a relation being represented as a table.

A binary relation can be represented as a table with two columns, a ternary relation with three columns, and an n-ary relation as a table with n columns.

> In a relational database, all information is represented by a collection of tables. But unlike a spreadsheet, every table in a relational database is given a name, and every column of every table is also named.
>
> In a relational database, every piece of information must be retrievable directly by identifying a specific row and column within a specific table.

6

A Simple Example: The ABC-Design, Inc. Database

ABC-Design, Inc. is building a database to help its business. The company wants to save information about clients and assignments and to identify color schemes that have been approved by some of its clients. Tables 6.1-6.5 show the database table and column names as well as some of the data that has accumulated.

TABLE 6.1   Client Information

CLIENT ID	CLIENT NAME	EMAIL_ADDRESS	PHONE
1	The Billings Group	admin@billings.com	555-1213
14	Ademco	mikew@ademco.com	555-3323
12	TR Fluff	accts@trfluff.com	555-1200
19	Mark Smith	msmith@localnet.com	555-7665

TABLE 6.2   PURCHASE_ORDER

PO_ID	CLIENT_PO_NUM	CLIENT_ID	PO_DATE	AMOUNT
1	P070	19	12-FEB-2001	2000.00
14	123454	14	04-JUN-2002	195.00
12	P087	19	18-FEB-2001	807.22
19	180201-A	1	13-AUG-2002	1800.00

TABLE 6.3   INVOICE

INV_NUMBER	INV_DATE	PO_ID
0001	14-MAR-2001	1
0014	22-FEB-2001	12

TABLE 6.4   COLOR_SCHEME

COLOR_SCHEME_ID	FOREGROUND	BACKGROUND	HIGHLIGHT
181	Violet	Taupe	White
2021	Med Blue	White	Purple
114	White	Dark Grey	Yellow

TABLE 6.5   CLIENT_APPROVED_COLOR_SCHEME

CLIENT_ID	COLOR_SCHEME
1	181
1	2021
14	114

> In a relational database, tables are arranged in columns and rows. Each column is an attribute of a table, or a more detailed breakdown of the data in the table. For example, the Client Information table has columns that allow for storage of specific client information. Each row in the Client Information table relates to a client record. Each row in a table is an occurrence of data.

Equipped with this new database, the management of ABC-Design, Inc. has the information available to answer several questions about its business. Some of the questions are

- How many outstanding invoices are there?
- What is the total amount of all outstanding invoices?
- What is the total amount of all invoices that have been outstanding for more than 30 days?
- What is the average number of days between purchase order and invoice?

As you can see, even with only a few tables, a number of questions can now be easily asked and answered.

Later you will learn how a person actually goes about posing such questions and retrieving answers from the database.

Keys

The ABC-Design database example shows how a carefully designed collection of tables (that is, a database) can be used to help a company answer questions about its business. To facilitate the task of getting those answers, every table and column has been given a name. Because tables and columns have names, it is easy to understand how tables and columns may be specified. However, a reasonable question to ask is how you might reliably distinguish one row of a table from another.

Although you don't actually name each row of a table, each row can be named by identifying one or more of the data values that are in the row. The column (or set of columns) that contains sufficient data to "name" a row is called a *key* of that table. A table must have at least one key, but there may be other columns (or sets of columns) that can also serve as a key. Therefore, one such column (or set of columns) is always designated as the *primary key*. The others—that is, those that were not selected—are called *candidate* keys.

NEW TERM   *Primary Key* is one or more rows in a table that cause the entire row to be unique.

6

NEW TERM   *Candidate Key* are the remaining rows not selected as or in the Primary Key.

Let's consider the example of the ABC-Design database. Notice that the CLIENT table includes a column called CLIENT_ID. This column is the primary key column for the CLIENT table. The CLIENT_ID column was introduced by the developer to assure that the row for any specific client can always be uniquely identified. Client names might not be unique, and email addresses and phone numbers can change.

For CLIENT_ID to be used as a key, a couple of conditions must be true:

- Every row must have a value for this column.
- The value for the CLIENT_ID in any row of the table must be distinct from all other rows in the table.

Another way of saying this is that to be a key, CLIENT_ID must be Never Null (NN) and Never Duplicated (ND).

It may be less obvious, but a requirement is that key values never be updated—that is, No Changes (NC). Why? Because this key may be referred to in other tables.

For example, the CLIENT_ID appears as a column in the PURCHASE_ORDER table. If you allow the CLIENT_ID value to be changed in the CLIENT table, you would need to track down all references to this key in the PURCHASE_ORDER table and modify them as well. Because a major concern of relational databases is to maintain the integrity of the data, such an update opens the data to unnecessary risk.

Notice that all the tables in the ABC-Design database have key columns. Even the COLOR_SCHEME spreadsheet that has been imported has a key column (COLOR_SCHEME_ID) that was added when the table was moved into the database.

To summarize, each table must have a column or set of columns that serves as a primary key. To be a candidate for this role, three conditions must apply: the values in the candidate key must never be null (NN), they can have no duplicates (ND), and they must never be changed (NC).

Indexes

An index is a database object that is used as a pointer to table data that makes access to a table more efficient.

Consider the simple task of looking up a friend's name in a large metropolitan telephone book. Even though the names are in alphabetical order, it would be impractical to always search for a name by starting with the first entry under "A" and proceeding name by name to find your friend. Instead, you commonly use what is called a *binary search*.

NEW TERM An *Index* is a pointer to a specific data in a table within a database.

Here is the recipe for finding a name in a phone book using a binary search: First, open the book near the middle, thus dividing the pages into a left and a right portion. By considering the alphabetized names, determine whether the name you are seeking is in the left portion or right portion of the divided book. If you determine that the name is on the left, find a page near the middle of the left portion of pages and repeat the evaluation. Is the name before or after the new page you have found?

Without too many steps, the name will be found. In fact, using a binary search, the correct page for any name in a 1,000-page listing can always be found in 10 cuts or fewer. What is even more remarkable, however, is that if the listing had a million pages, the number of required cuts grows to only 20.

Although a computer is a lot faster than a human being, searching a list of a million or more names or IDs one-by-one still takes some time.

By constructing an index for a key data column, it is possible to have the computer search for a name or ID using what is equivalent to a binary search. In fact, even more powerful ways of organizing an index allow names or IDs to be found in fewer steps than is possible with a binary search.

NEW TERM A *Binary Search* divides the possible locations of the data by two, ignores where the data could NOT be, then divides the remainder by two, and so on until the desired data is retrieved.

In addition to speeding searches, indexes are used in a RDBMS to enforce uniqueness, such as the required uniqueness of each table key.

For these reasons, when a RDBS is developed, it is standard practice to create an index on the key column of each table. Additionally, there may be other columns in a table on which efficient searches may be required. Such columns (or sets of columns) may also be associated with indexes.

6

Fortunately for the developer, the task of building each index is handled by the RDBMS. The developer generally needs to do no more than name the index and name the columns to be included.

An index in a database is much like the index in the back of a book. In a book index, keywords are listed alphabetically, providing fast lookup of commonly referenced or important terms. In a book index, each keyword or phrase in the index is associated with a page number, which allows the reader to navigate directly to the appropriate page in the book. Without an index, the reader would have to scan the entire book for sought information. An index in a database works conceptually the same and serves the same purpose as that in a book.

Understanding Relationships Between Data

Some people say that life is all about relationships. It is important to create good relationships with the people around you and maintain those relationships for a pleasant and successful life. In a relational database, relationships are equally important. Solid relationships must be established between data and maintained if your relational database is to be successful. A relational database with poor relational constructs is a recipe for a very unpleasant experience and, ultimately, an unsuccessful database implementation.

Introducing Entities, Attributes, and Relationships

In our earlier discussion of the mathematical notion of a relation, we stated that all databases store information about things, the characteristics of those things, and relationships among things. Within a relational database, these things, characteristics, and relationships are referred to more precisely as *entities*, *attributes*, and *relationships*.

When you develop tables for a RDBS, you must identify the appropriate entities to be represented within your system. How do you decide that something is worth naming? That is, how do you choose the entities that you need to represent? The short answer is that you name entities that you want to record information about. Of course, this leads you to ask yourself what information you want to record. This is both a practical matter based on the goals established for the database system and an art developed through experience.

You can categorize the information to be stored about the entities as one of two types: *attributes*, which are essentially descriptions, and *relationships*, which connect entities with each other. The identified entities, attributes, and relations for a database system are collectively referred to as the *data model* for that system.

It is important to avoid confusing the term *relationship*, meaning the relationship between entities, with the mathematical concept of a *relation*. A table in a relational database is always a mathematical relation. However, each table may represent a single entity or a relationship between entities.

As an example, consider the ABC-Design database introduced earlier. What are the entities? That is, what *things* does the company database record information about? By looking over the tables, it appears that the developer has identified clients, purchase orders, invoices, and color schemes as appropriate entities.

What descriptive information has been recorded for each of these entities? That is, what are the attributes? For the entity client, the CLIENT table has columns for an ID, a name, an email address, and a telephone number. For the purchase order entity, columns record the client's PO number, the client ID, the date of the purchase order, and the amount. Notice that in addition to the client's PO number, this table also contains a purchase order ID (PO_ID). This is a number that has been assigned by ABC-Design, Inc.

It is left to the reader to identify the attributes for the invoices and color schemes.

How Entities May Be Related

Looking further into the ABC-Design database example, you can identify a couple of relationships, between entities. For example, each invoice relates to a single purchase order. This is indicated by the inclusion of the purchase order ID (PO_ID) in each row of the INVOICE table.

Similarly, each purchase order is generated by a single client. Hence, each row of the PURCHASE_ORDER table contains a CLIENT_ID value.

These are examples of *one-to-many relationships*. That is, one client may be responsible for many purchase orders. However, each purchase order comes from only a single client. Similarly, a purchase order may result in many invoices, whereas each invoice applies to a single purchase order.

There is another relationship between entities in the ABC-Design database that is a little more complicated. This relationship can be seen in the CLIENT_APPROVED_COLOR_SCHEME table. Because each client may have approved more than one color scheme, and each color scheme may be approved by many clients, this is an example of a *many-to-many relationship*.

The CLIENT_APPROVED_COLOR_SCHEME table does not relate to a single entity; rather, it relates information about two entities. Its name has been chosen to reflect this fact.

6

How to Communicate with a Relational Database

An earlier section of this hour discussed the importance of establishing relationships with people around us. To establish relationships, a form of communication must exist. You can communicate with a relational database using a language, which is actually much more English-like than you might think.

Structured Query Language

Structured Query Language (SQL) has become the language of relational databases. In fact, the details of SQL that are spelled out in the ANSI standard are often taken as the definition of a relational database. Although this is not correct, it is close enough in the real world that it may be considered a justifiable approximation. SQL is a language that allows developers to implement database designs and to insert, update, and retrieve data from the resulting tables.

Structured Query Language (SQL) will be covered in later hours. It is mentioned in this hour because it is such an important part of relational database technology. In this hour, it is only important to understand the very basic concepts of SQL, not all syntax components.

The Structure of SQL

SQL can be logically grouped into the following three categories:

- *Data Definition Language (DDL)*—This is the part of SQL that is used to communicate the database design to the database management system. DDL operations are used to create objects in your database, such as tables, indexes, and integrity constraints. DDL commands usually start with the word CREATE.

  For example:
  ```
  CREATE TABLE COLOR_SCHEME (
    COLOR_SCHEME_ID NUMBER PRIMARY KEY,
    FOREGROUND VARCHAR2(20),
    BACKGROUND VARCHAR2(20),
    HIGHLIGHT VARCHAR2(20) );
  ```

- *Data Manipulation Language (DML)*—This is the part of SQL that is used to insert, update, and delete (in other words, manipulate) data in database tables. DML commands usually start with the words INSERT, UPDATE, or DELETE.

For example:

```
INSERT INTO COLOR_SCHEME (
   COLOR_SCHEME_ID,FOREGROUND,BACKGROUND,HIGHLIGHT)
VALUES (181,'Violet','Taupe','White');
```

- *Data Query Language (DQL)*—This is the part of SQL that is used to retrieve data from the database. That is, DQL is used to pose questions to the database and retrieve results. DQL commands typically start with the word SELECT.

For example:

```
SELECT FOREGROUND, BACKGROUND, HIGHLIGHT
   FROM COLOR_SCHEME
WHERE COLOR_SCHEME_ID=181;
```

Learning to Think in Sets

An important aspect in SQL is the capability (actually requirement) to query data based on *sets*. That is, rather than trace through data based on individual records, you use SQL to define the *set* of data you care about and let the DBMS do the work of finding and manipulating it.

When communicating the appropriate set of data using SQL, the word WHERE is used. For example, you can say effectively, "I want to see all the purchase orders where the amount is more than $2,000." As an SQL statement, this would look like the following:

```
SELECT PO_ID,CLIENT_PO_NUM
FROM PURCHASE_ORDER
WHERE AMOUNT>2000;
```

Joining Tables

Another important aspect of SQL is the capability to join tables in a single query. By joining tables, you access the power of the relationships between the entities defined in your data model. You might join tables to answer a question such as, "What are the names of the clients having purchase orders over $2,000?" An SQL statement to answer this question would look like the following:

```
SELECT CLIENT.NAME
FROM PURCHASE_ORDER, CLIENT
WHERE CLIENT.CLIENT_ID = PURCHASE_ORDER.CLIENT_ID
AND PURCHASE_ORDER.AMOUNT>2000;
```

Creating Applications Using SQL

An application is usually an executable program that allows a user to access data in a database. An application could be in the form of a compiled program that accepts input from a user, in the form of a client-server "Form" interface with fields and buttons, or in the form of an HTML document that appears in your Web browser (these are just a few

6

examples). A real-world example of and application with which we are all familiar would be one that a bank teller uses to look up your account information. The teller would use the application to query the database by account number, and the database would return the data result set for the targeted account back to the application on the teller's computer.

SQL alone cannot support all the logic that is required for all database applications, nor can it provide the rich interfaces and user environments that users have become accustomed to. To meet these needs, it is often necessary to imbed SQL into other technologies.

This is done in several ways. Many of the well-known suppliers of RDBMSs include a native procedural language that works with SQL to program and store essential database operations.

Some applications remain separated from the database yet still communicate with it. This type of communication is handled through the use of application call interfaces (APIs) or by referencing dynamically created database objects. Two APIs that are in common use are ODBC (Open Database Connectivity) and JDBC (Java Database Connectivity). ODBC and JDBC enable the program developer to communicate with a wide array of database types using a common set of procedures along with SQL.

Other database connectivity options are also becoming available using protocols based on XML.

Summary

In this hour, you first learned about the forces that brought about the development of relational databases. You then learned the fundamentals of relational database theory and the role of tables, keys, and indexes when applying relational theory to create usable systems. Finally, you looked at a few ways in which users and applications interact with data in a relational database.

Q&A

Q How do tables in a database get named?

**A Each table is named by the developers as part of the design process. Table names should identify the entity or entities to which the table refers.

Q Can different tables use the same column names?

**A Tables in a relational database often have columns with the same name as other tables. In some cases, the column may be a reference to the other table—for example, if the column contains primary key values indicating a relationship between entities. In other cases, column names may simply be similar attributes that have no direct relationship to each other.

Workshop

The following workshop consists of quiz questions and practical exercises. The quiz questions are designed to test your overall understanding of the current material. The practical exercises are intended to afford you the opportunity to apply the concepts discussed during the current hour, as well as build on the knowledge acquired in previous hours of study. Please take time to complete this workshop before continuing. You can refer to the answers at the end of the hour.

Quiz

1. Who is credited with publishing a paper in the *Communications of the ACM* that launched the development of the relational database?

2. What do all relational databases use as their primary storage structure?

3. In the mid 1980s, Dr. Codd proposed a set of rules by which a database could be considered relational. How many rules did he propose?

4. What is the term used to name the column or set of columns in a table that uniquely identifies each row?

5. To be considered a primary key, what three conditions must always be true?

6. What is the name of the ANSI standard language used to communicate with a relational database?

Exercises

1. Consider the following Table 6.6, T1, having generic column names (C1, C2, and so on):

TABLE 6.6 T1

C1	C2	C3	C4	C5
101	AA	A123	9	6
102	BB	B123	8	
103	AB	A124	7	7
101	CD	B124	6	
201	EH	C123	5	5

6

From the data that can be seen, which single columns do not qualify to be the primary key?

2. Again, considering Table 6.6 from exercise 1, assume that the primary key has two columns and that C1 is one of the columns. Of the remaining columns (C2 through C5), which ones might be the second part of the primary key?

3. A national company is in the business of leasing vehicles for corporate fleets. The company has a number of offices and keeps track of the vehicles and customers in a corporate database. Consider the following Tables 6.7-6.10 from this database:

TABLE 6.7 VEHICLE_TYPE

VEHICLE_TYPE_CD	COLOR	PASSENGER_COUNT	LEASING_OFFICE_ID
1212	BLUE	5	C12
13144	RED	2	C12
13117	RED	7	C14
13118	WHITE	7	C14

TABLE 6.8 LEASING_OFFICE

LEASING_OFFICE_ID	LOCATION
C11	Indianapolis
C12	Kansas City
C13	Chicago
C14	Virginia Beach

TABLE 6.9 CUSTOMER

CUSTOMER_ID	NAME	BUS_PHONE
3233	ABC Corp.	555-555-1112
3242	The Jackson Group	555-555-1234
3247	SRT, Inc.	555-555-5678

TABLE 6.10 TABLE CUSTOMER_LEASE

CUSTOMER_ID	VEHICLE_ID
3247	1212
3233	13144

What *things* is this database designed to record data about? In other words, what are the *entities* that appear in this database?

4. Consider the four tables in exercise 3; can you find a one-to-many relationship? Can you find a many-to-many relationship?

Answers to Quiz

1. Dr. E. F. Codd
2. Tables
3. 12
4. Primary key
5. Never Null (NN), Unique or Never Duplicated (ND), Never Changed (NC)
6. Structured Query Language (SQL)

Answers to Exercises

1. Column C1 (has duplicates), column C4 (has missing values).
2. From the data that you can see, you can combine either C2 or C3 with C1 to get a unique key. Column C4 is ruled out because it contains null values. Column C5 is ruled out because its values combined with C1 are not unique.
3. Vehicle, Leasing Office, Customer.
4. A one-to-many relationship exists between Leasing Office and Vehicle. A many-to-many relationship exists between Customer and Vehicle.

6

Hour 7

Using Tables and Keys for Fundamental Data Storage

It is impossible to touch a relational database and not touch a table in some way. In this hour, you will explore the role of the table in more detail and study how tables are related to each other through their keys. You will take a look at the important concept of normalization and consider how this process keeps table designs from going astray. Finally, you learn how tables are used in everyday life and how they must be managed to protect against loss or corruption of data.

NEW TERM *Normalization* is the process by which data is divided into smaller, specialized tables in order to reduce repeating or redundant data storage.

In this hour you will learn

- The different types of tables
- How to define tables

- How to use keys to define relationships
- What it means to normalize tables
- How tables are used
- How tables are managed

Types of Tables

As you have seen, all relational databases use tables to organize their data. In the ABC-Design, Inc. database example, you saw examples of tables used to represent individual Entities (CLIENT, PURCHASE_ORDER, INVOICE, and COLOR_SCHEME) and a table used to record the values in a many-to-many relationship between the CLIENT and the COLOR_SCHEME entities (CLIENT_APPROVED_COLOR_SCHEME).

In the previous hour, we touched on database tables as related to the relational architecture. In this hour, we will provide a more in-depth discussion and show more detailed examples of tables in a relational database. After this chapter, you should have a complete understanding of the table.

You could say that every table in a relational database represents either an entity (or perhaps a sub-entity) or a many-to-many relation. However, it is helpful to realize that there are many common uses of tables in which the underlying entities are not the concrete things that you are accustomed to picturing in a database.

Following are some of the types of tables that are often found in a production database:

- *Domain Tables*—Used to enumerate acceptable values for attributes in other tables.
- *Log Tables*—Used to record events such as updates, program exceptions, or various user activities.
- *History Tables*—Used to track changes in other tables.
- *Metadata Tables*—Used to record miscellaneous information about tables, such as descriptions of tables and table columns or notes on the database design.
- *Staging Tables*—Used as a temporary storage location when batch-loading data to insulate production tables from unexpected events that may occur during loading.
- *Process Control Tables*—Used to set up parameters and manage events for internal or external processes that may be managed by the database.

Defining Tables

The simplified version of the syntax for creating a table in SQL is

```
CREATE TABLE table_name (column definitions)
```

Here is an example from MySQL:

```
CREATE TABLE MY_DATA (
    MY_DATA_ID INT UNSIGNED PRIMARY KEY,
    ATTRIBUTE_1 INT,
    ATTRIBUTE_2 INT NOT NULL,
    ATTRIBUTE_3 VARCHAR(20) NOT NULL );
```

As you can see from this example, the portion of the statement that makes up the column definitions includes pairs of column names and data types as well as certain constraints placed on those types, such as NOT NULL and PRIMARY KEY.

Available data types depend on the actual database management system; however, in many cases, ANSI standard data types can be used and the DBMS will convert them to the internal types.

NEW TERM   **Data Type** refers to the attribute associated with the column of data, such as *date* or *number*.

MySQL has a number of data types available, many of them variations of fundamental data types. For example, there are five variations of the integer type in MySQL (TINYINT, SMALLINT, MEDIUMINT, INT, BIGINT) and three variations of real number type (FLOAT, DOUBLE PRECISION, REAL, DECIMAL, NUMERIC). Table 7.1 lists some of the important MySQL data types along with some related types.

TABLE 7.1   MySQL data types

MySQL Data Type	Example	Related Types
INT	INT	TINYINT, SMALLINT, MEDIUMINT, BIGINT
REAL(length, decimals)	REAL(5,2)	FLOAT, DOUBLE PRECISION, DECIMAL, NUMERIC
DATETIME	DATETIME	DATE, TIME, TIMESTAMP
CHAR(length)	CHAR(1)	CHAR BINARY
VARCHAR(length)	VARCHAR(20)	

7

Using Keys to Define Relationships

You have seen how the primary key, along with a table and column name, allows you to identify any single value in the database. In this section, you will look at the primary key in more detail and consider how primary keys in different tables may be used to allow tables to relate to each other.

The Primary Key

Every table can have an attribute (that is, a column) or set of attributes (that is, a set of columns) whose value uniquely identifies every row of the table. This attribute or set of attributes is referred to as the primary key for the table. You have already learned about three requirements for primary keys. These requirements are that they are Never Null, Never Duplicated, and Never Changed.

It is worth emphasizing that more than one set of columns could be designated as the primary key, but that only one set may be chosen. The columns that could serve as the primary key (columns that were not selected) are referred to as *candidate keys*.

Consider the COLOR_SCHEME table in the ABC-Design, Inc. database from the previous section. When this data was migrated from its spreadsheet into the database, the developer did three things. First, the table was given a name (COLOR_SCHEME). Second, each column in the table was given a name (FOREGROUND, BACKGROUND, and HIGHLIGHT). Third, the developer added a fourth column (COLOR_SCHEME_ID) to serve as the primary key.

Would it have been possible to use one or more of the existing columns (FOREGROUND, BACKGROUND, and HIGHLIGHT) as a primary key for this table? It is easy to see that no single column would work, because it is likely that the same color will be used in many rows for the FOREGROUND, BACKGROUND, or HIGHLIGHT. Similarly, you cannot define the primary key as the combination of any two of the columns (for example, FOREGROUND and BACKGROUND), because any pair of values may occur with many different values for the remaining attribute.

What about using all three values—FOREGROUND, BACKGROUND, and HIGH-LIGHT—as the primary key? Such a combination can easily meet the requirements for NN (not null) and ND (no duplicates). However, if you decide to modify the HIGH-LIGHT for one of these triplets, this would require violating the NC (no changes) requirement for a primary key. As a result, the developer chose to add a new column (COLOR_SCHEME_ID) to serve as the primary key attribute for the table.

The Value of "Artificial" Keys

The COLOR_SCHEME_ID is an example of an "artificial" primary key. That is, the numbers making up the key are arbitrarily assigned, having no derived relationship to the data.

Is this a good idea? What if the developer had decided to create a primary key by concatenating the first two letters of each of the three colors—something like this:

```
vi-ta-wh (for violet, taupe, white)
```

Such a key has a certain appeal because users who access the database can often learn to recognize the key as a shorthand for the data represented by the row.

The problem with this is that the designers may decide to change the highlight color from white to something else, such as gold. You are then faced with the decision to either live with a key that no longer matches the data or to update the key and all references to the key in all other tables. In a large database, such updates can entail a great deal of risk. Furthermore, if a number of printed reports have been created over the years, there is no easy way to correct these reports.

What about the CLIENT table? Again, an artificial key (CLIENT_ID) has been assigned. Surely you could use an abbreviated version of the client's name as a suitable key. Unfortunately, companies do change their name. Occasionally, the original entries in the database are spelled incorrectly and are corrected at a later date. If you had developed a primary key based on the incorrect spelling of a company name, what do you do with that key when the company name is finally corrected?

As a result, many developers prefer to use artificial keys, unless a well-established and permanent natural key can be identified. Although suitable natural keys do exist, they are not as common as you might expect.

> A bit more about **Natural Keys** versus **Artificial Keys**; A Natural Key is one that is based upon actual data that is being stored in the table. Primary Keys that are also Natural Keys are used, but should only be used on data that is not apt to have updates, such as social security number. An Artificial Key is NOT based upon the data that is stored in the table, but is still unique. A generated number or system assigned key (SAK) for each newly inserted row is a common Primary Key that is also an Artificial Key.

Representing One-to-Many Relationships with a Foreign Key

When you look at the PURCHASE_ORDER table in the ABC-Design database, you can see that the PRIMARY KEY for CLIENT (CLIENT_ID) has been included as an attribute of the purchase order. This is a special type of attribute called a *foreign key*.

7

A foreign key is an attribute in a table that is a primary key in another table. A foreign key establishes a relationship between the two tables and is used to represent a relationship between the entities represented by each of the tables.

The relationship between PURCHASE_ORDER and CLIENT is of a particular type called a one-to-many relationship. Each purchase order must be from a single client. However, each client may submit many purchase orders. You can use a diagram to represent this type of relationship, as shown in Figure 7.1.

FIGURE 7.1

Diagramming the one-to-many relationship between PURCHASE_ORDER and CLIENT.

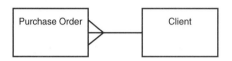

In Figure 7.1, the line connecting PURCHASE_ORDER and CLIENT splits into three little lines at the point where it connects to PURCHASE_ORDER. This split is called a crow's-foot and implies that PURCHASE_ORDER is on the many side of this one-to-many relationship.

A one-to-many relationship is represented in the database by placing the PRIMARY KEY of the "one" side of the relationship into the table representing the entity of the "many" side. The inserted primary key is called a foreign key.

In this example, you expect one client to have many purchase orders. Thus, you place the primary key for the client (CLIENT_ID) into the table representing the purchase order.

In the example, you also have one-to-many relationships between the purchase orders and the invoices (one purchase order to many invoices). As a result, INVOICE includes PO_ID as a foreign key.

 One-to-Many Relationship is such that one row from a given table may relate to more than one row in another table.

Representing Many-to-Many Relationships

The ABC-Design database also includes an example of a many-to-many relationship. Each client may approve many color schemes and each color scheme may be approved by many clients. We can represent this many-to-many relationship in a diagram, as shown in Figure 7.2.

Because a many-to-many relationship exists between the two tables, Figure 7.2 uses a crow's-foot attached to each of the tables.

FIGURE 7.2

Diagramming the many-to-many relationship between CLIENT and COLOR_SCHEME.

FIGURE 7.2

Diagramming the many-to-many relationship between CLIENT and COLOR_SCHEME.

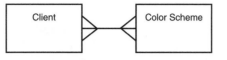

Can this type of relationship be represented using a foreign key, as in the one-to-many relationship? Consider the possibility of placing the COLOR_SCHEME_ID into the CLIENT table. That would allow you to identify only a single approved scheme for each client, unless you added a column for each color scheme approved. But how many columns should you add? What is the maximum number of approved color schemes you will allow?

Similarly, you cannot add the CLIENT_ID to COLOR_SCHEME, because that would restrict you to one client per color scheme. Again, this is true unless you arbitrarily add additional columns for each possible client approval.

NEW TERM **Many-to-Many Relationship** is such that many rows from a given table may relate to more than one row in another table.

Many-to-many relationships are resolved using a cross-reference or associative table. CLIENT_APPROVED_COLOR_SCHEME is an example of an associative table. The diagram in Figure 7.3 shows how an associative table has been introduced to resolve the many-to-many relationship.

FIGURE 7.3

Introducing the CLIENT_APPROVED_ COLOR_SCHEME associative table to resolve the many-to-many relationship between CLIENT and COLOR_SCHEME.

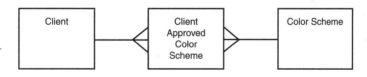

In Figure 7.3, you can see how the associative table (CLIENT_APPROVED_COLOR_ SCHEME) resolves the many-to-many relationship by creating two one-to-many relationships.

The associative table will contain foreign keys for each of the entities that are related. The combined set of foreign keys establish the primary key for the associative table.

7

In the CLIENT_APPROVED_COLOR_SCHEME table, CLIENT_ID and
COLOR_SCHEME_ID are foreign keys to CLIENT and COLOR_SCHEME, respectively. The primary key for the CLIENT_APPROVED_COLOR_SCHEME table is the
pair of columns CLIENT_ID and COLOR_SCHEME_ID.

Associative Tables, Subentities, and Compound Keys

CLIENT_APPROVED_COLOR_SCHEME is an example of a table having a compound
primary key. In this case, the primary key is composed of the pair of columns
CLIENT_ID and COLOR_SCHEME_ID. Neither column alone would be sufficient to
uniquely identify a row of the table because any client may appear with many color
schemes and any color scheme may appear with many clients.

Another case exists in which a table will have a compound primary key.

Consider a large school that maintains a database of available classrooms in a number of
buildings. Two of the tables in the database may look something like Tables 7.2 and 7.3.

TABLE 7.2   BUILDING

BUILDING_NUM	BUILDING_NAME
1017	Johnson Biology Center
1259	Markley Library
1003	Axton Arts and Sciences

TABLE 7.3   BUILDING_CLASSROOM

BUILDING_NUM	CLASSROOM_NUM	SEAT_COUNT
1017	102	27
1017	102a	29
1017	201	55

BUILDING_CLASSROOM represents the classroom entity; that is, each row represents
a single classroom. Because each classroom cannot exist outside of a particular building,
BUILDING_CLASSROOM is actually a subentity of BUILDING. In fact, the chosen
table name, BUILDING_CLASSROOM, serves to emphasize this subentity relationship.

As a subentity, BUILDING_CLASSROOM will have a compound key. The first part of
the key (BUILDING_NUM) is a foreign key to the parent entity (BUILDING). The
remaining part of the key (CLASSROOM_NUM) uniquely identifies the classroom

within the building. Both parts of the key are needed to form the primary key and uniquely define a room.

The Issue of Compound Keys

You have seen that associative tables and sub-entities may have compound primary keys. As a general rule, tables representing single entities should have simple (that is, single-column) primary keys.

This rule is not absolute. But in general, compound primary keys are more difficult to work with, particularly when using them as a foreign key and when involving them in queries that join related tables.

If you find yourself creating a table with a compound key, ask yourself if this table represents an association of entities or possibly a sub-entity. If so, what are the entities being associated? Or in the latter case, what is the parent entity? Do you have tables representing each of these other entities?

If the table having a compound key is not an associative or sub-entity table, ask yourself if a compound key is the best solution. Often, a single meaningless ID field will be the best solution.

Normalizing Tables

Is it possible to be unique and normal at the same time? It is in the world of the relational database. In this section, you will learn what it means to normalize a database and how the normalization process is used to assure that each value in the database is uniquely represented.

What Does It Mean to Normalize a Database?

Normalization is a process that is applied to a database design. The goal of the process is to assure that all attributes are assigned to appropriate tables and a suitable primary key has been identified.

From a practical viewpoint, the goal of normalization is to eliminate redundant data. Redundant data not only wastes resources, it creates the possibility of storing values that are not consistent across the database.

When a database is properly normalized, it is also easier to insert, update, and delete data because each attribute value is represented in a single location.

Finally, a normalized database provides a solid framework for modifying and extending the design of the database as future needs arise.

7

During the normalization process, the developer determines whether the design meets certain goals that are referred to as *normal forms*. The three most important of these normal forms are discussed next.

First Normal Form

To be in first normal form, the values of any attribute in any row of a table must depend on the primary key.

To understand this, consider Table 7.4 having STUDENT_ID as a primary key:

TABLE 7.4 TABLE STUDENT

STUDENT_ID	COURSE_NUM_1	GRADE_1	COURSE_NUM_2	GRADE_2	COURSE_NUM_3	GRADE_3
1011622	BIO101	95	SOC201	92		
2211244	MAT201	87	SOC201	85	MAT204	90

Now, consider how this table might be used to answer the following question: What grade did student 2211244 make in Math 204? Can the answer be determined on the basis of the primary key alone? No. To answer this question, in addition to finding the row having primary key 2211244, you must also determine which column contains course number MAT204 and then make the assumption that the appropriate grade will be in the associated column.

The value for the attribute you are seeking (grade) is not solely determined by the primary key (STUDENT_ID).

The problems get even worse if you consider the task of calculating the average grade in MAT204 for all students. The values to be averaged will not necessarily be in the same column for all students.

Another major concern is what to do if you find a student who decides to work a little harder and take four courses instead of the expected three. Do you modify your table design just for this one student?

The GRADE_NUM/COURSE_NUM pairs in this example are an example of what is called a repeating group. When you see a repeating column or group of columns in a table, you know that the table is not in first normal form.

Second Normal Form

To be in second normal form, if a table has a compound primary key, the value of any attribute in any row must depend on all columns of the primary key.

If, for example, the primary key of a table has two columns, an attribute is dependent on the entire key if neither of the primary key columns is sufficient on its own to determine the attribute's value.

This normal form concerns itself only with tables having compound keys. From the previous discussion, you expect this to apply to associative tables and tables representing subentities.

Consider Table 7.5 having STUDENT_ID and COURSE_NUM as primary key.

TABLE 7.5 TABLE STUDENT_COURSE

STUDENT_ID	COURSE_NUM	INSTRUCTOR	GRADE
1011622	MAT101	Susan Jameson	77
1011622	BIO101	Mark McKensey	95
1011622	SOC201	Terry Sanders	92
2211244	MAT201	Pat Ericson	87
2211244	SOC201	Terry Saunders	85

Each student has many grades. Therefore, STUDENT_ID alone cannot tell us the grade for any specific course. Also, because each course is taken by many students, the COURSE_NUM alone (without the STUDENT_ID) is insufficient to determine a grade. The GRADE attribute belongs in this table because it depends on the entire primary key.

Unlike GRADE, the value of the INSTRUCTOR attribute does not depend on the entire primary key. The instructor is determined by the course number. The STUDENT_ID is completely irrelevant. As a result, this table is not in second normal form.

When a table is not in second normal form, attribute values will be unnecessarily repeated. As a result, whenever the value of an attribute changes, multiple rows will need to be updated. In our example, if an instructor for a course is replaced, the instructor's name would need to be updated for every student taking the course.

When values are repeated in a database, there is a risk that the values may not be consistent. In this example, what is the correct spelling of the name of the teacher in course SOC201?

Third Normal Form

To be in third normal form, the value of any attribute in any row must depend on only the primary key and must not depend on any other attribute (or set of attributes) in that row except for candidate keys. To see why attributes cannot depend on other attributes, consider Table 7.6 having COURSE_NUM as primary key.

TABLE 7.6 TABLE COURSE

COURSE_NUM	COURSE_NAME	DEPARTMENT_ID	DEPARTMENT_NAME
MAT101	Algebra and Trig	16	Math
BIO101	Intro. to Biology	14	Biology
SOC201	Intro. to Sociology	12	Sociology
MAT201	Calculus II	16	Mathematics
MAT211	Intro. to Statistics	16	Mathematics

In this table, the value of the department name attribute depends on the value in the department ID column. Because each department ID will appear in the list many times, each department name will appear more than once, leaving open the possibility that it will be spelled inconsistently (as with the Math department) or worse, be entirely incorrect.

With the preceding table as defined, if the school decides to move a course to a different department, say from the Mathematics to a new Statistics department, it would be necessary to update both the DEPARTMENT_ID and DEPARTMENT_NAME columns. Failure to do so will result in inconsistent data.

Other Normal Forms

The normal forms listed previously were the three forms initially outlined by Dr. Codd. Although additional normal forms have been defined, the first three are generally viewed as the most critical to assure a good design.

The "Buzz" of Denormalization

A person does not need to be a database practitioner very long before the subject of denormalization comes up. The term is often accompanied by pronouncements that in the "real world," performance requirements make it necessary to design databases that are not fully normalized.

It is beyond the scope of this book to analyze the necessity or wisdom of denormalization. However, it is worth remembering that when encountering relational databases for the first time, it is often a little unsettling to have attributes distributed among many tables, even when the concept of normal forms is understood. Because of this, it is easy to be lured into the "wisdom" of denormalization without a complete consideration of the consequences.

Managing Tables

In a production database, tables must be carefully managed to meet a number of concerns. First, to avoid failures because of insufficient storage, you must monitor and plan table size while avoiding excessive waste of system resources.

Security is another major concern. The database manager must decide and enforce which individuals and processes should be allowed to access each table (or portion of a table) and in what manner.

A third area that must be managed is the capability to recover from system failures or human error. What is the acceptable level of data loss? What is the maximum acceptable time between disaster and recovery?

Although the DBMS is capable of automatically dealing with many of these issues at some level, production systems require the experienced hand of a knowledgeable database administrator (DBA) .

Summary

In this hour, you learned about the various ways tables are used within a relational database management system. You then looked at the syntax for creating tables and summarizing data types available in MySQL.

Next, you learned the fundamentals of database design, considering the use of keys to define relationships between tables and some important principles of normalization.

Finally, you looked at the way in which tables are used and summarized some of the typical database management concerns.

Q&A

Q If a table can have many sets of candidate keys, how is one set chosen as the primary key?

A Any candidate key is by definition a suitable primary key. There is no rule, but generally simpler keys, especially single-column keys, are the easiest to use.

Q Do tables need to be normalized?

A No. However, normalized tables eliminate redundant data and are easier to maintain. There are occasions when a developer might choose to denormalize selected tables, but this should only be done after a careful analysis of the trade-offs. Additionally, staging tables are often not normalized by design because they are used to rapidly load data, deferring clean-up to a later step in the process.

7

Workshop

The following workshop consists of quiz questions and practical exercises. The quiz questions are designed to test your overall understanding of the current material. The practical exercises are intended to afford you the opportunity to apply the concepts discussed during the current hour, as well as build on the knowledge acquired in previous hours of study. Please take time to complete this workshop before continuing. You can refer to the answers at the end of the hour.

Quiz

1. What is a foreign key?

2. Table X and Table Y have a one-to-many relationship. To represent this relationship, which table will hold the foreign key?

3. What type of relationship requires an associative table?

4. What are two situations for which you expect to use a compound primary key?

5. In his 1970 publication in the *Communications of the ACM*, how many normal forms did Dr. Codd define?

Exercises

1. Each of the following tables fails to meet the conditions for one of the three normal forms. For each table, identify the normal form violation.

TABLE 7.7   TABLE REPLACEMENT_PART

PART_ NUMBER	MANUFAC- TURER	LOC_ID_1	AVAIL	LOC_ID_2	AVAIL	LOC_ID_3	AVAIL
P10155	X-Corp.	Store-6	18	Store-3	27	Store-18	6
P22353	X-Corp.	Store-2	4	Store-3	3	Store-12	8

TABLE 7.8   TABLE STORE_LOCATION

LOC_ID	CITY	MANAGER_EMP_ID	MANAGER_LAST_NAME
Store-1	Indianapolis	3456	Smith
Store-3	Columbus	7898	Jones
Store-18	Cleveland	1876	Barney

TABLE 7.9   TABLE REPLACEMENT_PART_AVAILABILITY

PART_NUMBER	LOC_ID	NUM_AVAIL	PART_NAME
P10155	Store-6	18	Wheel Bearing
P22353	Store-12	8	Wheel Spoke
P10155	Store-3	27	Wheel Bearing

2. Consider the following two tables:

TABLE 7.10   TABLE EMPLOYEE

EMPLOYEE_ID	EMPLOYEE_NAME
123434	J.Brown
323232	M.Black
456454	C.Grey

TABLE 7.11   TABLE FACILITY

FACILITY_ID	LOCATION	NUMBER_OF_OFFICES
F12	Indianapolis	118
F18	Phoenix	200
F27	Las Vegas	104

Each employee is assigned to a single facility. Each facility will have many assigned employees. How would you modify these two tables to represent the relationship between facility and employee?

3. Consider the tables in Exercise 2. If each employee can be assigned to more than one facility, how would this information be represented?

Answers to Quiz

1. A foreign key is a column or set of columns in a table that is a primary key in another table. A foreign key is used to represent a relationship between the two tables.

2. The foreign key is always placed on the "many" side of a one-to-many relationship. In this case, the foreign key would be placed in Table Y.

3. A many-to-many relationship requires an associative table.

4. A compound primary key would appear in tables representing subentities and in associative tables.

5. Three.

Answers to Exercises

1. In Table 7.7, the repeated columns of location ID and availability are a violation of first normal form.

   Because the manager's name is dependent on another attribute (MANAGER_EMP_ID), Table 7.8 is a violation of third normal form.

   Because the part name depends only on the part number (and not on the location ID), Table 7.9 is a violation of second normal form.

2. Add the FACILITY_ID column to the EMPLOYEE table. This is the "many" side of the one-to-many relationship.

3. A new associative table having columns EMPLOYEE_ID and FACILITY_ID would be needed.

HOUR **8**

Optimizing Data Storage with Indexes

A table in a database allows you to store from one to millions of rows of related information. In fact, the size of a table is limited only by the space available on your hardware. Database developers must plan for efficient data retrieval. When a query needs to retrieve a row from a table, the query has to find where the row is located. When a table has many rows, the time spent to find that row increases as the table grows in size. A fast computer can spend minutes processing a query in a large table, which may yield an unacceptable response time in which data is returned to the requesting user. It is essential in most databases to provide a method for efficient and speedy data retrieval. In most databases, this is handled by using an index, which can be compared to the index in the back of a book.

After this hour, you should understand

- The need for indexes
- The different classes of indexes
- The different types of indexes

- Objects used to supplement the use of indexes
- How indexes work
- How indexes are used
- Database optimization

Understanding the Need for Indexes

When a query has to look through an entire table to find the specific row or rows it needs, it is called a full table scan. In the database world, a full table scan should be avoided in most cases.

One way to facilitate a query is to use a database object called an *index*. Simply stated, an index is a sorted list of the records and where the records reside in a table. If the rows in a table were stored in sequential order, there would be little use for an index. However, data is not stored this way. It is entered randomly and, if need be, sorted out as it is retrieved. The index keeps a specific order of the indexed column values, which reduces a search that would have taken minutes to one completed within seconds, sometimes fractions of a second. This is analogous to the index at the back of the book, which helps the reader find an entry in the book much quicker than looking through each page one at a time.

When an index is created, the database makes a copy of the indexed column or the column that the index will use as the key to find records. It will sort it, attach a name to it, and create pointers to where each index entry resides on the table (see Figure 8.1).

FIGURE 8.1

The sorted index list shows where each row is located in the table.

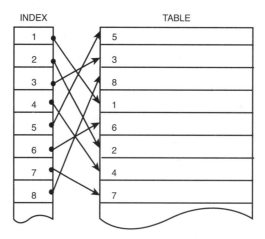

By the end of this hour, you will have learned about the different types of indexes and how and when to use them. You will also learn that full table scans are not always bad.

You will know what to do when your query takes longer than expected. At the end of the hour, an exercise in creating and using an index is included in the workshop section.

Classifying Indexes

There are two classes of indexes: single and concatenated. In a single index, the values of one table column are used as entries on the index. On a concatenated or composite index, more than one column is used in an index to produce unique values.

For example, suppose that you are creating a table with information about the residents of several neighborhoods. You want it to be unique so you can select a single record using their indexed columns. Not all residents have telephones, so you cannot use phone numbers in the index. You could use the house number, but you may end up with repeated values. You cannot use the first or last name because of the high probability of redundancy.

NEW TERM In a *Single Index* the values of one and only one column of the table are used as entries on the index. The *Composite Index* utilizes the values of two or more columns to create the index.

However, if you could use all three columns of the first name, last name, and house number, you can have a combination that has a very high probability of being unique. How many homeowners with the same name live in a house with the same number? That would be highly unlikely. The index will contain all three columns. The order in which to place those columns in the index has been the subject of many debates. Many opinions favor placing the most selective columns first (in this case the house number). However, the way a query uses an index is probably more important. The speed of the query is driven more by how the index is used in the query than by which column is placed first in the index. Here is an example that illustrates this type of query:

```
select * from neighbor_table
where first_name = 'Juan'
  and  last_name = 'Gonzalez'
  and house_number = '2343';
```

The * in the SELECT statement represents "all columns" from the neighbor_table. The WHERE clause is limiting the results to all first names that match Juan, all last names that match Gonzalez, and all house numbers that match 2343. If all of these conditions are not met, no results will be returned by the query. If one of the items in the WHERE clause is false, no results will be returned. Only rows that match all of these conditions will be returned.

The order of the columns in the composite index that will provide for a more efficient search is first_name, last_name, and house_number.

However, if you already made the index using, for example, house_number, last_name, and first_name, in that order, the query that will provide fastest results is the following:

```
select * from neighbor_table
where house_number = '2343'    and last_name = 'Gonzalez'
  and first_name = 'Juan';
```

Types of Indexes

There are several types of indexes, and many of these types vary according to each database vendor. Logically, all indexes work the same way, but some are more efficient than others depending on how the data is stored and accessed. To some degree, you have control over how data is stored, but for the most part, data is physically stored as designed by each database vendor. If you are using the Oracle database, for example, some index types may not be available in Microsoft Access. In any case, it is important to understand some of the most popular and widely implemented indexes.

The types of common indexes discussed in the following subsections include:

- Binary tree index
- Bitmap index
- Reverse key index

Binary Tree Index

The binary tree index is the most commonly used index. In databases such as Oracle, this is the default index. Therefore, if you create an index and do not specify what type, this is what you will get. The binary tree index is a memory structure that stores the values of the primary key in its "leaves." In the concept of the binary tree index, the leaf is reached by dividing the search in terms of two—thus the binary terminology. After the leaf is reached, the table row is found.

For example, to find any number between 1 and 16, the tree in Figure 8.1 searches its way by moving to different levels. It takes the index four steps to find a number between 1 and 16. The number of steps to find a row is given by $\log_2 16$, which is the same as $\log_{10} 16$ divided by $\log_{10} 2$. Figure 8.2 illustrates the number of steps, or levels of the tree, to reach a leaf.

FIGURE 8.2

Representation of a classical binary tree.

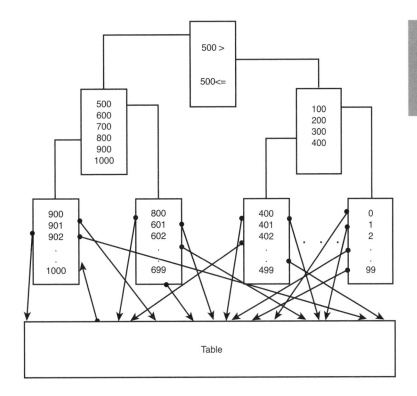

Currently, most indexes have no more than three or four levels, even for those with millions of indexed records. That is because the binary trees no longer look for records basing their search in $\log_2 x$ alone, but also mix a sequential search. The index finds its way from one level to another, and then the index looks sequentially within the leaf to find the desired row. Figure 8.3 illustrates a modern binary tree index structure for a table of 1,000 rows.

The binary tree index works well with small and large tables alike as long as most of the indexed column entries are unique. When the values of a column have many distinct values, it is known as having a *high cardinality*. When the column values have a great number of repeated entries, or low cardinality, the binary tree is not very useful in finding the desired table rows quickly. Another type of index, the bitmap index, helps in this situation.

Bitmap Index

As stated previously, the bitmap index is used when many of the values on the indexed column are repeated. For example, a column that holds values M for masculine and F for feminine has a cardinality of two (only two different values) and repeats a lot. Figure 8.4 shows a binary index.

FIGURE 8.3

*Modern binary tree
index structure.*

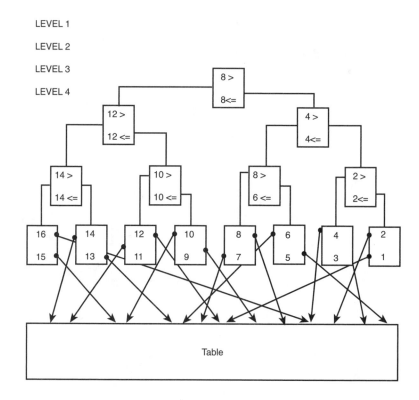

LEVEL 1

LEVEL 2

LEVEL 3

LEVEL 4

Table

FIGURE 8.4   Row1234567891011121314151ValueM110000001101011F001111110010100

*Bitmap index
representation.*

The binary index creates a bitmap for the table rows where the values of either F or M
are located in the table. Different from the binary tree index where an entry in the index
maps to a row in a table, a bitmap index entry maps to many table rows. In the case of
Figure 8.4, the index points to rows 1, 2, 9, 10, 12, 14, and 15 having the value M and
3–8, 11, and 13 having the value F.

Bitmap indexes are used in tables that are rarely updated. These can be found in applications such as data warehousing, where data is stored and seldom updated. One example
is food market applications. Here, a database stores all items bought by customers for
data analysis of consumer purchasing patterns.

NEW TERM   ***Bitmap Indexes*** map to many rows in the table where there are repeating values,
generally where there is a high degree of cardinality (either value A or value B)
and the data is very seldom updated.

Because an entry in the bitmap index contains many pointers to a table, if one row is updated, all rows on that bitmap are prevented from being updated or locked until the bitmap index is updated. This creates delays and it is quite inefficient when many users need to update the table. SQL Server and Sybase do not support bitmap indexes at this time.

Reverse Key Index

The reverse key index is similar to a binary tree index, but its values are stored in reverse. As you can see in Figure 8.5, if an index is created on a table and its entries are added with sequential orders, the right side of the tree will be filled before any entries are written to the left side. Therefore, because of the nature of the data, the index is not being used efficiently. A reverse key index will reverse the entries to spread the values along the index leafs. Figures 8.5 and 8.6 show the new values in the reverse key index.

 NEW TERM *Reverse Key Indexes* operate in reverse of the binary tree index in order to better utilize the indexing on the table when sequential transactions are made.

FIGURE 8.5
Reverse key index representation for numbers.

Entryreverse key index value1000011011011022011033301...

FIGURE 8.6
Reverse key index representation for character strings.

EntryReverse key index value
PATTERSONNOSRETTAPPAULLUAPPENCEECNEPPENSSNEP...

Other Objects That Optimize Storage

Although the index is the primary object in a relational database that is used to optimize the retrieval of data, other objects can be used in conjunction with the index that may further streamline data access.

Some other common database objects that may be used to supplement the use of indexes are

- Index organized tables
- Clustered tables
- Table partitions

As stated earlier, each database vendor varies according to how data is stored and the types of indexes available. Some vendors may not provide some of the objects discussed in the following subsections, such as clustered tables or partitions.

Index Organized Tables

The organization of data according to an index key is a common way to store data among different database implementations. In Sybase and in SQL Server, it is known as a clustered index. In Oracle it is known as an Index Organized Table (IOT). This is a table in which its structure is organized in the manner of the binary tree index. Whereas the example of a binary tree index is the index at the back of a book, an example of an IOT is a dictionary. Usually, dictionaries do not have an index because words are sought in alphabetical order and because the book is organized that way. This enables you to look for the specific word because you know where it should be.

If you have a one-column table—the serial numbers of a product, for example, or tables that translate a code, such as those that translate telephone area codes to states or airport codes to airport names—you have a candidate for an IOT. In the case of the one-column table, because the table values are already in the index, the table is not necessary. Actually, the existence of the table is pure overhead that slows down the query.

IOTs are used in any case where the primary key is used to access the table frequently. The leaves of the tree contain the primary key and the remaining row columns. When the rows of an IOT become too big for the IOT to be effective and a user-defined threshold limit is reached, the row continues to be stored in an overflow area. This overflow limit is defined at IOT creation.

Clustered Tables

The index clustered table—not to be confused with the Clustered Index—is a way to store related sets of rows in the same memory block for fast retrieval. Tables that are frequently joined, such as the example in Tables 8.1 and 8.2, are good candidates to be stored in clusters.

TABLE 8.1   Student Table

STUDENT_ID	FNAME	FNAME	MAJOR
50975657	ERICKA	FOX	3
18815042	LINDA	FARIES	3
88095482	WADE	STEEN	3

TABLE 8.1 continued

STUDENT_ID	FNAME	FNAME	MAJOR
577722	MARSHA	FERGUSON	3
83348488	MARSHA	RUNNELS	3

TABLE 8.2 Major Table

DEPT_ID	NAME
1	Health Sciences
2	Fine Arts
3	Dentistry
4	Education

Because of normalization, student information has been divided between two tables. However, the sole information of either one is incomplete. A table join is a regular operation that would occur to gather "who is studying what" at the school. A clustered table prejoins the tables. In other words, it stores the information, as it would have been queried with a join. To find out the students' major, the query can be the following:

```
Select * from students a, major b
Where a.major = b.dept_id
And dept_id = 3;
```

The preceding query returns which students have major number 3. The clustered table stores information as it would have been retrieved by the preceding query.

Figure 8.7 shows which students' major is number 3, Dentistry. When a query is made that joins tables A and B, rather than read the student table and figure out who is where, it reads the clustered table in a block of memory where the information has already been preselected.

FIGURE 8.7
Clustered table.

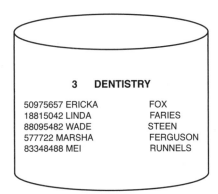

An obvious benefit is faster information retrieval with minimal input-output operations. On the other side, if you wanted to list all the school's students, the query would be faster if the data did not form part of a cluster. Also, because they are more complex structures than a simple table, repeated modifications to the information in the cluster are not very efficient and affect database performance.

Table Partitions

Table partitioning is the division of a table into sections that allow the query of a part of the table rather than the whole. It also makes a table more manageable because storage, backup, and recovery are possible in a table partition. These sections are divided according to a *partition key* that defines how the table is partitioned.

Partitions are not designed to enhance performance. It is possible that a slight performance improvement may result from a proper way to implement partitions in the most accessed tables. However, if you decide to partition your largest tables, do it because it provides an easier way to manage data. If partitions are not properly implemented (using a good key, good local or global indexes, and the like), they may be more of a drag than a help.

You can use several methods to partition a table. One that is commonly used is called range partitioning. Here, a classical partition key is by date periods. Data that belongs to a specific year can be stored in a partition.

A query such as

```
Select * from loan_table where year = 2002;
```

will look only at the partition with a key with the date equaling 2002. However, once there, the search will continue using a partitioned index. In essence, a local index is concerned with only one table partition. All the entries of a local partitioned index point to the indexed column of a given partition alone.

The advantage of the local index is that it is easier to manage. When a partition is moved to another location, only the local index associated with such a partition needs to be created again, or rebuilt. If the partition is deleted, the index used on that partition will be deleted as well, and you do not have to do anything else because the other local indexes are independent of each other. SQL Server and Oracle support local partition indexes. Figure 8.8 shows the setup of local indexes.

A *global* index is also partitioned; however, one partition of the global index contains entries for all table partitions. This type of index is suited for On Line Transaction Processing (OLTP) where many small read and write transactions take place. An airline reservation database is an example of an OLTP system. If a partition is moved to another location, or deleted, the entire global index must be rebuilt. If your table has millions and millions of rows, it can take a while to rebuild an index. Figure 8.9 illustrates the concept of the global index. Global partition indexes are supported only by Oracle.

FIGURE 8.8
Local indexes.

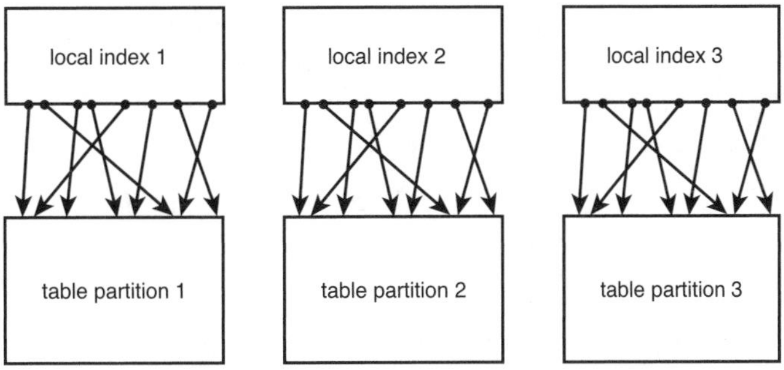

FIGURE 8.9
Global indexes.

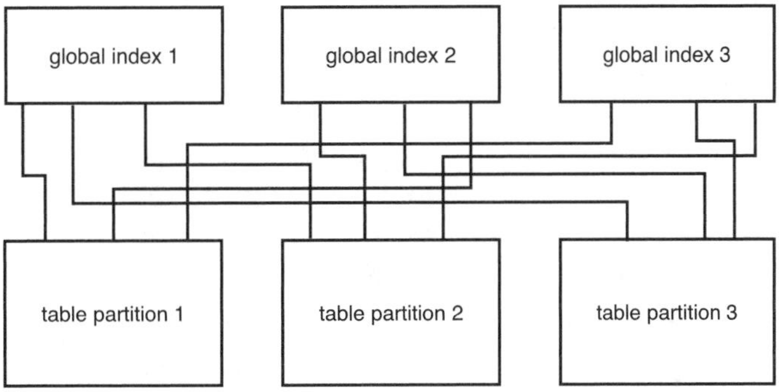

How Indexes Are Used

Indexed columns are usually used when joining tables. Indexes increase the performance of update, select, and delete operations. However, insert operations take longer on indexed columns because every time an insert operation occurs, the existing index has to be updated with the new rows and values. This is the reason why having too many indexes in a table can be detrimental to query performance. On every insert, all the indexes on the table have to be updated. On the same line, having indexes on columns that are never referenced contributes to slower queries and do nothing to speed queries.

If an index does not exist, the query traverses the entire table on a full table scan, looking to satisfy the query made. If an index exists and the query returns one row, it can be very fast. However, a query can return more than one row. The question is, how many rows can be retrieved by a query and still be faster than a full table scan? It is our opinion that if less than 10% of the total table rows are returned by a query, the query will be well served in having an index.

If more than 10% of the rows are returned, not having an index can produce faster results. The best way to decide whether an index will work for you is to try one. Make an index and design a query that returns various table percentages and a full table scan. Then you will be in a better position to decide whether to use an index. Also, if you decide not to use an index, having objective proof of your decision will help when your colleagues tell you that you need one. Some people think that indexes should be used whenever they can fit one, but in reality, indexes will not always help you. By making a test you can decide that for yourself.

If you have a small table, in all probability having an index will not provide significant improvement to the query speed, unless the percentage of rows returned is 1% or less. A table with fewer than 1,000 rows falls into the category of small tables.

One of the problems you will encounter with indexes is inefficiency. Suppose that you build a new binary index. After lots of inserts, updates, and deletes, the values of the table heavily weigh on one side of the index tree. For example, if in Figure 8.3, the values on the indexed column average below 500, most of the values will reside on the right branch and your index will not be very efficient.

The more spread out the values on an index, the faster it will find the queried values. The fix for this type of problem is to rebuild the index. The new index will have the column values spread throughout the index for higher efficiency. How do you know if your index starts to get skewed? The data dictionary of your database has tables containing a variety of index parameters where you can find how your index is structured, how many levels it has, and much more information.

Cost Optimizer and Hints

The optimizer is the component of the database software that determines the execution plan to process a query. Not all queries are created equal; therefore, they are individually processed by the optimizer and will find the most efficient way to run a query. Most implementations, such as SQL Server, Sybase, and Oracle, have their own flavor of optimizer.

There are two kinds of optimizers, the rule based and the cost based. The rule-based optimizer was the first one introduced. It bases its decisions of executing a SQL statement on a specific set of rules. For example, using an index to retrieve data from a table has priority over scanning the table fully. The rule-based optimizer checks for the existence of indexes and uses them when possible.

NEW TERM   The *Optimizer* is a construct within a relational database that determines the best method to execute an SQL statement.

The cost-based optimizer finds a query execution path based on the resources used to retrieve the information. The execution plan with less processing required will be chosen.

8

Because the cost-based optimizer needs to know its data before it can formulate a plan of action, the tables that will be accessed need to be analyzed beforehand.

When the command to analyze tables is given, the database gathers statistics on the table data, which will help find the best way to execute a given query. An example of this gathered data is finding out how many rows a table contains. This result is stored until the table is analyzed again. An environment where tables change rapidly requires periodic table analysis to keep the cost-based optimizer working efficiently. Otherwise, it makes execution decisions on new data with old information, which may not represent the actual state of the table.

Hints

Users make use of "hints" to control the cost-based optimizer so that it does certain things. Explaining the use of hints could take an hour by itself, but it will be enough to mention that one of the many things they can do is turn on and off the use of an index. Suppose that you have a big table (a few hundred thousand to a million rows) and the column you can index has half the table with unique values and the other half repeating one identical number.

If you make a query that will return a few rows based on the unique value of the indexed column, the index will go to great lengths to make an efficient query. If you happen to query the value that is repeated in half the table, the existing index will be more of a hindrance than a help. It would be to your advantage to look at every row of the table rather than use an index. Here is where hints become handy. The hints tell the query whether to use the index, and this is where you can control the query efficiency. The following query shows the use of a hint turning off the index.

```
Select /*+ FULL(table_name) */ column a, column b
From table_name;
```

The full hint (written between slash and star signs) specifies a full table scan of the table defined in parentheses; therefore, it does not use the index. You can also force the use of an index in those cases in which you believe that your query should run faster and suspect that the optimizer is not using your index. This can be done as follows:

```
Select /*+ INDEX( table_name  index_name */ column a, column b
From table_name;
```

Summary

This hour covered what is an index and what it can do for you. It can make the difference of running a SQL statement from minutes to seconds, sometimes fractions of a second. When a query is running slow, see whether it is using an index. Perhaps the table does not have one.

If you think a table needs an index, do not just add it. Consult with your colleagues first. It may make your query run faster, but someone else's query may unexpectedly (and mysteriously) start dragging. It is to your advantage to keep an updated record of the tables and objects in your database and their location. This might help your investigation, in case someone placed an unexpected index without telling you and your blazing query suddenly tanks.

Some of the most popular indexes and their uses have been explained, and this hour briefly covered the database optimizer. The optimizer is your friend, and if you make its job easier by analyzing the tables and providing appropriate indexes, it can help you run SQL statements most efficiently.

Q&A

Q As a general rule, should you create an index on every table to improve database performance?

A Indexes are not appropriate for all database tables. Sometimes an index will actually decrease database performance. For instance, very small tables should not have indexes. Another example is that you would not index the GENDER column in a table, because every data value is either MALE or FEMALE (that would be like having the words "the" and "it" in a book index). There is not always a defined line between the benefit of creating an index and not creating one. As much as most DBAs hate to admit, database performance tuning involves a certain amount of "intelligent" trial and error.

Workshop

The following workshop consists of quiz questions and practical exercises. The quiz questions are designed to test your overall understanding of the current material. The practical exercises are intended to afford you the opportunity to apply the concepts discussed during the current hour, as well as build on the knowledge acquired in previous hours of study. Please take time to complete this workshop before continuing. You can refer to the answers at the end of the hour.

Quiz

1. What is a full table scan? Should a full table scan always be avoided?
2. What is cardinality?
3. Can an index have repeated values?
4. What is an index organized table?

5. How many rows should your query return to merit the implementation of an index?

6. What is the optimizer and why is it important?

Exercises

In this exercise, you will prove that an index does make a query run faster. The script to use is chp8wkshp.SQL. This script creates two tables: Students and Major. Then it will populate both with data. The Students table will have about 25,000 records, so let the query run for about a minute, until it finishes loading all the rows. You will run a query and note the results.

1. Log in to MySQL (go to C:\mysql\bin and type **mysql**). Type **use test;** to use the test database.

2. Run the script chp8wkshp.SQL. Assuming it resides on drive J, type

   ```
   \. J:\chapter8\chp8wkshp.SQL.
   ```

   Let the query run until it shows a description of the Students and Major tables.

3. Choose four or five entries from the Students table and make note of their student_id numbers. You can select them from all students whose last name is "French," (`select * from students where lname = 'FRENCH';`) or those studying Mathematics (`select * from students a, major b where a.major = b.dept_id and b.dept_id = 23;`), or any other method you like.

4. Create a table like this one:

Student_id
Time With Index
Time Without Index

5. After you have the student ID numbers, write them in the student_id column of the preceding table and run the query:

   ```
   Select * from students
   Where student_id = student_id_number;
   ```

   Example:

   ```
     select * from students
       where student_id = 58037281;
   ```

   The query will return the number of rows retrieved and the time it took to do it. Write this time on the Time Without Index column for all numbers you chose.

6. Create an index on the Students table. Type **create index stu_indx on students(student_id);**

After the index is created, log out from MySQL and close the window. This is necessary because after you run a query, it remains in memory in case you need it again; therefore the same query will run and there would be no difference in the retrieval time. If you try running any of the queries you just did, you will find that they run faster than before. However, if you change anything in the query, it will be different from the one in memory and the query will have to parse the query again, just like it was run the first time.

7. Log back into MySQL and run the same queries on the student_id numbers in your table. Does the query run faster? How many times faster?

8. If you want to try again without the index, drop the index as follows:

```
drop index stu_indx on students;
```

Then log out from MySQL, close the window, and log back in to ensure that the queries are not in memory anymore. Run the queries again and write your result.

Answers to Quiz

1. A full table scan occurs when a query looks at every row in a table to find the information it requires. Although full table scans are usually avoided because they generally take longer than using an index, that is not always the case. There are times when using an index slows down a query—for example, when you're querying a small table and in the case of a code look-up table, which can be made into an IOT.

2. Cardinality is defined as the number of records in a table. High cardinality is having a high number of distinct values in an indexed column, whereas low cardinality is when there are many repeated values. The more distinct the values, the higher the cardinality.

3. An index can have repeated values. However, if it does, its values cannot be elements of a primary key, because they should uniquely identify a row within a table.

4. An index-organized table basically is a table organized as an index. It is used on one-column tables and code tables (like the one translating area codes to states). On this table, it is quicker to find the information from the table organized as an index than to look at the index and later look at the table.

5. To be a candidate for an index, a query should return no more than 5%–10% of the total rows of the table.

6. The optimizer is the component of the database software that decides how best to execute a query. It is important because the efficiency of your query depends in part on how it decides to execute the query.

Hour 9

Organizing Data Appropriately in Databases and Schemas

One of the primary responsibilities of a database administrator is to properly organize the database. All predominant database vendors have different ways of organizing their databases. Although the terminology is different, the idea is still the same. Some product vendors, such as Oracle and Microsoft, might call an object owner "schema" or "schema owner," whereas other vendors might just call it an owner. These proprietary differences will not be addressed in this basic text. We will instead focus on the importance of properly organizing a database. The purpose of this hour is to introduce you to basic concepts of properly organizing a database.

The first considerations in organizing a database are "How is the database going to be used and what type of information will be stored in the database?" Advance planning and preparation at this stage can save you a lot of time later and make the implementation of the database much easier.

The objectives in this hour are

- Learn the difference between database and database schema.
- Learn about different types of database objects and their role in the database.
- Learn the concept of database organization.
- Learn different types of databases and their applications in business.
- Apply the concepts presented in this hour to a sample database request.

Understanding Database and Schema Terminology

Before you get into the specifics of database organization, you need to know some of the terminology and keywords that are going to be used in this hour. Having an understanding of these terms will help you get more out of the hour.

- *Users*—A person authorized to perform tasks on a database.
- *Application*—A collection of related objects designed to perform a specific task. End users use the application to interact with the data in the database.
- *Schema*—A collection of objects owned by a single user account. The user account that owns these objects is called the *schema owner*. The schema owner has full control of the objects in the schema. Users require access privileges to schema owner objects to view or manipulate the schema data. Schemas are the primary means of organizing data and application code in the database. It is common to have separate schemas for development, testing, and possibly even production within the same database. You should isolate these environments, if possible, for clarity and ease of administration.
- *Graphical User Interface (GUI)*—Graphical interface for the end user to access and manipulate the database.
- *Front end*—Text-based forms or graphical forms that the end user accesses to make changes to the data within the database.
- *Back end*—A database running behind the scene. The database is considered back end because the end user does not have direct access. The database is only accessed through the front end.

A schema is simply a group of objects (most often tables and indexes) that are owned by a single database user, but used by many end-users through a database application. The owner of the objects in a schema is called the schema owner.

Schema Terminology

When dealing with database schemas, certain principles are necessary to understand. The principles of primary key, foreign key, and record will be useful in this discussion.

A primary key is a unique column or combination of columns that identifies a record in a table. In other words, it is what makes each row a unique record. An example is a social security number or part number and possibly even an automatic database-generated sequence number. Primary keys are necessary to prevent duplication/redundancy of data within a table.

A foreign key is a column or combination of columns in one table that matches the primary key in another table. This match creates a relationship. Foreign keys are necessary so that data in one table that matches data in another table is not duplicated.

A record is a row of data in the database. A record consists of columns of data.

Database Organization at the Database Level

A database from the database administrator's logical point of view is a set of objects, relationships, and processes that represent business rules. However, to store the objects in a database, schemas have to be created. A *schema* is a database entity that contains all the tables, relationships, processes, and so on of a certain database. From the end user's point of view, a database is the application that the user runs to process data.

Naming Conventions

Before you get started on the database objects, you should know about another important topic—naming conventions. Databases and the objects in the databases should follow a nomenclature standard. How this standard is set depends on each database vendor and the businesses that create the database. There are two schools of thought about naming conventions. Some people say that the database and its objects should be named in such a way that they should not make logical sense to outside persons who gain access to the database. This naming system exists to improve security. It prevents hackers from recognizing tables that contain crucial information. For example, to securely name a human resources database, name it something ambiguous, such as WASI587.LD. If you were a hacker, you would have no clue that WASI587.LD is a human resources database. If you had named the database HR_PROD, any malicious user who gained access to the system would immediately know that this table contains human resources data. Then name the tables as table1, table2, table3, and so on.

The other way is to name the database something that is meaningful to the business. For example, name a production payroll database PAYROLL_PROD, and name tables something meaningful, such as EMPLOYEE_TBL and SALARY_TBL. There is no right or wrong way of doing this. One of these or a combination of both will work fine, as long as it is consistent.

There should also be some standard for using abbreviations. I always name my databases with an extension at the end. For example, production is always named with a name followed by PROD, development databases are always named with a name followed by DEV, test with TST, and training with TRNG. This helps in identifying the database and ensures that you are working in the right database environment.

Database Organization at the Schema Level

In this section, you will learn about commonly used relational database objects. You will notice that different database vendors have different naming conventions for these database objects. But the principles of organizing the database schema remain the same. The ANSI standard for SQL specifies a basic naming convention. Not all database vendors use this standard. This hour adheres to the current SQL ANSI standard. Note that some of the database objects mentioned here are discussed in previous hours. Although some of the information is redundant, the examples should help with understanding how the database should be organized.

Tables

Tables are building blocks of a database. A table is a logical object within the database that holds the actual physical data. A table consists of multiple columns and rows known as records. Each column has a name and a specific data type associated with it. A database consists of one or more tables. How the tables are designed and how data is divided up is covered in Hour 7, "Using Tables and Keys for Fundamental Data Storage."

Views

Views are another type of logical object in the database. They allow end users to look at the data from a different perspective. Views, like tables, contain columns and rows. An important difference between tables and views is that views do not contain stored data. The data from a view is generated by the query that created the view. This data is refreshed each time the view is requested. They can be created from columns and rows of a single table or a combination of tables. Views are created to give users access to information, without giving them the capability to change the data.

Views allow multiple users to access a collection of data, and even process the data according to their individual needs, but not modify it. Views provide a read-only snapshot of the specified data collection. Another benefit of views is that they allow the database administrator to control access to sensitive data. A database administrator can create a view that contains only the columns of data the user is authorized to see. Because views consist of columns selected from tables, they are dependent on those tables. If one of the tables is accidentally deleted or removed, the view becomes invalid.

NEW TERM   A *View* is a customized way of looking or *viewing* data from one or more tables.

9

Indexes

Indexes are used to increase the performance of the database. They can be created on one or more columns of a table. As the database grows in size, more and more data is stored within the tables; it becomes a performance issue to select values within a table. Indexes allow a huge collection of data to be searched efficiently. Consider the index commonly found at the back of a book. If a reader wants to review all pages containing a certain word, the reader could do one of two things: search every page in the book for the word or use the index and jump immediately to the relevant pages.

Creating indexes increases the database performance, but a cost is associated with indexes. Creating too many indexes on a table can slow down the update process for the table. When a new row is inserted into the table, all associated indexes will have to be updated.

Functions

Functions are blocks of code in the database. When executed, they return a value to the user. There are built-in functions —for example, mathematical functions—already defined in the database. There are also user-created database functions for specific uses in the application.

Procedures

A procedure is a block of SQL code stored in the database for use by different users and applications. It stores application-specific logic frequently used by the application. Procedures are also used to process data in tables or for presentation of data in reports. Procedures, unlike functions, do not return any value to the user.

Packages

Packages are objects used to arrange procedures and functions into groups. After the package is called, it executes all objects in the package in order of their placement in the package.

Triggers

Database triggers are blocks of code executed when a specific database event occurs. For example, a trigger can be created to execute every time a table is updated or a procedure is executed. This execution is completely transparent to the end user.

Triggers can also be used to audit tables. For example, as an application administrator, you may want to know every time changes have been made to the payroll table. A trigger can be created for this purpose and when executed, it inserts the user's name making the changes and the changes made to the payroll table to another table within the database application. The administrator then checks for newly inserted rows and ensures that the changes are valid and authorized.

Synonyms

Synonyms are alternate names for the objects. When accessing objects in different schema, the schema owner's name needs to be prefixed with the object name.

For example: HR.Employee or PR.Salary, in which HR and PR are the schema owner's name and Employee and Salary are tables being called on. If synonyms exist, the schema owner prefix is not required. One point needs to be clear—that even if synonyms are created, proper privileges are still required to access the data in the other schema.

Constraints

Constraints are conditions put on a table. Every value in the table must meet these conditions before the record can be written to the table. Constraints help keep the data consistent in the tables.

Other Objects

Databases may also contain other objects, such as Java objects, graphics, text documents, shared libraries, and tool kits unique to the application, as you can see in Figure 9.1.

Now that you have a general understanding of what is in a database, let's talk about how a schema is organized. There is a common misconception regarding database creation. An end user may call the administrator requesting the creation of a database. The end user commonly thinks that the database administrator will be creating the entire database, including tables, relationships, indexes, and so on. This is not the case! The reality is that a schema needs to be created to hold those tables.

Many times, creating a new database is a resource-intensive task. Most of the time, small applications do not need a database of their own. In cases like this, a schema will suffice. The decision whether to use a full database or a schema in a shared database should be based on the type of application, the quantity of data, and the number of concurrent users who will access the database

FIGURE 9.1

A Database may contain many objects.

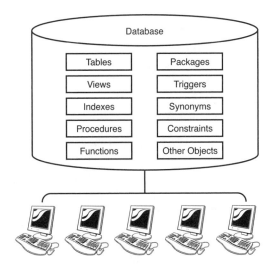

There are times, however, when the applications are so large that they require separate database processes of their own to implement the database.

Single Schema Applications

To create this type of application, a schema is created in the database shell. In this schema, all the application objects, such as tables, views, procedures, and packages, are created. This schema becomes an application schema, which will be used by the end user to interact with the data. This is shown in Figure 9.2.

FIGURE 9.2

All application objects are created in the schema.

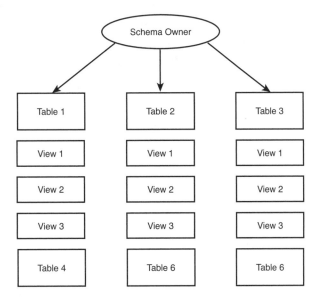

Multiple Schema Applications

Another type of application environment occurs when two or more schemas are accessed by a single application. In these database applications, a set of synonyms is created in each schema. This allows all schemas involved to access data in each other's area without using long names. Object privileges are still required by the accessing schema to access objects from other schemas. You can see this in Figure 9.3.

FIGURE 9.3

Some applications access multiple schemas.

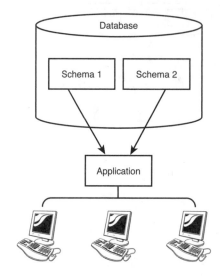

Shared Data Applications

Data is commonly shared by several applications at the same time. In such cases, the database tables, procedures, packages, and other objects are placed in unique schemas. The database user who owns these schema objects is called the schema owner, or data owner. The data owner assigns the required data access privileges. These privileges are assigned to individual roles and then these roles are assigned to individual schemas or users.

Schema-based organization is common in data warehouse type applications in which the data is shared by several applications. This type of organization allows multiple applications to access the data with limited select and update privileges, as you can see in Figure 9.4.

FIGURE 9.4

*Multiple applications
accessing a single
schema.*

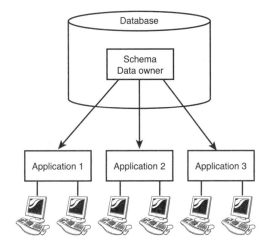

9

Distributed Databases

Another way of organizing the database occurs when the data is shared between several databases or the data is brought over from a different database in the network. The common term for this type of application is *distributed* databases. In situations like this, a user is created on the source database with the required privileges. (These privileges can be select or full privileges of insert, update, and delete.) To get the data from the source database, a database link is created for the source database in the target database. A database link stores the source database's name, user ID, password, and network location in the target database. This database link is then used to access the source database. A select statement is used to select the required data and update a set of local tables. An example of a linked database is shown in Figure 9.5.

FIGURE 9.5

*Linked schemas are
used often in distrib-
uted databases.*

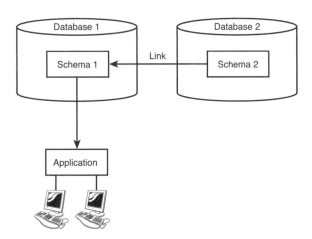

Application of Covered Concepts to a Sample Database

In this section, you can apply some of the concepts you just learned to a database. The company is World Trading Company, and it has a database, named WTC_PROD, that holds different applications for the company. The database contains three applications called Human Resources (HR), Payroll (PR), and Benefits (BF). Each of these applications has a variety of tables.

For security reasons, the DBA has decided to create several views for the end users. These views are created with the capability to select only the data the end user is authorized to see. For example, the human resources administrator and the manager are able to look at all the data in the Employee Information table, the Department Information table, and the Personal Information table. On the other hand, the Human Resources secretary's ability to view the data is limited. The same principle is applied to the Payroll Department. The payroll administrator is able to see everyone's salary via a view created especially for him; the manager, on the other hand, is able to see everyone's salary except the administrator's.

Based on job responsibilities, the database administrator also set roles in the database. These roles prevent managers from giving themselves a pay raise. Only the payroll administrator is allowed to makes changes to payroll tables. The database administrator can also monitor the updating of payroll tables. Several triggers have been created for this purpose; they execute every time a payroll table is modified and updates another set of audit tables. The company's president can monitor these audit tables. This creates checks and balances within the company.

Let's take a look at a hierarchical chart of a sample World Trading, Inc. database as the database gets organized.

World Trading, Inc.   (database)
   ☐   Human Resources   (schema)
      ☐   Employee Information   (table)
         ☐   Administrator View
         ☐   Manager View
         ☐   Secretary View
      ☐   Department Information   (table)
         ☐   Administrator View

☐   Manager View

☐   Secretary View

☐   Personal Information   (table)

☐   Administrator View

☐   Manager View

☐   Secretary View

☐   Payroll   (schema)

☐   Salary Information   (table)

☐   Administrator View

☐   Manager View

☐   Secretary View

☐   Taxes Information   (table)

☐   Administrator View

☐   Manager View

☐   Secretary View

☐   Audit Information

☐   President's View

☐   Benefits   (schema)

☐   Insurance Information   (table)

☐   Administrator View

☐   Manager View

☐   Secretary View

☐   Expense Account   (table)

☐   Administrator View

☐   Manager View

☐   Secretary View

Summary

The key to organizing a database is preplanning. Determining what type of information is going to be stored and how the database is going to be used by the end user are factors to be considered when organizing the database.

Q&A

Q **What is the difference between a database and a database schema?**

A A database is a tool that is used to store data in an organized manner. A database schema is a part of a database. A database schema is a grouping of related objects, such as tables, indexes, constraints, views, and procedures within a database.

Q **What is the difference between a primary key and a foreign key?**

A A primary key is a combination of one or more column values in a table that can identify a certain unique row of data in a collection of rows. A foreign key is a combination of columns in a table that reference the primary key of another table.

Q **How can an index improve the performance of a database query in a database with an enormous amount of data?**

A A database index contains shortcuts that allow the data to be queried much faster. For example, when you search the yellow pages for a painter, you jump immediately to the P section, then Pa, then Pai, then Pain, and so on, until you reach the Painters section. Okay, maybe you don't really look for Pai or Pain when looking for a Painter, but the database does. By beginning a search at P and narrowing it with each consecutive letter (Pa, Pai, Pain, Paint…), the indexed database search avoids searching all irrelevant data. Thus, much time is saved.

Workshop

The following workshop consists of quiz questions and practical exercises. The quiz questions are designed to test your overall understanding of the current material. The practical exercises are intended to afford you the opportunity to apply the concepts discussed during the current hour, as well as build on the knowledge acquired in previous hours of study. Please take time to complete this workshop before continuing. You can refer to the answers at the end of the hour.

Quiz

1. Describe database schema.
2. Name three types of database objects.
3. What are the main types of databases?
4. In which database object is the data stored?
5. Which database object executes in response to a particular event?
6. Which database objects are used to look at information but not update it?
7. What is the difference between a table and a view?

Exercise

As a database administrator, you have been assigned to organize a database being developed for an upcoming retail store. The Information Technologies department head has contacted you and the following information has been provided:

- A database needs to be created.
- This database should contain three applications: Sales, Marketing, and Inventory.
- The IT head expects to have 10–15 tables per application.
- All the data will be produced locally and will not be brought over from anywhere else.
- The sales department head has requested that sales information should not be available to anyone except for a few key people on his team and the company president.
- The company president wants complete, unrestricted access to the database.

Based on the information given, how would you design a single schema application structure?

Answers to Quiz

1. A schema is a collection of objects owned by a single user.
2. Tables, views, and procedures.
3. OLTP—Online Transaction Processing

   OLAP—Online Analytical Processing

   DSS—Decision Support System
4. Tables
5. Trigger
6. View
7. The information being looked at via a view is not updateable.

9

HOUR **10**

Welcome to Object-Oriented Databases

In previous hours, you concentrated on relational database architecture. The relational database architecture is quite popular and useful in industry, but the relational architecture is not the only type of database system on the market. Another type of database architecture, the object-oriented database, is becoming available and offers many unique benefits. As a beginner in the database world, you might not be familiar with object-oriented databases (a.k.a. object databases). At the time of this writing, object-oriented databases have not yet fully penetrated the mainstream corporate environment. As object-oriented programming continues to grow and object-oriented database management systems continue to emerge and be developed, you can expect to see greater use of object-oriented databases in industry. This hour will provide you with an overview of object-oriented databases. After reading this material, you should be able to impress your boss with OODB talk.

If you intend to use object-oriented databases in the future, then knowledge of an object-oriented programming language is prerequisite. Common object-oriented programming languages include C++, Java, and Smalltalk.

Feel free to pick up a reference book, attend a workshop, or take a Computer Based Training (CBT) class to learn one of these languages. Note that learning object-oriented programming is not necessary for this hour, but it is required to use an object-oriented database.

The highlights of this hour include

- An overview of object-oriented databases
- The benefits of object-oriented databases
- Basic object-oriented database theory
- Basic elements of the object-oriented database

Overview of Object-Oriented Databases

Before you begin learning about object-oriented databases, let's talk about what objects are and why objects require special storage.

This hour is intended to provide a basic understanding of object-oriented databases. Few full object-oriented databases are in production today. However, it is important to stay up with technology and understand some of these concepts as object-oriented features are starting to be incorporated into relational databases.

What Is an Object?

An object, simply put, is a programming entity—a collection of attributes (variables) and behaviors (functions) packaged together. The functions contained in an object are used to operate on the data stored within. Objects provide an advanced means of storing data within a program and can perform useful work by exchanging messages with other objects. In a program, an object is laid out in a class. A class is like an object blueprint. A class describes the variables and the functions that are stored inside an object.

As an example, consider two objects: a Circle and a Square. Presume that the Circle has a radius attribute. The Circle has the following behaviors: calcArea and calcCircumference. Different instances of the Circle object might have different radii and therefore would return different values for circumference and area. The Square has one attribute, length, and the following behaviors: calculateArea and calcPerimeter. These two objects are represented in Figure 10.1.

FIGURE 10.1

This figure shows the structure of two objects: a Circle and a Square.

```
Object: Circle
  Attributes:
    radius
  Behaviors:
    calcCircumference
    calcArea
```

```
Object: Square
  Attributes:
    length
  Behaviors:
    calcPerimeter
    calcArea
```

The code representing these two objects might look like the following. Note that attributes are represented by variables, and behaviors are represented by functions or methods.

```
class Circle
{
public:
   float radius;
   float calcArea();
   float calcCircumference();
}

class Square
{
public:
   float length;
   float calcArea();
   float calcPerimeter();
}
```

If the program needs to access a behavior or an attribute of an object of type Circle, the program sends a message to that Circle object. This message contains information on the attribute or behavior that is desired and any additional data that needs to be transferred, such as parameters or values that would be used in determining the outcome of a behavior. Figure 10.2 demonstrates the communication that occurs between different objects in a program.

10

FIGURE 10.2

This model depicts communication between objects in a program.

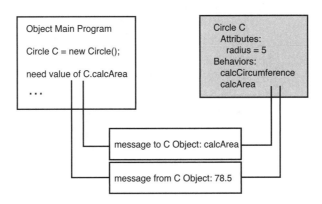

This may seem a strange concept to grasp at the moment. Have no fear! You do not need to completely understand objects or object-oriented programming at this time. The point of this section is simply to introduce objects as data structures that combine both variables and functions and to demonstrate that objects are complex data types that can be made up of many data items. A DBMS designed to store objects must be designed with these complexities in mind.

Other aspects of objects make the object-oriented DBMS complex in nature. Objects can contain other objects in addition to variables and functions. Figure 10.3 represents an object that contains another object in addition to variables and methods.

FIGURE 10.3

An object within an object.

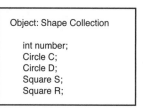

```
Object: Shape Collection

    int number;
    Circle C;
    Circle D;
    Square S;
    Square R;
```

Inheritance is a widely used practice to reduce development time. Objects can inherit variables and functions of other objects. Figure 10.4 represents two objects that both use inheritance to obtain the attributes and behaviors of the single "super" class. The shape class is the super class. The circle and square classes inherit the attributes and behaviors of the shape class. When inheritance is used, the super class description and the subclass description are combined to create a blueprint for the subclass.

 **NEW TERM**   *Inheritance* Just as someone might take on or inherit eye color or another attribute from their parent, objects are able to take on the attributes of other objects.

FIGURE 10.4

An inheritance diagram.

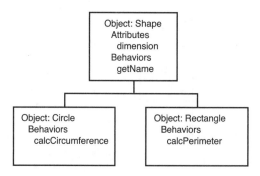

The code to create the preceding inheritance scheme might look as follows in C++.

```
class Shape
{
public:
    int dimension;
    String name;
    String getName();
}

class Circle: public Shape
{
public:
    calcCircumference();
}

class Square: public Shape
{
public:
    calcPerimeter();
}
```

In this code, the Square class inherits the Shape class. This means that the Square class contains the item's dimension and getName(). In other words, the Shape class is a fundamental part of the Square class. The Shape class is also a fundamental part of the Circle class.

A Circle object might contain the following items:

```
dimension: 5
name: Big Circle
getName()
calcPerimeter()
```

A Square object might contain the following items:

```
dimension: 4
name: Little Square
getName()
calcPerimeter()
```

Notice that the Square and Circle objects both contain the items that are specified in the Shape class. The Shape class is used in the formation of the "blueprint" for the Circle and the Square objects.

What Is an Object-Oriented Database?

Earlier, you learned that objects are complicated data types. Standard primitive data types such as integers, floating-point numbers, and string values can easily be stored in traditional databases. Objects cannot be stored directly in traditional databases. The data

10

stored within an object in a program must be parsed and exported to a typical relational database. Object-oriented databases provide a means of storing this data without parsing. The entire object is stored within the database.

Object-oriented databases came about in the 1980s, but without a well-defined standard. The object-oriented database specification was developed relatively recently by the Object Database Management Group (ODMG). This specification provides for a more efficient means of storing data from object-oriented programs while maintaining the cross-platform and cross-language data storage and retrieval benefits of relational data-bases. With object-oriented databases, the object-oriented programmer no longer has to write lengthy import or export code. Objects are stored intact.

The ODMG standard provides major benefits to the object-oriented programmer. Object database management systems that comply with the ODMG standard allow objects to be stored and retrieved using different programming languages and platforms. This means that using a compliant object-oriented DBMS, an object created and stored using Smalltalk can be retrieved and used from C++.

Why Are Object-Oriented Databases Needed?

Current relational database technology is great for many industry applications. However, relational database technology does not take into account the unique data storage model provided by object-oriented languages. Certain problems are inherent when using rela-tional databases with object-oriented applications. This section discusses those problems and the solutions provided by object-oriented database technology.

Problems with Pre-Object-Oriented Databases

Up to now, you have seen how data is organized into databases using the relational model. The relational model is the most popular type of database management system in use today. This model works well and is quite practical when you're using procedural languages such as C or PL/SQL. The relational model also works well with object-oriented languages, but it is not as practical. Relational database management systems (RDBMS) are not designed to store data as objects. Therefore, the data located within objects in an object-oriented program must be filtered, modified, and, in essence, exported through a custom-built export process to a relational database. Figure 10.5 demonstrates the process of exporting data from an object to a relational database. This filtering process takes time and money to develop and accounts for a large percentage of the execution time in these applications.

FIGURE 10.5

This figure demon-strates the relation-ships between objects and relational data-base tables.

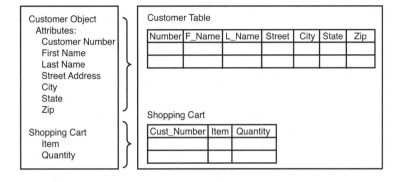

Notice in this simplified example that the Customer object data does not fit naturally into a single table in the relational database. Each time a Customer object needs to be stored, the Customer table data has to be extracted and saved in the database, and then the Shopping Cart data has to be extracted and saved in the database. Often, objects hold data that span many tables. Each table has to be updated with relevant data separately.

The same holds true in the case of importing data from the relational database to the object. Data from the database has to be obtained—in some cases from many tables and passed through a custom import process to rebuild the object in the program. It is, in fact, more common that the data stored within an object does not map correctly to one single table in the relational database. When this occurs, data must be imported into the object(s) via queries with joins—sometimes multiple joins. Figure 10.6 demonstrates the process of importing data from tables in a relational database to an object.

FIGURE 10.6

Joining relational tables for object storage.

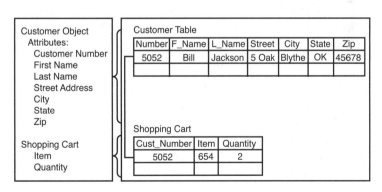

For more complex objects, the task becomes more involved. Consider an object that inherits the properties and behaviors of another object. To re-create this object at a later time, all the necessary data must be stored in the relational database. This includes data from any super classes. Figure 10.6 demonstrates a simple case of mapping and storing inherited object data into a relational database.

10

One other problem with integrating object-oriented programming and relational databases is flexibility for system evolution. If changes are made to relational database tables that affect the manner in which data is stored, changes have to be made to the program to compensate. This scenario requires additional coding time and is not flexible for the object-oriented programmer.

Solutions Provided with Object-Oriented Databases

Object-oriented databases offer many benefits to object-oriented programmers. The greatest benefit is the decrease in development time needed to deploy a solution in which an object-oriented program communicates with a database. This development time decrease translates directly into money saved per project.

Another benefit is an increase in application execution speed. Because of the omission of thousands of lines of code traditionally used to relate objects to database tables, the object-oriented application using an object-oriented database will execute much more quickly.

Understanding Basic Object-Oriented Database Theory

As you have learned so far, the purpose of object-oriented databases is to provide a storage mechanism for objects. As with any DBMS, it is important that the data be stored in a robust, correct, and secure manner. It is also important that the complex communication between the client and server be as transparent to the programmer as possible. Relative ease of use is crucial. Traditionally, most widely used database management systems allow data to be stored in a multi-platform, language-independent environment. These aspects are also important for object-oriented database management systems.

How are these lofty goals met? Current multi-platform and language-independent object-oriented databases offer programming interfaces for different languages. Using these programming interfaces, the programmer can add object database functionality to applications of certain languages. Certain objects within the database are assigned handles by the programmer. These handles are then used to refer to the object and access the data stored within.

Basic Elements of an Object-Oriented Database

This section briefly discusses a few necessary elements of an object database. These elements include Object Definition Language (ODL), Object Manipulation Language (OML), and Object Query Language (OQL). These "languages" are actually specifications. Each of these specifications is provided by the object-oriented programming language that you decide to use. These examples use C++.

Object Definition Language (ODL)

Object Definition Language (ODL) is a tool similar in functionality to Data Definition Language, but ODL uses an object-oriented programming language. Data-definition language describes the way data is stored in a relational database. Object-definition language describes the characteristics of the objects stored within the database.

ODL differs between languages. C++ has been chosen as the sample language for this topic. To use ODL to define a database object from C++, you write a C++ class. This class should inherit the Persistent_Object class. The Persistent_Object class contains functionality that is used by the object database when storing objects. The following code example demonstrates the use of Object Definition Language from C++. In this example, a class Person inherits the Persistent_Object class. A class Employee inherits the Person class and therefore can store public data described in the Person class.

```
class Person: public Persistent_Object
{
public:
    String name;
    String address;
}

class Employee: public Person
{
public:
    Ref (Location) office_location;
}
```

In the preceding example, the Person class stores a name and address value. The Employee class inherits the Person class and adds a reference to a Location object. This Location object is another object stored inside the database and will refer to the location of a certain employee's office. Figure 10.7 demonstrates how references work inside the database.

Figure 10.7

References link objects in an object database.

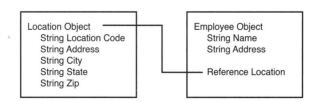

More specifically, an Employee object will reference a Location object, as shown in Figure 10.8.

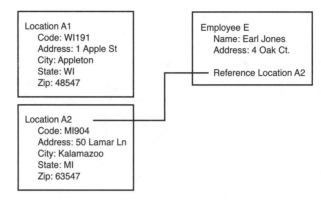

FIGURE 10.8

Explicit references in a database.

From the preceding example, you can see that the Employee with the name "Earl Jones" is associated with the Location with the code "MI904."

These classes—Person, Employee, and Location—describe objects that can be stored inside the object database. The code to describe these two classes can be stored inside the database or external to the database. The location of the code depends on the specific object database vendor.

Object Manipulation Language (OML)

Object Manipulation Language (OML) is used to modify the state of object data inside the object database. Object manipulation is achieved using an object-oriented language that can address the object-oriented database. The following code example is a C++ function that creates an Employee object stored within the object database and stores data in this Employee object.

```
int create_employee (String _name, String _address)
{
Database *Datebase;
Transaction *T;{

Database = Database::open("Employee-DB");
T.begin();

Ref (Employee)employee = new (Database) Employee;

employee->name=_name;
employee->address=_address;
T.commit();
}
```

You can see right away that the process of manipulating data within an object database is quite different from manipulating data within traditional relational database models.

Object Query Language (OQL)

Object Query Language (OQL) is used to retrieve data stored within the object database. You may be surprised to find that Object Query Language resembles SQL. The following is an example of how one might search for employees with the name "John."

```
Select e.name
From employees e
Where name='John'
```

> Notice the use of an alias for the employees table. For this query only, the table has been renamed to e.

10

This is a simple query. What if you want to query more than one class? Joins can be formed as in normal SQL. The following code is an example of how two objects could be joined to retrieve data.

```
Select l.city
From employees e, e.belongs_to l
Where e.name='John'
```

This code finds employees with the name "John" and obtains the city in which they work. Assume that "l" refers to the Location table briefly referred to in the ODL example.

This has been a brief overview of how data is managed and retrieved with an object database. If you plan to use an object database, it would be wise to refer to the documentation for the ODBMS that you will be using for specific information on how your ODBMS handles data management.

Understanding Relationships Between Data

You have learned that object-oriented databases store data in a manner different from traditional relational databases. Object-oriented databases store data in the form of raw objects. These objects can be interrelated by reference or by relation. Relationships can be created using pointers or references between objects or by using a Primary-Foreign Key relation, as in standard relational databases.

Let's look at an example in which several objects are interrelated. Consider a hypothetical online shopping system. You'll define a Customer object, a Shopping Cart object, a Transaction object, and a History object. The Customer object will store data relevant to tracking the customer. This might include such things as first name, last name, street address, city, state, ZIP code, customer number, and so on. The Shopping Cart object will be used to store items pending payment. The Transaction object will be used to record information about the current transaction. The History object will be used to record information about previous transactions. Figure 10.9 demonstrates graphically the relationships between these objects.

FIGURE 10.9

Relationships between object data.

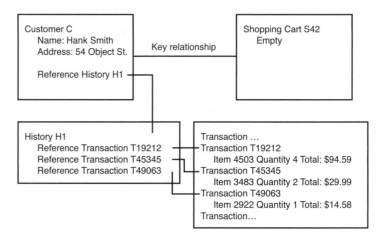

The main object in our hypothetical online shopping system is the customer object. The customer object contains a shopping cart object, and a history object. There are references within the customer object to each of the other objects: shopping cart and history. Thus, these objects are related.

Now consider how difficult it is to model these four objects and these relationships using a relational database. Many objects in a relational database could be represented by a single table. The shopping cart object and the transaction object, for example, could be represented by single tables. The transaction table might contain a transaction number and various details about the transaction. A single table and a related table can represent the history object. The history object table might contain customer numbers and transaction numbers. The customer table might contain information such as a customer number (primary key), first name, last name, address, and so on. In a relational database, the data is related using Primary-Foreign Key relationships. In an object-oriented database, the data is related via references.

Object-Oriented Databases in the Real World

Object-oriented databases are an emerging technology; there are at least two major object database vendors, Versant and Excelon. Object-oriented databases have been integrated into the daily operations of many high-profile companies. Operations ranging from online commerce to telecommunications, manufacturing, and software development companies are using object databases.

Object databases are making an appearance because of the reduction in cost possible when using this technology. Development time is decreased because of the absence of a need for mapping existing objects to a relational table system. Products that use object-oriented databases and object-oriented languages have shown higher transaction performance than their counterparts that use relational databases. Higher performance means that the object-oriented systems offer the capability to support a larger volume than previous systems.

Summary

This hour introduced an emerging technology—object databases. You were introduced to the concepts of object databases and read a brief overview of their evolution. This hour began with a basic discussion of objects and communication between objects. This helped explain the rationale behind the development of object-oriented databases. The benefits of object-oriented databases and the drawbacks of relational databases when used with object-oriented programming languages were then discussed. You were introduced to and given simple examples of ODL, OML, and OQL. Relationships between objects within the object database were described.

Armed with this knowledge, you should be able to give a supervisor or peer an overview of object databases and how they offer performance superior to relational databases.

Q&A

Q If object-oriented databases are so great, should we expect them to replace relational databases?

A No. Object-oriented database systems probably will become more popular as time goes on, but the relational model is very well suited for many tasks. In fact, most companies that use object databases use them in conjunction with other relational databases.

Workshop

The following workshop consists of quiz questions and practical exercises. The quiz questions are designed to test your overall understanding of the current material. The practical exercises are intended to afford you the opportunity to apply the concepts discussed during the current hour, as well as build on the knowledge acquired in previous hours of study. Please take time to complete this workshop before continuing. You can refer to the answers at the end of the hour.

Quiz

1. An object-oriented database is a database that stores data in object form from object oriented programs. True or False.

2. What benefits does an object-oriented database provide when using object-oriented programming?

    a. More code

    b. More efficient storage

    c. Faster development time

    d. Less code

3. What are some drawbacks when using relational databases with object-oriented applications?

    a. Relational databases require code to perform importing and exporting of object data.

    b. Simple object data can be stored efficiently in a relational database.

    c. When storing objects in relational databases, the application runs slower and requires more resources, development time, and code.

4. What is ODL?

    a. ODL is Object Definition Language, which is used to define objects that will persist in an object database.

    b. ODL is Object Manipulation Language, which is used to change data within objects inside an object database.

    c. ODL is Object Query Language, which is provided as a convenient and familiar means of retrieving data from an object-oriented database.

Exercises

1. When an object-oriented database is integrated into an infrastructure, there will usually be existing relational databases that will cooperate with the OODB. Think of an instance where this might be true. Sketch out the information system for your instance that uses the following components: an application layer, relational database(s), object database(s).

2. Imagine a company that offers products for sale on the Web and wants to use an object-oriented database in its shopping system. An existing relational database contains tables of product information (name, description, quantity on hand, selling

price). The object-oriented database will be used to store customer and order information together. What objects will be needed? What attributes and behaviors should each of these objects demonstrate to get the job done in the most efficient, effective manner? How should these objects be related?

Answers to Quiz

1. True.

2. Object databases provide

    b. More efficient storage

    c. Faster development time

    d. Less code when used with object-oriented programming languages

3.   a. Relational databases require code to perform importing and exporting of object data. Objects do not fit naturally into relational databases.

    c. When storing objects in relational databases, the application runs slower and requires more resources, development time, and code.

4.   a. ODL is Object Definition Language, which is used to define objects that will persist in an object database.

10

PART III

Design, Implementation, and Management

Hour

Hour 11

Understanding the Basics of Database Design

There is more to a database than creating it. Any database must be designed, which involves the identification of a need for a database, the definition of the database's purpose, and the careful selection and arrangement of the data that will be stored in the database.

The following elements of database design are introduced in this hour:

- Planning for design
- Design tasks
- Post-design tasks
- Design methodologies

Defining Database Design

Let's take a moment to define database design (we have taken some excerpts from one of our other Sams titles, *Database Design*). *Webster's* dictionary uses the following phrases to define the term design:

- "To prepare the preliminary plans or sketch for"
- "To intend for a definite purpose"
- "The combination of details or features of something constructed"
- "To plan and fashion artistically or skillfully"
- "Adaptation of means to a preconceived end"

"To prepare the preliminary plans or sketch for" implies that there is more work in database design than what is obvious on the surface. Before the actual design of the database occurs, much planning is involved. The "definite purpose" of the database should be clearly defined. Many "details and features" are involved during the design of any database.

After the purpose of the database has been established, the design team should study all the details and features that compose the business. These details and features, after they are gathered and are often "sketched," are eventually formatted into a database structure using a predetermined database model.

During the actual design of the database, these details and features are "fashioned artistically and skillfully" into a database model, which will most likely be modified numerous times before the design process is complete.

"Adaptation of means to a preconceived end" is an excellent phrase used to describe the activities of database designers in many situations. You must be able to adapt the phases and tasks in database design to roll with the changes and meet the customer's needs. Often, you may find that the customer's needs for a database are refined throughout the design process, or even changed drastically.

Planning for Database Design

Before a database is designed, a need for a database must first be established. The need for any database deals with the requirement to store data. Storing data is not the end it is the beginning. Typically, the real need for a database occurs because of the requirement to use stored data in some manner to operate a business, conduct analysis, and make intelligent business decisions. Determining the need for a database is always the first step to database design. After the need for a database has been established, you can begin planning for database design.

The following items represent actions that should be taken during the design planning process:

- Defining a mission statement (purpose)
- Defining design objectives

- Devising a work plan (to keep everyone on track)
- Setting milestones and deliverables
- Establishing project deadlines (or nothing will ever get done)
- Assigning tasks (distributing accountability)

Before a database can be designed, all the requirements for the database must be gathered. A database can be created quickly, and perhaps poorly, and may not meet the customer's needs. The process of carefully gathering requirements is imperative to the successful design of any database.

Two types of requirements are used to design an information system:

- Business requirements
- System requirements

Business requirements refer to those details that are related to how a business functions on a daily basis. System requirements are those details, many of which are associated with business requirements, that are used to actually design the database system.

Gathering Business Requirements

Business requirements relate directly to the tasks performed by individuals within an organization. Business requirements deal with how the business functions currently, as well as how the business plans to work or conduct business in the future.

It is the responsibility of the development team to find out what the data is and how the business uses the data. Data and processes within an organization are always closely related. Processes can be used to determine data, and data can be used to determine processes. It is important to compare processes to data during modeling to ensure that all requirements have been completely gathered. Individuals who belong to organizational units perform processes. An organizational unit is normally a department within an organization.

During the business-requirements gathering portion of the design process, the main goal is to decompose an organization's tasks as much as possible so that all data to be included in the database can be completely defined. Some business processes that are performed can be specific to a particular organizational unit or can be shared between organizational units.

After the basic data and processes are determined, business rules must also be determined. Business rules are directly associated with data and processes that are used to manage the data. Business rules established affect the way data can be accessed for operations such as queries, inserts, updates, and deletions. Business rules also help determine how data relates to other data and will eventually be used to design entities and their relationships. Business rules are also the greatest factor in determining the use of referential integrity in a database.

The following are a few miscellaneous sample business rules:

- Applications must be processed before licenses are granted.
- A customer record must exist before an order can be placed.
- An employee can receive only one discount per month.
- An employee cannot receive more than one promotion per year without a waiver.
- All products must be inspected before being introduced into inventory.
- Funds must be verified before they are transferred.
- A person can have only one spouse.
- A person can have only one primary address.

Gathering System Requirements

System requirements cannot be determined without the existence of business requirements. This is because business requirements are used to establish the needs for an information system. With the assumption that all business requirements have been completely gathered, the development team should feel confident about the conversion of business needs into system needs.

Often the most difficult part of designing a system is outlining the requirements and devising a plan in which to design the system. The process of defining system requirements should, without question, simplify the process of physically designing the database. If business needs have been converted accurately into system needs, the physical design of the database should go smoothly.

Modeling Entities and Relationships

In database design, an entity is simply a representation of data. Entity modeling is basically the process of drawing sketches that represent data and how data is related to other data. Modeling entities is one of the fundamental concepts of database design; it simplifies the design process, summarizes data relationships, and promotes accuracy. Entity modeling is also the first major step of data modeling.

There are two basic types of data modeling:

- Logical modeling
- Physical modeling

Understanding Logical Modeling

Logical modeling deals with gathering business requirements and converting those requirements into a model. The logical model revolves around the needs of the business, not the database, although the needs of the business are used to establish the needs of the database. Logical modeling involves gathering information about business processes, business entities (categories of data), and organizational units. After this information is gathered, diagrams and reports are produced including entity relationship diagrams, business process diagrams, and eventually process flow diagrams.

Understanding Physical Modeling

Physical modeling involves the actual design of a database according to the requirements that were established during logical modeling. Physical modeling deals with the conversion of the logical, or business, model into a relational database model. When physical modeling occurs, objects are being defined at the schema level. During physical modeling, objects such as tables and columns are created based on entities and attributes that were defined during logical modeling.

Entity Modeling

11

Entities represent an organization's data. An occurrence of data in an entity can be related to a record in a file cabinet. Suppose that one file cabinet stores resumes, each folder in the cabinet containing a resume for an individual. Suppose that another file cabinet maintains files containing employee information.

We know that all resumes kept by a company don't correlate to the hiring of an employee. Yet, we don't want to store an employee's resume in the employee file if we already have a resume file. That would be nearly twice as much paperwork to store resumes for employees. Instead, the files in both cabinets are stored alphabetically. If you wanted to pull an employee file along with the employee's resume, you would refer to both file cabinets using the employee's name. Thus, the information (resume data and employee data) stored in both cabinets is related by the employee's name.

Entity relationship modeling is the process of visually representing entities. The entity relationship diagram (ERD) is an iterative tool and process that models logical data structures during the analysis phase of system development. The ERD is the sketch of data that we referred to earlier in this section.

ERD components include the following:

- Data entities
- Attributes of those entities
- Relationships among the entities

The complete ERD is used later in database design to physically design database tables. The creation of an ERD first involves the identification and definition of entities.

Entities are the nouns of your database. EMPLOYEE, CUSTOMER, PRODUCT, and INVOICE are all probable examples of entities. An entity is not a single individual or example, but a class or category of things. A single, specific occurrence of an entity is an *instance*. In physical design, a logical instance will become a physical row. For example, John Smith, the employee, is an instance of the entity EMPLOYEE.

After entities are defined, attributes are assigned to each entity. Attributes categorize the data that will be associated with each entity. For example, the CUSTOMER entity may have the following attributes: CUSTOMER_NAME, ADDRESS, CITY, STATE, ZIP, and PHONE. Attributes eventually complete the definition of the data that will be stored in the database.

Finally, relationships are defined (this process may actually begin before all attributes are defined). Relationships tell how different entities are related to one another. For example, the CUSTOMER entity may be related to the PRODUCT entity because customers place orders on products.

ERDs contain *metadata*, or data about other data. For example, ERD data include boxes, names, and lines. The data that a line represents is the relationship between two entities in the ERD. An entity name represents a table that will be created later, which will also contain data of its own. Simple examples of basic ERDs and data relationships are shown in the next section.

NEW TERM An **ERD** is an Entity Relationship Diagram. The ERD maps the tables in the database, details how they are related, and provides information on those attributes of the columns in the tables.

> The advantage of the ERD is that it is simple enough that both technical and nontechnical individuals can quickly learn to use it to communicate productively about data requirements. Yet it is enormously powerful in its capability to capture and communicate data about data (metadata) on an evolving information system's data requirements.

Sample ERDs

The intention of this section is to show a few simple examples of entity relationship diagrams (ERDs) that can be easily related.

Figure 11.1 shows an entity called INSTRUCTOR. This entity represents information about instructors, such as name, contact information, skill set, and so forth. This is a simple entity illustration. A more detailed entity diagram might list attributes such as the instructor's name, address, phone number, and other personal information.

Figure 11.1
An entity.

Figure 11.2 depicts an example of a simple illustration of a data relationship in an entity relationship diagram. In this ERD, the following story is told: an automobile is powered by an engine. An engine powers an automobile. This is a simple story, but simple stories are best told with pictures.

Figure 11.2
ERD relating automobiles and engines.

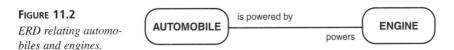

In Figure 11.3, multiple relationships are shown. These relationships involve customers and product orders. Each customer may place multiple orders. Each order may have multiple line items. Each line item corresponds to one product, although each product may exist as a line item in multiple orders.

Figure 11.3
ERD explaining product orders.

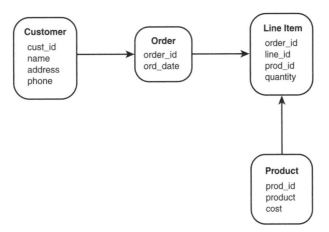

Designing Tables

Tables are the fundamental logical building blocks of relational databases. A table is a grouping of columns of data that pertains to a single, particular class of people, things, events, or ideas in an enterprise about which information needs to be stored or calculations made.

For example, the phone book is a table containing data about phone numbers and about people or businesses that have phones. The phone book table's columns would represent peoples' and businesses' names, addresses, and phone numbers. The phone number and other columns of information pertaining to a specific phone is a row in the table. There are other terms that are used to describe columns, rows, and tables, depending on which relational database system (RDBMS) you're using.

In database design, tables are derived from entities that were defined during logical modeling. Likewise, columns are derived from these entities' attributes. So, you can see the importance of the care taken during information gathering and logical design.

Figure 11.4 illustrates the basic structure of a table in a relational database. This is how an end user visualizes a table.

FIGURE 11.4
The structure of a table.

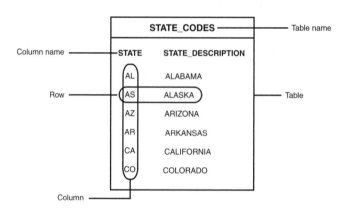

The data dictionary language (DDL), an integral part of the SQL language, is used to create the database (tables and columns) and is derived from the ERD. DDL is discussed in more depth in Hour 16, "Creating Databases and Database Objects."

The four types of tables found in a relational database are

- Data tables
- Join tables
- Subset tables
- Validation tables

These tables are briefly discussed in the following sections.

Data Tables

A *data table* contains rows of information about a person, place, event, or thing of importance to an enterprise. This is by far the most common type of table. The other classes of tables described are data tables as well. The following table types are placed into additional classes because of some database function they meet in addition to holding data.

A data table represents a single class of things of significance in the database. A data table has a primary key column or combination of columns (a composite key) that uniquely identifies each instance of the class. All other table columns are dependent on that primary key and only on that primary key. A data table should have no columns that consist of data derived from calculations or concatenations on other data columns.

New Term   *Data Tables* represent a single class of things of significance in a database.

Good candidates for data tables include the following:

- INSTRUCTORS
- CUSTOMERS
- STUDENTS
- COURSES
- MATERIALS
- EMPLOYEES
- PRODUCTS

11

Join Tables

A *join table*, also known as an *intersection table* or *linking table*, is used to resolve a relationship between two other tables (that would otherwise have a single many-to-many relationship) into two one-to-many relationships. Because many-to-many relationships are initially pretty common in the logical design and must be resolved prior to creating tables, most databases will have some join tables.

New Term   *Join Tables* are used to resolve a relationship between two tables.

For example, an instructor will teach many courses during his or her career and many instructors may teach **a** course.

Here's an example:

INSTRUCTORS	COURSES
INSTRUCTOR_ID	COURSE_ID
INSTRUCTOR_LNAME	COURSE_NAME
INSTRUCTOR_FNAME	DPT_ID
INSTRUCTOR_SSN	

The following statements are true about these tables:

- Instructors will teach one or more courses.
- Courses will be taught by one or more instructors.

A COURSE_SCHEDULE intersection (join table) can be placed between COURSES and INSTRUCTORS, with the primary keys from the COURSES and INSTRUCTORS tables in it as foreign keys.

You can then add columns to the intersection table so that each row in the join table will support a unique connection between the two tables with the many-to-many relationship.

In the following example, you need COURSE_ID, SECTION, SEMESTER, and ACADEMIC YEAR columns to uniquely identify a particular presentation of a course. These columns compose a composite primary key for COURSE_SCHEDULE.

INSTRUCTORS	COURSE_SCHEDULE	COURSES
INSTRUCTOR_ID	COURSE_ID	COURSE_ID
INSTRUCTOR_LNAME	INSTRUCTOR_ID	COURSE_NAME
INSTRUCTOR_FNAME	SEMESTER	DPT_ID
INSTRUCTOR_SSN	SECTION	
	ACADEMIC_YEAR	

The following statements are now true about the previous tables:

- A course section during a particular semester and academic year will be taught by one and only one instructor.
- A course section during a particular semester and academic year will be a presentation of one and only one course (a course may be taught during many semesters) .

Subset Tables

In some cases, a general-purpose table will have columns that do not apply to some subclasses or subsets of all the instances of the table. In the following example, instructors in INSTRUCTOR_CATEGORY classified as "adjunct" or "associate" would be primarily employed elsewhere than the college. This information would need to be captured for them, but the columns involved would be null for all the full-time instructors.

NEW TERM   *Subset Tables* exist to resolve data that is not easily classified in existing sets. They also help to reduce the amount of null values in columns.

INSTRUCTORS

INSTRUCTOR_ID

INSTRUCTOR_LNAME

INSTRUCTOR_FNAME

INSTRUCTOR_SSN

INSTRUCTOR_CATEGORY

PRIMARY_EMPLOYER

PRIMARY_POSITION

By creating a new subset table called ADJUNCT_EMPLOYMENT, which can be joined to INSTRUCTORS by INSTRUCTOR_ID, you can avoid all those null columns. The common columns for all instructors, whether a university employee or adjunct instructor, remain in INSTRUCTORS. Only those unique to the subset and the linking primary/foreign key relationship column used with the join are moved to the subset column, as shown next:

INSTRUCTORS	*ADJUNCT_EMPLOYMENT*
INSTRUCTOR_ID	INSTRUCTOR_ID
INSTRUCTOR_LNAME	PRIMARY_EMPLOYER
INSTRUCTOR_FNAME	PRIMARY_POSITION
INSTRUCTOR_SSN	
INSTRUCTOR_CATEGORY	

Validation Tables

A *validation table* or *lookup table* contains a list of acceptable values for the columns of some other table or tables. It is used to support data integrity or business rules by providing a list of acceptable values to the user or to check input against the validation table to ensure that the input is in the range of acceptable values. Validation tables are often called *code tables* as well.

NEW TERM   *Validation Tables* are also known as look-up tables. These tables contain code values and their definitions and are also used to ensure data integrity.

Good candidates for validation tables include the following:

- DEPARTMENTS
- POSITIONS
- STATE_CODES
- MARITAL_STATUS

For example, data in the STATE_CODES table might appear as follows:

STATE_CODES

STATE	STATE_DESCRIPTION
AL	ALABAMA
AS	ALASKA
AZ	ARIZONA
AR	ARKANSAS
CA	CALIFORNIA
CO	COLORADO

The application may query the STATE_CODES table to validate a state that is input by the user. Additionally, the STATE_CODES table may be joined to the EMPLOYEES table, for example, by the STATE column.

Note the structure of the following table that references the STATE_CODES table:

EMPLOYEES

EMP_ID
LNAME
FNAME
MNAME
ADDRESS
CITY
STATE
ZIP

Normalizing Data

Normalizing data is one of the final steps of physical database design. The normalization process is fundamental to the modeling and design of a relational database. Its main purpose is to eliminate data redundancy that can occur in databases that have not been normalized. Normalization is the application of a set of simple rules called FIRST, SECOND, and THIRD NORMAL FORM to assign attributes to entities in the ERD. Although there are additional levels of normalization beyond THIRD NORMAL FORM, such as Boyce-Codd, FOURTH, and FIFTH levels of NORMAL FORM, normalization of a production relational database generally stops at the THIRD NORMAL FORM. For more information on normalization, refer back to Hour 6, "Understanding Relational Database Architecture."

Understanding Post-Design Tasks

You may think that after database design, most of the work is done; but in many cases the work is just beginning. For any successfully designed database, the following post-design tasks must occur:

- Building and testing the database
- Implementing the database into a production environment
- Managing the database after implementation

Building the database involves its creation according to the design, which involves many tasks such as the selection of database software, installation of software, creation of the database, and creation of database tables based on the entity relationship diagrams (ERDs). Testing the database is the post-design tasks that will ensure that all database features function properly and as intended. After successful database test results, the database is implemented in a production environment in which real users access the database. Then, of course, you have management. Database management involves many things, from basic database administration to managing changes and versions to a database and a database application.

These concepts are discussed in greater detail in Hour 13, "Managing the Database Life Cycle."

11

Understanding Database Design Methodology

Simply put, a *methodology* is a set of guidelines for performing some process. A database design methodology is a set of guidelines for designing a database. The following common sense principles must be considered during the design and implementation of any database:

- Determining the need for a system
- Defining the goals for the system

- Gathering business requirements
- Converting business requirements to system requirements
- Designing the database and application interface
- Building, testing, and implementing the database and application

These principles are applied by most database design methodologies.

The Barker method is one of the most common methodologies used for relational databases; it involves the following seven phases:

1. Strategy
2. Analysis
3. Design
4. Build
5. Documentation
6. Transition
7. Production

Strategy involves planning the design effort. In the analysis phase, the development team interviews key employees to gather all the business requirements that will be used as a model for the system. During the design phase, a physical model is designed based on the logical model that was designed in the analysis phase. After the design is complete, the database is built. The use of documentation is extremely beneficial, both for system users and application users. During the transition phase, data is prepared for a move into the production environment. The end-user application is tested against the database with real data to ensure that all components of the application function properly and that the integrity of the data as stored in the database is consistent. Finally, the database is ported into a production environment, where it is available to the end user for daily use.

Figure 11.5 summarizes the seven phases of the Barker method:

A design methodology can and should be adapted to meet an organization's needs during a specific database design effort. To expect the most out of a database design effort, the participating individuals should understand the fundamentals of database design and then select a methodology by which the design will occur. Then, it is a matter of carefully applying design concepts to the situation at hand.

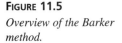

FIGURE 11.5
Overview of the Barker method.

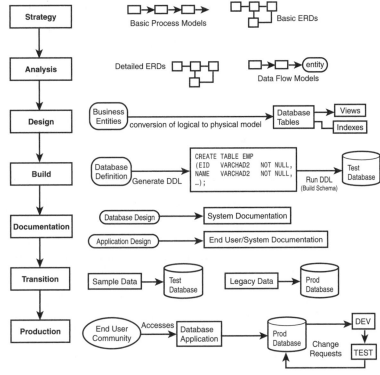

11

Summary

Database design is the most important step in the creation of a high-quality database. Unfortunately, the design process is often taken too lightly and is not given the attention it deserves. In this hour, you just barely scratched the surface on database design. The intent was to make you aware of some of the basic concepts that are imperative to understand if you ever become serious about designing a database. If you ever get to that point, seek further guidance on the database design process, such as our Sams title, *Database Design*, which takes you through all the stages of database design, from idea inception to requirements gathering to implementation. In any case, take database design seriously and realize that the more work put into design, the better the end product.

Workshop

The following workshop is composed of quiz questions and practical exercises. The quiz questions are designed to test your overall understanding of the current material. The practical exercises are intended to afford you the opportunity to apply the concepts discussed during the current hour, as well as build on the knowledge acquired in previous hours of study. Please take time to complete this workshop before continuing. You can refer to the answers at the end of the hour.

Quiz

1. What are the two types of data modeling?

2. Name the common database design methodology discussed in this hour.

3. What are the two types of requirements that must be gathered before designing a database?

4. From where are tables normally derived in database design?

5. What are the three main elements illustrated in an ERD?

Exercises

1. Define three or four possible entities that would be involved in a human resource database.

2. Define attributes for each entity that you defined in exercise 1.

3. Identify the relationships that might exist between the entities that you have defined.

4. List a few business rules that might exist in your human resource database.

5. Sketch a simple ERD based on your human resource database.

Answers to Quiz

1. Logical and physical modeling.

2. The Barker method.

3. Business and system requirements.

4. Tables are derived from the ERD.

5. Entities, attributes, and relationships.

HOUR 12

Learning Basic Database Administration

Administration is necessary for any database, regardless of the implementation, purpose, or size. A database is not a self-sufficient entity—it requires guidance and management through its life, from design to implementation to data management. Although database administration specifics may differ between database implementations, the tasks involved in administering a database are fairly standard. They vary from software installation to storage management to performance tuning. The intent during this hour is to make you familiar with the basic fundamentals of administering a modern database.

The objectives of this hour include

- Learning about database administration
- Learning roles and responsibilities of database administrators
- Learning about database creation and configuration
- Understanding the basics of database security
- Exploring database monitoring

- Understanding the basics of backup and recovery
- Understanding database space and resource management
- Understanding basic database performance tuning

Understanding Database Administration

Database administration is the maintenance of a database to ensure that the data is available, reliable, and secure at all times. Database administration should also ensure that the data has been backed up properly for recovery purposes in the case of any unfortunate loss of data. Loss of data is normally related to database failures that are caused by hardware problems, human error, accidents, and natural disasters. Loss of data is one of the greatest fears in database administration. Thus, database administration revolves around the protection of data. Database administration is performed by the database administrator, commonly referred to as the DBA. In the following sections, you will learn about some of the most typical tasks of a DBA, which should provide you with a good overall understanding of database administration.

Relating to the DBA

Many tiers of responsibility are associated with the tasks of a database administrator. Each year, technology grows, especially in the world of relational database systems. New tools are constantly made available to the DBA to aid in overall job effectiveness. However, no tool can equal the importance of a knowledgeable DBA who not only installs, implements, and configures a database, but monitors the database and its users, combines database concepts with business rules, and makes the best decisions for the maintenance of a database to keep it in tune with itself and other systems.

The DBA is the person responsible for managing and maintaining the databases for an organization. This person is also responsible for ensuring that the data is available at all times and that it is secured and reliable.

NEW TERM   *Database Administrator (DBA)* is the person who plays a major role in the creating of the database, maintaining the database, ensuring that the data is available and secure.

Reviewing a DBA's Tasks

The primary responsibilities of DBAs include, but are not limited to, creating the database, sizing the database, design and development, security, performance tuning, and backup recovery. In addition to their duties to maintain databases, database administrators also provide technical guidance to application developers, database designers, and the end users.

In a smaller organization, it is not uncommon for the database administrator to have multiple roles. At times, the database administrator may fill in for the system administrator, either part-time or full-time. Most database administrators have previous database-related experience working with a variety of vendor products or job roles. A database administrator may have worked as an application developer or database designer before getting involved in database administration. Having such experience enables database administrators to be versatile and helps with job performance.

It is a database administrator's ultimate responsibility to ensure that the data is available and protected at all times. In the case of a disaster or database failure, the data must be recoverable with the least amount of data loss and downtime.

Creating the Database Environment

One of your preliminary tasks as a DBA is to create the database environment and the database itself. After all, you cannot manage a database that does not exist! Before creating the database environment, you must do your homework. The database should be well planned, just as the database design effort should be well planned, as discussed in Hour 11, "Understanding the Basics of Database Design." Before creating the database, you must know answers to questions such as

- What hardware/computer will be used to host the database?
- What is the operating system?
- What database software will be used?
- How much disk space will be required?
- How much memory (host computer) will be available for the database?
- How many databases will be on the host computer?
- How many users will there be?
- What are the growth expectations of the database?

These are just a few of the questions that must be answered. After you know the answers, you must perform the following steps to establish the database environment:

1. Install the database software.
2. Create and configure the database.
3. Control database availability.

These steps are covered in the following sections.

12

Installing Database Software

DBAs are responsible for installing the database software on the host machines. This involves creating proper directory structure and assigning proper permissions to all database files. Most database vendors require root (Unix) privileges or membership in the administrator's group (Microsoft NT/2000) to install the database software. These permissions can be either permanently or temporarily assigned depending on the situation. Before installing database software, you must be sure that all the requirements are met, such as the operating system version and minimum amount of memory required to support the software.

> Later in this book, you will use the MySQL database for basic hands-on practice to become familiar with the standard database language, SQL. In Hour 15, "Understanding the Standard Database Language: SQL," you will learn how to download and install MySQL.

Creating and Configuring the Database

After the database software has been installed, the database can be created. In terms of database administration, the database is the mechanism that is created in which tables and indexes can later be created. Usually, the database is created first and tables and indexes are added later. However, it is possible to create the database and all database objects at once. Realistically, the database will exist before the objects do, in the database design.

The complexity of creating a database depends on the product vendor. For example, in Microsoft Access and SQL Server, it is very easy to create a database using a graphical interface. It is a matter of clicking a few buttons, and a database is created. On the other hand, in Oracle, creating a database is a more complex task. There are two ways a database can be created in Oracle. The first uses a GUI-based tool called Oracle Database Configuration Assistant. The database administrator is asked a series of questions as the database is created. The other method is creating a database by manually issuing commands or using a script with embedded commands. This method allows a database administrator flexibility to customize the database. This method is also the most preferred method by many database administrators.

> Hour 16, "Creating Databases and Database Objects," discusses in more detail the concepts and processes of creating databases and database objects. Hour 16 deals with a database called MySQL, which is an open

source database that is easy to download and install. MySQL does not have many of the features of other databases, such as Oracle, but it is appropriate for learning how to interact with a database. Some organizations find that MySQL sufficiently serves their database needs.

Controlling Database Availability

After the database has been created, the next step is to be able to control availability. The database is made available by starting it, or running a program to open it up for use. Oracle offers a simple command, called "startup," to start up the database. Some database implementations simply require you to double-click an icon, which invokes software that allows access to data stored in data files.

When starting the database, the DBA needs to ensure that the right database is being started with the right values for the database parameters. Starting the database with the wrong parameters not only affects the database being started, but also can affect the other databases on the host machine. For example, if, by mistake, too much memory has been allocated to a particular database, the whole machine will be affected by this decision. This step will take away resources from other, and maybe more important, databases on the host machine and slow down machine performance.

DBAs are responsible for starting up and shutting down the database. The commands to shut down a database are not difficult in any database vendor product; anyone can issue these commands, but there is much responsibility attached to shutting down the database. Database administrators need to ensure that the target database to shut down is the correct database and that the database will restart. If the database does not restart, a plan should be in place to take the necessary steps to recover the database. Before shutting down the database, the database administrators also need to ensure that no active users are in the database or that the database is not active making an update via a large batch process. Shutting down the database at the wrong time can destroy work that someone has put a lot of time into creating.

Managing Database Security

After a database is created, it must be secured. The most secure database is one that has no users and has no network connection—but let's be reasonable. A database is meant to be used, and breaches in security are risks inherent in making data available to one or more users. After database creation, it is one of the DBA's foremost responsibilities to ensure that the database is secure, using methods that enable users to access their data

12

appropriately while providing the highest level of protection possible. The sections that follow discuss database security at these levels:

- Managing user accounts
- Password authentication
- Security at the database level
- Security at the application level
- Security at the system level
- Security at the network level

Managing User Accounts

User processing is the primary justification for any database. Within the realm of user processing, a multitude of actions may be taken by a user against the database. Limiting database access is one of the most effective methods for protecting the data within a database and the database itself. Although most users would not maliciously harm a database, an accident can be just as devastating as sabotage. In fact, most "sabotage" incidents are the end result of an accident.

Database administrators are responsible for creating users in the database. Administrators need to ensure that proper procedures are being followed when creating users. For example, a proper naming convention for the user ID and a proper password is assigned to users to create their own database objects. The database administrator needs to verify that the users are authorized to access the data in the database and at what security level.

New Term *Naming Conventions* for our purposes is a standardized set of rules and practices that govern how database objects are to be named.

After user accounts have been created, the DBA can assign privileges to users that allow them to interact with the database and access certain data. There are two types of privileges: system privileges and object privileges. System privileges allow a user to interact with the database—to issue database-level commands. Object privileges allow users to access certain objects (data) in the database. These privileges are the basis of anything that a user can do while connected to a database. Privileges also form the building blocks of database roles, which provide a means for the DBA to group together sets of similar privileges and grant them to a single user or a group of users.

New Term *User Accounts* are login identification names associated with a password that allow individual users to access a given database.

> What a user wants is not always what he or she needs to accomplish his or her job. Determining the level of access that users need to use the database appropriately happens on a site-by-site basis. It is generally best to give too little access at first and to add privileges as needed. Determining user access levels should be well planned and should take place preferably in the database design phase. As discussed in Hour 11, "Understanding the Basics of Database Design," proper design and planning eases the tasks of database administration.

NEW TERM   *Privileges* are a series of rights or permissions that can be granted to a user account in order to allow that user the ability to perform various actions.

NEW TERM   A *Role* is a database construct, usually created by a DBA, that can have privileges assigned to it. Then that role is subsequently assigned or granted to a user or group of users. The users are then automatically granted the permissions of the Role.

Password Authentication

As a rule, databases do not have an open-door policy that allows everyone access. Therefore, a database needs a way to authenticate users—to determine their identity and make certain that they have authorized access. The concept behind password authentication is the same as the traditional password method used on other databases, operating systems, network servers, and so on. Under this concept, the user supplies a connect string to the database, which includes a username and password. The username is a way of identifying the user to the database, and the password authenticates, or verifies, that each user is who he says he is. Upon valid entry of a username and password combination, the database allows entry and also allows the user to perform tasks as specified by privileges and roles that have been granted to that user.

Integrating Security at the Database Level

Security in the database is enforced via roles and by assigning privileges to these roles. When a user is created in the database, a role is assigned to the user based on his or her job responsibility and the type of work the user will be doing in the database. It is the DBA's responsibility to manage roles in the database. These roles are then assigned to the users. For example, a role called Manager is created in the database. This role is assigned to all the managers in the company. There are 20 managers in the whole company. If these managers are given additional privileges, it is much easier to assign the privilege to that one role than to give privileges to 20 managers. This greatly simplifies the process of assigning privileges. Figure 12.1 illustrates internal database users and security using privileges and roles.

12

Privileges can be granted that primarily allow the following access to database tables: creating data, updating existing data, and deleting data from tables. Roles are simply groups of privileges that allow users to access tables in certain ways.

FIGURE 12.1

Database security.

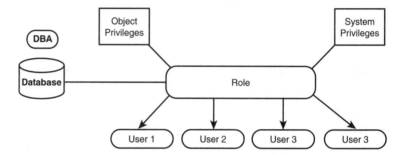

Integrating Security at the Application Level

Although the DBA is not always responsible for application security, it is good to have a solid understanding. Application security is handled mainly in two ways: through the application interface and by using stored procedures in the database. The application interface may also have a login for the user and may have built-in edits that control what kind of data can be entered. Furthermore, the application itself may have roles, or profiles (external from the database), that determine which tasks each user can perform. Stored procedures can be used by the application interface to manipulate data in the database, rather than allowing a user full access to the data. Using stored procedures, you can control exactly how the user is manipulating data. Figure 12.2 illustrates database application users.

FIGURE 12.2

Application users and security.

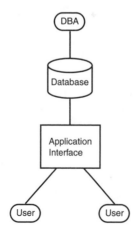

Integrating Security at the System Level

Some users with operating system access may also need direct access to the database. For example, DBAs need access to both the operating system and the database. All databases store data files at the operating system level on a host machine. Therefore, the DBA should have to supply login information to the operating system as well as to the database. Other users, such as software developers, may also need access to both the operating system and the database. At the operating system level, access is controlled by user authentication and permissions (Unix systems) or user authentication and password-protected folders (Windows systems). Figure 12.3 illustrates the operating system security layer.

FIGURE 12.3

Operating system security layer.

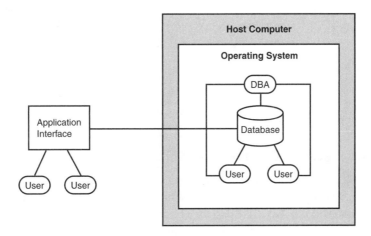

Integrating Security at the Network Level

Most databases are connected to some sort of network environment. Because a multitude of users often have access to the network, great care must be taken to control access. First, all users should have to authenticate themselves to the network (username and password). Another precaution is the use of a firewall on the database host computer. A firewall controls allowed connections based on information such as the location of the client computer. Other precautions include the division of users into workgroups, using secured shell logins, and data encryption. Network security is normally the responsibility of the network administrator, although the DBA may be heavily involved. Figure 12.4 illustrates the network layer of database interaction.

12

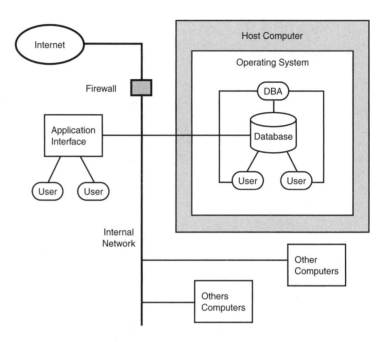

Figure 12.4

Interacting with the database through the network.

Monitoring the Database

All databases have flaws, both in the structure, at the application level, and definitely in the accuracy of user activities. Yes, most database users are human, and they do make mistakes. Databases are designed by humans and deficiencies will inevitably exist. Databases are implemented, problems arise, and the management wants results—now! Throw the growth factor into the equation, as well. Database objects grow with increased data, and often the user community grows, too. This is where database monitoring comes into play.

Take a proactive stance! Database monitoring is knowing what is happening in your database at all times. Seeing is knowing, and knowing is the ability to act in a proactive manner and make intelligent decisions.

The following types of monitoring envelop the responsibilities of a DBA:

- User auditing
- Space and resource monitoring
- Session (user) monitoring

Some databases automatically monitor major database events, such as startup, shutdown, user activity, and internal errors, and record information pertaining to these events in the database itself or in an external operating system file.

In addition to the tools that are provided by database vendors, many third-party products that are tailored specifically for an Oracle database have been made available to the DBA. Be sure to check all your options to optimize the task of monitoring database activity.

Auditing Users

One of the most dominating fears of a taxpayer is the chance of being audited by the IRS. Yes, we need to be audited because some of us cheat the system. Likewise, database users also must be audited, because sometimes users make mistakes or get into data they shouldn't out of curiosity, or they get angry and try to make the organization they work for pay by destroying data. And sometimes, user productivity must be audited.

Auditing can happen all the time or be turned on and used periodically—sort of a spot check, like that of the IRS. If malicious activity is suspected, the DBA may decide to turn on auditing, and upon acquired evidence, action may be taken to reprimand the offending user. The IRS does not audit every individual because of the costs involved—costs such as additional personnel required to handle the workload and of course, more capital, along with any other resources required to run the organization. Likewise, auditing in a database has costs as well because of the extra processes involved.

Typical reasons for database auditing include

- Monitoring overall concurrent user activity/load on the system
- Pinpointing misuse of user IDs/passwords
- Pinpointing malicious activity
- Measuring employee productivity
- Monitoring database changes on specific objects
- Monitoring activities executed by privileged accounts

Various types of auditing may be integrated into a database. Audit information can be retained from general login information to specific changes that occur within specific database objects. All actions can be audited and the task of auditing can be (and should be) tailored specifically to the needs of the database system to ensure proper use of the

12

system, to discourage unauthorized database activity, and to do so in a cost-effective manner. Some databases provide a means for auditing user activity. In any database, scripts can be used to audit users.

Monitoring Resource Utilization

Inherent with any database is a considerable amount of system processing that takes place behind the scenes. Every database has a significant amount of overhead, much of which is composed of background processes that require certain amounts of a computer's CPU and memory. Another important system resource is disk storage. Resource monitoring is important to the DBA because if resources are not managed properly, the database may not operate efficiently or may not even function. As data gets bigger, and workloads increase, proactive resource monitoring provides a means for the DBA to justify the allocation of additional resources to allow the database to function as originally intended. Data growth and space management is discussed in more detail later in this hour.

 Resource Utilization is how the Central Processing Unit (CPU) and memory are being used in the course of everyday activity.

Managing Backup and Recovery

Your database has been created. It is running smoothly and the users are happy. The customers are happy and so is management. Your database is the most secure database in the entire world and your company's IT department was featured on the front page of the business section in yesterday's issue of the *Wall Street Journal*. Today is another day, and while you are getting ready for work, you notice on the news that a tornado has taken out a business complex. Your company's building was completely flattened.

First, you are concerned that nobody was hurt, and you are relieved to find out that the tornado occurred before anybody got to work. Then your stomach sinks when you realize that all your computer equipment has been destroyed. Your business relies on data, and your data is gone. Sure, insurance will replace your office and equipment, but the only insurance you can provide for your data is a solid backup and recovery plan. Maybe you were backing up your database regularly, but maybe you were not using offsite storage for your backups. You hope that you will be able to recover your data; otherwise, you might find your company featured in the *Wall Street Journal* for a more grim reason.

NEW TERM *Backup and Recovery Plan* is a detailed and strictly adhered to plan for making regular backup copies of the database, storage of the backup (both on site and off site), and how to recover your database should the need arise.

This sounds like a nightmare, but it is reality in the database world. Nothing is more important to the DBA than protecting the data, and a good backup and recovery plan is the only solution.

Backup and recovery are among the most important considerations on any system, but they generally receive less than 1% of the total planning, developing, and testing effort. In the event of a catastrophe, it is imperative that the data be recovered. Two factors are critical for success: accuracy and timeliness.

If a backup does not properly record all the information necessary to recover the database, it is worthless. A backup that fails to provide a critical piece of information, such as a required database file, cannot be used to restore operations. It is essential, therefore, that all the necessary database components be part of scheduled backups. Likewise, recovery of a mission-critical database that takes several days is, in most cases, unacceptable. A backup must expeditiously and completely restore the database after a failure occurs.

Three types of backups will be briefly discussed in sections that follow:

- Cold backups
- Hot backups
- Logical backups

Conducting Cold Backups

One of the simplest backup methods is the cold backup, also known as the consistent backup. In a cold backup, the database has been closed, but preferably totally shut down, and all the physical files associated with the database are copied by means of normal operating system utilities. The backup copies of the database files are typically stored on a tape or a disk drive on a separate computer. Because the database is not in operation, changes are not made to the physical files, and there are no conflicting integrity or consistency problems. Depending on the size of the database and the speed of the copy utility used—copies to disk are faster than copies to tape—a cold backup can take anywhere from a few minutes to several hours or even several days. Thus, a cold backup is not always an option. Many sites supplement weekly or monthly cold backups with other backups on a nightly basis. They think that they have 24/7 operations, when in reality, large windows of time are available in the evening for a cold backup. This is, of course, site specific. It is up to the DBA to evaluate the needs of the user community versus the needs of the operations staff.

New Term   *Cold Backups* are performed when the database is closed.

12

Conducting Hot Backups

Some databases provide a means for taking hot backups. A hot backup is one that is taken when the database is up and running. During hot backups, users can access the database. Because of this, the database must keep track of all changes to the data that occur during the backup. Hot backups are appropriate when the database cannot be shut down for any amount of time. Many production databases are like this and cannot be shut down without making prior notification of the downtime. In cases like that, a hot backup utility is used to perform the backup.

 Hot Backups are performed when the database is up and running and users are accessing the database.

Most modern RDBMS vendors have a hot backup process. For example, in Oracle, a hot backup can be taken of the database. A tablespace can be placed in a backup mode and then the operating system's copy command is used to make a copy of the database files. After the copy is done, the tablespace is returned to its normal state. This process is for the most part transparent to the end user and does not affect usage of the database. Although the hot backup process is meant to provide increased database uptime to the end user, the cost is possible degradation in database performance if the backup process is long or the amount of data being backed up at any given time is very large.

 Tablespace refers to a portion of the computer disk that has been allocated for user tables.

Conducting Logical Backups

Many database vendors provide a means for taking exports of the database, also called a logical backup. Database exports are a quick way of logically backing up the data, meaning that the data files themselves are not backed up, only the data as it is stored in the database. All exported data is stored in a file, usually referred to as an export file or a dump file. In case of a database failure, the file can be moved to any database host server and the schema can be re-created. This can be done in a very short amount of time. Exports are quick solutions for small databases, but at a cost. One problem with exports is that they are good only for the time the export was taken. An export is basically a logical snapshot of the database at a given point in time.

 A *Logical Backup* is a point in time backup of database data that is exported or copied to another location.

For example, if the export was taken at 10:00 a.m. and the database crashed at 12:00 p.m., the database can be returned only to the last good export, which is 10:00 a.m. Manual entry of all transactions made between 10:00 a.m. and 12:00 p.m. must be done to bring the database to its current state before the crash. Some database products support incremental exports to handle these situations.

Exports are also good for moving the application between two database servers. For example, HR_Application database currently resides in HR_Host database server. The company decides to upgrade the HR_Host machine with a newer machine called AC_Host. Exports can be used to move all the applications from HR_Host to AC_Host.

> If an export is used for recovery, everything in the database that has been added, deleted, or otherwise changed since the last export is lost. For this reason, exports are used only to facilitate quick, point-in-time recoveries, such as when a static reference table is truncated. They do not provide the level of recovery that most mission-critical operations require.

Recovering a Database

Backups should be a daily part of the life of a DBA. Hopefully, recoveries are not. However, time should be spent to ensure that, if a recovery is needed, it will work. Too often, DBAs get comfortable with backup routines and don't really know how well a recovery will take place. In fact, some DBAs do not know how to recover a database. Therefore, it is important to test backups, and the only way to test them is to simulate database failure or disaster. That doesn't mean burn your office building down, but it does involve having a test environment in which you can destroy the data and try to recover it.

There are several methods for performing database recovery. Each method offers a trade-off between speed and simplicity. Typical recovery types include

- Cold restore of database files
- Complete, up-to-date recovery
- Point-in-time recovery
- Logical recovery (import from an export file)

Planning for Disaster Recovery

Disaster recovery involves providing a working plan to successfully recover a database after the occurrence of a disaster, such as a fire, a tornado, or a hurricane. If a disaster occurs, often entire information systems are destroyed, including all hardware, software, and data. A plan must be in place to reinstate the damaged or destroyed information, its

12

software, and data. Database administrators play a key role when planning for disaster recovery. Following are some of the key points to consider for disaster recovery:

- Uninterrupted power supply
- Media storage
- Key systems
- Testing

Uninterrupted Power Supply

In planning the recovery from failure, one of the most obvious pieces of hardware that is overlooked is the uninterrupted power supply (UPS). Having a quality UPS can save businesses from a lot of extra work when there is a power failure. Buy a quality UPS and test it.

> Commonly a UPS provides only a few minutes or a few hours of power. Most companies running a large "warehouse" of databases or mainframes prefer to have a fuel-powered generator, sometimes more than one.

Media Storage

Store disk or tape media offsite. Many people have created elaborate disaster recovery plans but did not think about the media and stored it next to the machine. Store tapes at a different site and always have a plan for how the tapes are going to be brought to the site and who is going to bring them. Natural disasters do happen.

Identify Key Systems

The DBA, in consultation with management, should identify key database systems that need to be running for the company to operate at a bare minimum. Furthermore, these systems should be identified in term of priority. Which system needs to come up first? This is usually documented in Service Level Agreements (SLAs).

Testing the Plan

The DBA should also test the disaster recovery plan before the actual disaster occurs. A lot of times, database administrators create elaborate recovery plans, but never test the plan. Overlooking minor details can make or break a great disaster recovery plan. The DBA should become an expert at restoring databases. All the plans are a complete waste if the data cannot be restored in a timely fashion.

Managing Space Utilization and System Resources

Capacity planning is one of the key responsibilities of the DBA. A DBA must allocate disk space to the application in the database based on the number of records and the size of the records. Furthermore, based on the number of concurrent users accessing the database application and the times the database will be most used, the database administrator allocates memory to the database. When managing storage and naming database files, standard naming conventions and descriptive names should also be used all across the database. This will help the administrator identify the files for each database running on the host system.

When discussing space utilization, the database objects that cause the most problems are tables and indexes. Because transactions are constantly extracted from and inserted into database tables and indexes, problems such as chaining, migration, dynamic extension, and fragmentation can occur regularly. Because they occur often, most DBAs wait until these problems exceed a threshold, or they follow a maintenance schedule.

Managing Basic Data Storage (Projection, Sizing, Allocation)

Whenever you create a table, you must decide how large it should be, how fast it should grow, and how often its data will change. Unfortunately, the only way to gauge a table's growth is to rely on experience and trends. For that reason, you must deal with dynamic extension. Every database object is created with an initial size. Information is added to the table or index until no more room is left in the initial space allocation. Then the size of the table is incremented by a fixed amount. This is called dynamic extension.

Managing Data Growth (Projection, Resizing, Purging)

After space has been allocated, you have to assume that data will grow and more space will be required eventually. As data grows, more space is required, and the database often becomes fragmented. Fragmentation occurs when database objects grow and pieces of the same object are located in different physical locations on disk.

As with data sizing, projecting data growth relies heavily on trends and experience. Suppose that a new business doubles its customers and the products that it sells to its customers the next year. This could mean that the database has doubled in size. There may be no accurate way of projecting growth, but the DBA must ensure that data growth is possible. It is not only the DBA's responsibility to project data growth, but it is the DBA's responsibility to make data growth projecting a priority.

12

Purging of data is a consideration in the life of many databases. Suppose that after several years, a company's data is 100 times larger than its original size. It may be a good decision to purge data that is no longer needed, or have a routine that rolls old data into a historical area. This way, historic data can be accessed if necessary (perhaps via tape storage), but does not take up so much space in the database itself. Therefore, space is freed for new data that will be accessed more frequently.

Tuning the Database for Optimal Performance

People don't like to wait. They want information and they want it now. Improving database performance is also one of the responsibilities of a database administrator. Numerous books have been written on the topic of performance tuning, and most of them are vendor specific.

 Tuning is the process by which the DBA makes adjustments to the database in order for it to perform at the best of its abilities.

 When tuning a database, the first and most crucial step is gathering statistics on the current database performance. These tools give a benchmark of how the database is currently performing and enable the DBA to gauge progress by measuring improvement.

Four basic steps are involved in any kind of database tuning:

1. Gathering information
2. Determining optimal changes
3. Implementing changes
4. Monitoring the database

 For all tuning, the more proactively the process is done, the more effective it is. The process is seldom effective when it is done on-the-fly or without the proper amount of research.

When a DBA considers tuning a database, it is important to distinguish between the two levels of performance tuning: applications tuning and database tuning. They are distinct areas of expertise and are often handled by different people. The DBA should have at least an overview of the importance and functions of each type of tuning. At the base of both levels is the operating system, which drives the physical functionality—such as how to access the physical disk devices.

The following sections discuss tuning at the following levels:

- Database
- Application
- System
- Network

Performance Tuning at the Database Level

DBAs are expected to monitor their databases regularly. The purpose of monitoring is to identify any problem areas before they become big and end up crashing the database. Administrators should also monitor space in the database or if the database is up or down. Nothing is worse than hearing from management that the database has run out of space or to find out through a third party that the database is down. It is better to be proactive than reactive in database administration. DBAs must recognize and correct problems before noticed by others.

As a DBA, you can monitor by executing shell scripts at the command prompt. These scripts can be written in Shell for the Unix environment or via NT scripting for the Windows NT environment. A shell script is a set of commands in the form of a file. When the file executes, all the commands in that file get executed. Monitoring scripts are either executed manually or scheduled via a Unix Cron or Windows Scheduler.

12

There are all types of monitoring scripts available from different database vendors for purchase or as freeware on the Web. These scripts can be easily modified for a specific use. Some of the common tasks that can be done via monitoring are space availability and utilization, and performance history.

There are also graphical tools available on the market that make monitoring a simpler task. For example, Quest Technologies has a tool available on the market called TOAD. TOAD is a graphic that can be used to perform a variety of database administration tasks. Oracle Corporation has a tool called Oracle Enterprise Manager. OEM is an Oracle-specific tool and can be used for all database administration tasks, including monitoring. Microsoft also has a SQL Server-specific tool called Enterprise Manager to perform administration tasks and monitoring.

Outside of proactive monitoring of resources and space utilization, tuning at the database level is a bit of a hit-and-miss process. It concentrates on things such as enlarging database buffers and caches by increasing database parameters or attributes and by balancing database files to achieve optimum throughput.

Performance Tuning at the Application Level

Applications tuning deals with how the various applications (forms, reports, queries) are designed to interact with the database. Essentially, an application is nothing more than a program or collection of programs that issues calls to the database, which, in turn, are interpreted as physical reads and writes from the physical data files. Application code can be tuned to more efficiently access the database. Much application tuning involves restructuring embedded SQL code.

Each organization has its own specific problems and issues that affect the problems that occur in applications. More often than not, it is the duty of the developers to tune and modify their own programs without the involvement of the DBA. Because of perceived responsibility, however, the DBA must work with the applications development staff to resolve these problems.

Performance Tuning at the System Level

System-level tuning is usually the role of the system administrator, not the DBA. However, it is often the role of the DBA to offer suggestions. At the operating system level, paging and swapping are used to efficiently allow numerous processes to share system memory and resources. Paging involves moving the pages (virtual memory areas of program code and/or data) of one or more programs out of main memory to a special disk area. Swapping is where the memory manager "swaps" entire programs out of main memory to disk. The DBA should expect to see both paging and swapping occur on his system. It is up to the system administrator and/or the DBA to tune the system appropriately so that the database has all necessary resources to operate efficiently without adversely affecting other applications that reside on the same system.

Performance Tuning at the Network Level

The DBA should always consider network performance when evaluating the application environment. Specific tunable parameters, if set incorrectly, can cause serious performance problems for the application. Reliable performance statistics should be gathered and maintained so that proper workload determinations can be made. Keep in mind that if the network environment cannot sufficiently support your user community, no amount of operating system tuning will resolve your performance problems. Also keep in mind that an application will more than likely perform differently when operating in a wide area network (WAN) than in a local area network (LAN). This is because your applications data is traveling greater distances (often called hops) through special equipment (routers) designed to manage the WAN. Additionally, a WAN environment (such as the Internet) will have a higher possible number of concurrent users. If you begin to experience poor performance with your databases, consider including your network administrator in your efforts to resolve the performance problems.

Summary

Database administrators hold a key position in any organization. This job comes with the huge responsibility of managing databases. They perform a variety of tasks, from initial planning of how to lay out the database and objects to creating and managing users. Developers and designers of the database also look to database administrators for answers. Database administration is an ongoing task and is never complete. New applications get added to the databases all the time. As these applications are being added, new work for the database administrator is also being created.

Database maintenance involves the regular monitoring of the database. To perform good, wholesome maintenance, you must be proactive, studying the activities that occur in the database, such as space utilization, database growth, user functionality, and so on. Understanding the database is imperative to providing a better environment for the end user. Understanding is derived from study, and study is enabled through manual monitoring and database auditing.

Workshop

12

The following workshop is composed of quiz questions and practical exercises. The quiz questions are designed to test your overall understanding of the current material. The practical exercises are intended to afford you the opportunity to apply the concepts discussed during the current hour, as well as build on the knowledge acquired in previous hours of study. Please take time to complete this workshop before continuing. You can refer to the answers at the end of this hour.

Quiz

1. What is the definition of database administration?
2. Name five of the primary responsibilities of a database administrator.
3. Name two primary types of backups and describe how they differ.
4. Why is it important to have a backup plan of the database?
5. What is the significance of testing the disaster recovery plan?
6. What is the purpose of creating roles?

Exercises

1. Go to the following Internet links of three database vendors and identify their database backup strategy and recommendations.

   `http://oracle.com/ip/deploy/database/oracle9i`

   `http://microsoft.com/catalog/`

   `http://www-3.ibm.com/software/data/`

2. Choose a database vendor, go to its Web site, and identify different training recommendations.

3. Some of the most popular database vendors are listed next:

   Oracle

   Microsoft SQL Server

   IBM DB2

   MySQL

   Informix

Answers to Quiz

1. Database administration is the maintenance of a database to ensure the data is reliable, available, and secured at all times.

2. Installs Oracle software

   Creates the Database

   Starts up and shuts down the database instance

   Manages database storage

   Manages database users

3. Hot backup and cold backup.

   Hot backups are conducted while the database is up and being used by the users.

   Cold backups are conducted after shutting down the database.

4. To minimize loss of data and downtime for the database applications because of a natural disaster or a deliberate act.

5. Overlooking minor details can make or break a great disaster recovery plan. All the plans are a complete waste if the data cannot be restored. The plan has to be tested to ensure that it works.

6. Creating roles and assigning them to the users greatly simplifies the process of assigning privileges.

HOUR 13

Managing the Database Life Cycle

The previous hour presented topics associated with database management, including database creation, configuration, and resource management. This hour generalizes the discussion of administration to include all activities associated with the maintenance of a database throughout its life.

The objectives of this hour include

- Understanding the typical software life cycle
- Understanding the typical database life cycle
- Gaining an overview of the life cycle and roles of participants
- Learning about change management

Understanding the Software Life Cycle

Software life cycle refers to the period of time in which a software product is in use, from design until the termination of its use. The software life cycle depends on many factors, some of which include technology progression, the changing needs of an organization, and the usefulness of the software after a period of time. Databases are managed by software products therefore it is important to understand the basics of the software life cycle (which applies to any type of software) and then apply those concepts to databases.

Generally, software type has a profound impact on its life cycle. Embedded software, designed for hardware control, often has a life span of 10 or more years after initial release. Desktop applications may survive for only two years. Database designs may be intermediate between these extremes. Regardless, the expected life of the software product is a critical consideration in life cycle planning.

NEW TERM   *Life Cycle* is for the purposes of our discussion the period of time that the software or database can reasonably be expected to be in use.

The notion of software components is a basis for this discussion. Subsequent discussions offer a more general definition, but when applied to a database system, the components might be the following:

- Execution environment (operating system, hardware resources, helper programs)
- SQL engine (database software)
- SQL applications (database application interface)
- Data

Managers involved in software upgrades often insist on reuse of existing code. Historical evidence from many programs, large and small, proves convincingly that source code reuse offers only small gains in development time. When working with preexisting code, the developer must first study its original objectives, sometimes relearn the code, struggle with logic, then make modifications to modernize the software. However, requirements and documentation reuse can offer considerable efficiencies. For this reason, though, this discussion does not assume software reuse as a program goal.

This section explores five topics in general terms. These are

- The database life cycle
- Requirements management
- Configuration management
- Release management
- Software change control

The discussion concludes with a summary that provides a brief synopsis of these topics, as well as an example.

The discussion of the general software life cycle leads into the database life cycle and should help provide an understanding of how the database life cycle is a subset of the software life cycle.

Relating the Software and Database Life Cycle

A life cycle model captures the development, deployment, and maintenance of a typical software element. Development is the construction phase. Deployment is a formal release of the software. Maintenance consists of testing and tracking activities. Different models may apply to the various stages as well as to different software components.

Formal models become crucial as a risk reduction method for complex systems. Waterfall and spiral life cycle approaches are common. The waterfall method consists of discrete steps, whereas the spiral model is iterative. In practical terms, most projects are a combination of these methods. No manager is willing to continually revisit early design decisions, yet requirements changes often demand a return to previous plateaus.

In addition, managers may control different software components using different formal models. For example, upgrades to a user interface might involve the spiral model, whereas changes to an execution environment could follow a waterfall approach. The spiral approach is probably better in the former case because user interface requirements may continue changing during the upgrade. The latter approach might be better for an execution environment because it may consist of pieces that must work properly to install and test the next piece.

In many organizations, quality standards apply to software as well as to hardware. It is the responsibility of an engineer who participates in such an organization to understand the project life cycle model and to know in which stage the current project lies.

As the introduction describes, database projects often consist of an execution environment, SQL engine (database software), application interface, and data. Revisions of either the execution environment or the SQL engine typically result in major changes to at least the applications, and possibly the data itself. Therefore, these upgrades represent major milestones in the life of a database. Problem fixes and change requests usually impact only the applications and data. Therefore, these events may have less impact on the system as an entity.

13

Requirements Management

Software requirements capture the intended system behavior necessary for efficient use. Requirements categories include

- Function
- Interfaces definition
- Performance

Functional requirements relate to the behavior of the system. Interface definitions formalize the connections between major pieces of the system, as well as the interface to the user. Performance requirements define needed execution speed, memory usage, and mass storage limits.

Requirements management consists of analysis, tracking, and testability. The goal of the analysis task is to verify that requirements are technically achievable and produce the intended result. This activity may involve prototyping. Testability demonstrations prove that it is possible to establish tests that prove that the software meets the stated requirements. This is usually a precursor to formal definition of system-level tests. A requirement tracking is a broadly based task that extends beyond the development stage.

New Term   *Requirements Management* is determining how the new software is to function efficiently, how the software works with and between major components of the overall system, and determining if it will meet needed performance needs.

Requirements managers establish a process by which engineers, managers, and customer representatives can submit change requests. The management team approves or rejects the submissions based on relevance, cost, and schedule impacts. Approved changes then undergo the analysis process just described.

Mapping requirements to specific software components is a crucial part of this analysis. This has the effect of assigning the change request to the proper software author. This engineer does not only implement the change, but usually must also accept and validate the cost and schedule estimates of the change. Experience shows that historical data are the most reliable basis for this estimation. Therefore, this represents another example in which a responsible developer must keep a careful diary of work performed.

New Term   The *Change Request* is the formalized request to change something about the system. It is analyzed using Requirements Management concepts.

Requirements change throughout the database's life, even beyond the development stage. However, the largest number of changes to requirements typically occurs during design and just after initial release. Beyond this, the number of requirements changes tends to decrease. The exception to this happens if a software upgrade incorporates new interfaces, functions, or must execute on a new system. Most often, though, users tend to get comfortable with a system that functions as it should.

Configuration Management

For several reasons, the architecture of a complex software system may consist of components. For example, this structure might be a reflection of a software development approach called divide and conquer. In this method, the designers break a complex system into individual pieces. Managers then assign teams to develop dedicated elements. Another factor could be the intended usage. Components may correspond to members of usage classes, such as operating system support, execution environment, or user data. The test strategy may also be a consideration. Information security could be another factor.

NEW TERM	*Configuration Management* is the development of separate pieces or components of a complex software system.

It is possible to manage each component separately. This approach is common when many projects rely on some component, perhaps an execution environment. The key to this type of support consists of two activities:

- Documentation of software changes for each component
- Assignment of software version numbers for groups of changes

Change Documentation

Change documentation is project specific, but it might be as simple as a development log. This is simply a diary in which each engineer keeps a record of work performed. In larger systems, the engineers must submit the change records periodically. The documentation experts assemble these changes into a Version Description Document (VDD).

Versioning

Version numbers identify changes to a component. A version number consists of a major number and a minor number. Major version numbers reflect significant changes, whereas minor numbers account for incremental modifications. As an example, 2.12 represents major version 2, minor version 12.

NEW TERM	*Versioning* is the documenting of changes to a component or the entire software package as a whole.

13

A system software configuration is an assemblage of components of specific version numbers. Test engineers must verify that the various components of a specified version actually operate correctly as a system. In formal processes, the test engineers must submit a report that documents the tests completed and the results of testing.

Release Management

The definition of a software release is a key issue for those involved in configuration management. The release might be to an external software customer or a user within the same company. The rules for a release depend on the end user. However, in either case, a release involves

- A catalog of files and components, usually documented as a VDD
- Test results assembled into a test report
- Software, either source code, object code, or executable on some transferable medium such as magnetic tape or disk

For large systems, especially those supporting high-reliability applications, a Change Control Board (CCB) approves changes to requirements, documents, and software. In addition, the CCB authorizes release of a configuration.

 Release Management is the series of procedures and rules that govern a new software version being made available for use.

 A panoply of automated tools exists for support of configuration management. This includes software that can track changes to the components and even can assign the major and minor version numbers. Other tools might connect changes to requirements, software, and documentation. Regardless, teams should perform tool selection after establishing formal methods. Teams should never use automated tools as a shortcut to define a process.

Change Control

Software change management is an element of configuration management. The distinction is that configuration management includes requirements, documents, test software, and software components. Software change management refers specifically to modifications to the code base.

As in many of the other topics, there are industry and military standards that describe formal models for software change management. The goal of such models is to offer team members the opportunity to identify who made a particular change and the reason for the change. The larger the team and the more complex the software create a greater need for formal models.

 Change Control is the system of procedures that must be followed in order for a change to be initiated.

For an existing database or software application, the software change cycle often begins with a collection of problem reports. Usually, the end user submits Software Problem Reports (SPRs). The SPR contains a description of the problem and the circumstances that led to its detection. The standards described earlier offer templates and management methods for SPRs. Often these methods lead to a database application in which a help desk agent enters the information. For many products, it is also possible to submit an SPR electronically.

An important distinction exists between trouble and problem reports. As just mentioned, an end user generates a problem report whenever the system behaves unexpectedly. After analysis, it is possible to assign the behavior to a software component, at which point it is possible to produce a Software Trouble Report (STR).

To establish systematic procedures, managers should insist on a standard format for an STR. A document template is helpful for this purpose. The format of the template might be project specific, but usually includes the following (remember that it is a technical support engineer who generates this report, not the end user) :

- System description
- Software description
- Submitter
- Time and date
- Observed behavior

The system description is a list of components of the software environment. Operating system, including version number, is often a critical piece of information. The type of hardware might also be relevant. Other support components, such as network interfaces or helper programs, could be significant to problem isolation.

The software description is the version number of the product. This description should also note any software patches that administrators might have installed.

The submitter is the technical support engineer. However, some indication of the end user should also be provided. The technical support staff usually generates a tracking number so that the end user who provided the problem report can follow its resolution. The date and time of the STR submission allow for use with quality metrics such as response time.

The observed behavior is a description of the problem. Again, this is from the perspective of the technical staff. If the technical staff is unable to reproduce the problem (this happens more than you might expect), the technical staff can either request more information from the end user or ask management to close the issue.

13

An STR tracking system might itself be a database application. Key fields could include

- Tracking number
- Date of entry
- Title
- Responsible person
- Status

Most of these elements correspond to the discussion earlier in this topic. However, the application itself might automatically generate the tracking number. Also, the responsible person is the engineer working on a fix to the problem. Status could include milestones such as initial entry, problem assigned (to the responsible person), work in progress, fix proposed, and fix installed. A tracking system might also provide status reports that show the status of each tracking number and a total for each status category.

The STR database interfaces to, but is distinct from, the SPR tracking system. Data security is at least one reason for this split, because outsiders from the development group can enter an SPR. However, STRs are an important element of development planning, so it is important to keep this information accurate and current.

Finally, the version documentation should address the status of each relevant STR. Within this document, typical subcategories are a list of problems fixed and known problems.

It may be helpful to consider a final example. Consider an inventory tracking system. The goal is to identify material within a shipping center and to also identify when it arrived and when it was shipped.

Requirements management for this system controls, among other issues, the interfaces. These include data entry using bar-code scanners and menu systems for inventory agents. The interface is also likely to contain authentication information because accuracy demands limits on the access to the inventory. Use of an employee identification badge might be one such method. Finally, the interface is likely to include a report generator that produces documents from which managers can examine trends.

Quality Assurance

Quality Assurance (QA) planning involves establishing procedures that verify correct operation of the software prior to release. Testing plays a key role in most QA programs. However, code walk-throughs and formal reviews may also play a role. Some processes require formal reviews not only during development, but also as part of the software release process.

NEW TERM *Quality Assurance* is the process by which the entire system, and each component, is tested to ensure that it performs properly prior to release.

There are various kinds of software tests. Unit tests apply to a low-level software element, such as a function or subroutine. The software author usually is responsible for formulating and maintaining unit tests. Component tests apply to software components such as libraries or classes. An integration team is often responsible for these tests. System tests evaluate the operation of the entire assemblage. These tests are often distinct for the development team and QA engineers. Regression tests are an important subcategory of system tests.

Regression tests are a library of execution conditions designed to demonstrate that the entire system behaves correctly. For extremely complicated systems, the design of tests may involve statistical methods based on failure modes analysis. For less complex systems, there is often a suite of tests for each component and the entire system. Two common types of regression tests are validation and performance. In addition, regression tests may contain test conditions based on code fragments from earlier trouble reports. This is an attempt to ensure that previously repaired problems do not creep back in.

Validation tests are a suite of known inputs and outputs constructed to validate a release or component. An individual test feeds the inputs into a component and then compares the outputs to the expected results. If the results do not conform to expectations, the test team documents the test conditions as a software trouble report. If the results and expectations agree, the test team documents the success in a Software Test Report (STR).

Performance tests demonstrate that the software executes within system limits. This might involve response from a user interface or measurement of execution time for a component. Performance tests also can include code size comparisons to available system memory and storage.

Problem report tracking is the purview of the configuration management group. However, QA engineers must review open trouble reports prior to a release. This review verifies that there are no severe problems that are unresolved.

Finally, QA may involve an entirely separate team known as Independent Validation and Verification. This is often a safety mechanism for systems requiring high reliability, such as military or medical applications.

13

Managing Changes to the Database Throughout Its Life

Change control is the process used to manage the inevitable changes that will occur to a database after implementation. This process takes all components of the database into consideration—and possible effects on business operations—before database changes are allowed.

A database system must evolve in order for errors to be corrected and new features to be added. It is usually most cost effective to make such modifications in an evolutionary manner. New designs are often cost prohibitive. However, there is no counterpart for natural selection. Either the database works and is efficient, or it is not. Consequently, some mechanism for achieving a smooth transition between database versions is essential to avoid disrupting the work of users. Change control, also called change management, is this method.

Change management is applicable to a database system, referring to a back-end database and a user front-end application used to access the data. It is important to discuss change management from the viewpoints of both the database and the user application because they are both used together by the end user. Changes that are requested typically have an impact on both the database and the application, so these issues must be addressed together.

Two basic origination points for changes are required to improve a system or, more specifically, a database:

- Changes in business needs
- Changes in system needs

As the next three subsections discuss, changes to a database, or virtually any software, is managed with the following three environments:

- Development
- Testing
- Production

Managing Development

A database is initially developed in a development environment. Likewise, any future changes to the database should be made in the established development environment. The database development environment is established by the database administrator. It is important for the database-development environment to mimic the production environment so that changes and their impact can be expressed accurately. In development, real data is not important, it is the structure of the database that is. The development environment for the application developers may consist of a single-user personal computer or a multiuser, multitasking system such as Unix. The application-development environment is usually connected to the database-development environment. Again, the focus is on making necessary changes to the structure of the database and application features. The development environment is in a sense a staging area for any elements introduced into a new or existing database.

Managing Testing

After work has been accomplished in the development environment, all appropriate files, compiled programs, and scripts to build database structures are applied to the test environment. The database test environment should mimic the latest development environment. Real data is created in the test environment so that users can test the application against the database. Changes should never be tested in a production environment. Sometimes it is difficult to foresee all the effects of a small change before testing. The latest version of the application may be installed on test computers, where assigned end users try to make the database and application break. Testing is the last chance to unveil imperfections in the database or application interface before release into production. The whole point of testing is to handle any issues that are unveiled by making necessary changes in the development environment and retesting before production changes are made available to the database user.

Implementing Changes into Production

After changes have been tested, two conclusions may be drawn: Either the test was successful because all changes were made and the system works as expected (which is rare the first time around), or the test was not successful because changes were not completely made or the system does not function properly. If the end users are not satisfied with the test results, the development team must redirect its efforts back to the development environment with the new data that was gathered during testing. It is important that the project manager and test users sign off (approve changes) when testing is successfully completed. If the users are satisfied with test results, the changes made may be propagated to the production environment—but never any sooner!

> The development, test, and production environments must always be in synchronization with one another, which is simply part of the change-management process. There is simply no other way to effectively manage changes to the database.

13

Figure 13.1 illustrates the flow of changes from development to testing to production.

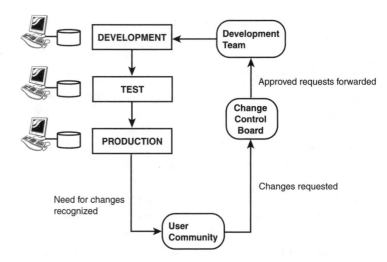

FIGURE 13.1

Managing database changes from development to production.

Redesigning the Database

You may have heard the term *legacy database* or *legacy system*. "Legacy" commonly describes old databases that were developed using third-generation languages and early RDBMS versions. The term *legacy* implies that the technology used to host a database is old. In information technology, generally anything that is old is out of date or obsolete.

When something is out of date, it might still function as originally intended, but may lack functionality that current business requirements may demand. Even if a database functions as intended, it might not fully optimize the use of the end-user's time to effectively perform on the job. If a database is obsolete, it might no longer be of use, or its original purpose might have been modified to the point that the database no longer meets the current needs of an organization.

Some situations that might prompt a database redesign are

- An organization changes the way it does business, which changes processes, data storage, and data access.

- An organization that is successful usually grows, which means more customers and more data. As an organization grows, new business processes might surface, along with requirements for new data.

- New ways are discovered to use data to streamline business functionality.

Understanding the Impact of Changes on Database Components

Now that you have learned about the database life cycle, it is possible to apply the general discussion toward a better understanding of the impact that changes have on database components. Remember that the components of a database include the following:

- Execution environment
- SQL engine
- SQL applications
- Data

Execution Environment

The machine execution environment refers to the operating system, drivers (such as the network interface), and helper applications that the SQL engine uses. As an example of the last item, many SQL engines use secondary applications, such as HTML browsers, document readers, multimedia extensions, and others. The environment is crucial because nearly everything associated with the database depends on it. An operating system major upgrade could render all components, even the SQL engine, inoperable. Fortunately, the developer involved in an upgrade probably does not have this worry. A manager, though, should avoid such changes while an upgrade is in progress.

SQL Engine

The SQL engine is the software that converts application source code into executable programs. This component also includes a user interface. Increasingly, this is a visual interface that provides for rapid design of applications. Application developers usually do not make changes to the SQL engine. However, a major revision, or even an outright change, can have a significant impact to developers. Applications that run on earlier versions might require significant work to execute with the new SQL system. Again, the safest course for the management team is to avoid version changes while an upgrade is in progress.

As just suggested, application developers can experience surprises when there is a new version of the environment or SQL engine. Database administrators and program managers should perform considerable analysis and testing prior to such changes in order to minimize cost and schedule risk.

13

Application Interface

The application developer is responsible for generation of SQL code. Although subsequent chapters introduce the SQL language, it is possible to offer a general description of database applications. In the classical model, software performs inputs, processing, and outputs.

Interacting with the Application

The inputs to SQL applications are usually search requests (queries) and related commands. The commands often relate to formatting of results, such as printing tables or more complicated results.

Processing Data

Processing involves interaction with the data entities using the SQL language. This might involve data retrieval, data checking, calculations, and similar activities. Data retrieval copies information from database storage. Data checking might verify the results of the retrieval or calculations. For example, it could validate that the information lies between maximum and minimum values that are context unique. Another type of checking might rely on scheduled events that involve time or date checking. Such checking is very common in accounting applications, such as payroll processing.

Entering Data

Data-entry support persons are usually responsible for populating the database with information. Limiting the number of persons who have this authority is usually a key step in information security. The larger the database, the more crucial change tracking becomes.

Although the tracking systems might be common, it is common to track changes to data and applications separately. There are several practical reasons for this approach. First, the frequency of data changes is usually much higher than that of applications. A typical financial software system might involve volumes of data each day, but the applications might change only for problem fixes. Another reason is that, as just suggested, different teams might be responsible for data entry and application support. Finally, separate change tracking can often reduce the time required for problem isolation.

Summary

The database life cycle refers to the period of time that a database and/or its application interface are useful to an organization. A database may continue to exist in its original form or may be modified or even redesigned throughout its life. Change control is the process of managing changes that occur during the life of a database system. This book refers to the database and the end-user application as a database system.

When discussing changes, it is important to discuss both the database and end-user application because changes to one often affect the other. You have learned that changes are necessary for a variety of reasons, such as changes in business requirements and changes in system requirements. When a change is made, other database components may be affected. The simplest form of database change control involves three environments: development, testing, and production. The database is designed or modified in the development environment, tested in the testing environment, and implemented into the production environment for use. Following these basic steps optimizes the usability of any database and may extend its life.

Workshop

The following workshop is composed of quiz questions and practical exercises. The quiz questions are designed to test your overall understanding of the current material. The practical exercises are intended to afford you the opportunity to apply the concepts discussed during the current hour, as well as build on the knowledge acquired in previous hours of study. Please take time to complete this workshop before continuing. You can refer to the answers at the end of the hour.

Quiz

1. What are the three environments that should be used to manage database change control?

2. What are two types of requirements that may change and provoke database changes?

3. What are the four major components of a database environment?

4. Who holds the primary responsibility of database change management?

5. What is the best way to identify different functional states (versions) of a database?

6. Under which database environment must any changes first be applied?

7. Who is responsible for the generation of SQL code?

8. Under which database environment does end-user data entry occur?

Exercises

For the following exercises, consider the following database and application interface: human resource system for an organization, including components to manage payroll and employee benefits such as 401k, retirement planning, and health care.

13

1. Who are the users?

2. Who are the customers?

3. Who may be affected by database changes?

4. What are some possible negative impacts if changes are not properly tested?

Answers to Quiz

1. Development, testing, and production

2. Business and system requirements

3. Execution environment, database engine, application interface, and data.

4. The database administrator.

5. Version control.

6. The development environment.

7. The application developer.

8. The production environment.

Answers to Exercises

1. The users are probably internal users, such as HR staff and personnel used for data entry and reporting.

2. The organization's employees are the customers of the HR system.

3. The users may be affected if the database application interface does not function properly. The employees (customers) may be affected if personnel information is lost or not properly managed.

4. Application interface no longer functions properly.

   Employees are not paid the right amount.

   Employees are not paid on time.

   Employees' retirement contributions are incorrect.

   Employees may not have access to their personnel data.

   Employer may not be able to forecast expenses.

   Manual processes must be used until database and/or application interface is corrected, causing more man hours and higher cost to employer.

PART IV

Accessing Databases

Hour

HOUR 14

Understanding Basic Database Connection Methods

As you learned in previous hours, databases are used for storing and manipulating data. Databases can serve their purpose in a wide array of settings, from the single user who tracks his household valuables to the multibillion-dollar corporation that tracks its business with multiple large databases.

Whether you are the single user tracking household inventory or the huge corporation, you must connect to the database to do your work. In this hour, you will explore the different ways to connect to databases and learn when those connection methods are appropriate.

In this hour, you will learn about the following:

- Native connections to databases
- Remote connections to databases
- Web connections to databases

- Database driver installation
- Database driver setup
- Database connection software

Overview of Database Connection Methods

When users of an application need to do work in a database, some type of connection must be made to the database so that data can be added, changed, or deleted. Users who use databases at their place of work usually don't see the actual machine on which the data they are using resides. These database servers are tucked away in some faraway, secure room. The users must connect to the database with a remote connection over a network.

NEW TERM   *Remote Database Connection* is a connection across a network to a database that resides in another physical location.

When a user is using desktop database software such as Microsoft Access or Borland's Paradox, the database is on the hard disk of the computer being used. Using desktop database software gives the user the capability to connect to the database using the same methods as connecting to databases remotely. The more common connection method to desktop databases is a direct or native connection.

NEW TERM   *Native Database Connection* is a connection that is to a database that resides on the hard disk of the machine the user is working on.

While you are on the Internet, you may connect to many databases indirectly via Web sites you visit without even knowing it. For the person surfing the Web, this appears as a remote connection when the user is not really connected to the database at all. The computer where the Web site is located usually has the actual connection to the database.

Remote Database Connections

When connecting to a database that does not reside on the PC you are using, a remote database connection has been made. For a remote connection to work, both the computer on which the database resides and the PC accessing the database must be on a local area network or a wide area network.

NEW TERM   A *local area network (LAN)* is a group of computers that are connected via cables, or in the case of wireless networking, radio signals. A LAN is usually confined to a single building.

NEW TERM   A *wide area network (WAN)* is a group of computers that are much farther apart than those in a LAN and are connected via telephone lines or radio waves.

A WAN allows the computers to "talk" to each other. A remote connection to a database from a PC requires that special software be installed on the computer where the database resides and on the computer the user is accessing the database from. The software used to let the user and database interact is sometimes proprietary, but not always. This connection software is discussed in more detail later in this hour. Figure 14.1 illustrates a remote database connection.

FIGURE **14.1**

A remote database connection.

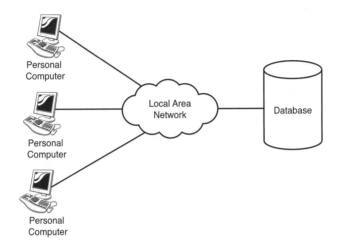

- Personal Computer
- Personal Computer
- Personal Computer
- Local Area Network
- Database

Native Database Connections

If you use the software the database vendor provides to connect to the database, you are probably using a native database connection. Usually, a native database connection does not require any type of extra software, such as ODBC or JDBC drivers. These are intrinsic to the vendor's database software. An example of a native database connection is using Microsoft's desktop database software, Access. When you create and use an Access database, no special software is being used other than the database software itself.

Client Software Database Connection

Most vendors of database server software, such as Oracle or Microsoft SQL Server (both of which are discussed in Hour 22), provide client software as part of their database package. This software is the "client" side of client/server database architecture. The client's main job is to connect the user to the database by using database-specific protocols and drivers or by using a driver written to serve many kinds of databases, such as ODBC.

| NEW TERM | *Client Software Database Connection* is software that is installed on the users machine that provides for the database connection. |

14

Another type of client used to connect to databases is software that has been enabled or written to use other database connection software to make its connection to the database. These applications usually allow a database connection as a feature of the software, not as a primary purpose. A good example of client software of this type is Microsoft Excel. Excel can be set up to connect to a database and run a query, which will input data into the spreadsheet, which will then be able to be seen graphically in chart form if desired.

A third type of client software used to connect to a database is specific to the database. This type of software is sometimes written in-house by programmers of a company that requires a graphical user interface, or GUI, to its data, making manipulation easier. More commonly, this type of client software is written by vendors who provide the database along with their GUI software. These clients and databases are usually geared toward a specific purpose, such as Customer Relationship Management software by Oracle or Peoplesoft, which is very popular right now.

Telnet Session into Database Server

Sometimes a database user will be working at his desk when he needs to connect to one of the company databases. He just wants to run a quick query to find out some information about a user of the database. To do so, he could use a program called Telnet. Telnet is client software used to connect remotely to another machine hosting the database that you want access to. Telnet software is used primarily by system administrators and database administrators. This type of remote database connection is a hybrid between a remote database connection and a native database connection. The user is not working directly on the computer the database runs on, but he is connected to the database as if he were sitting at the console of the database server machine.

NEW TERM   *Telnet Session* is software that is used predominately by administrators that combines the aspects of both native and remote connectivity.

Email-Based Queries

Some of the more expensive database server software packages provide a feature that allow users to email a query to a database server and have the database email the results back to the sender.

Web Database Connections

With the popularity of the World Wide Web today, it is no wonder that so many companies and individuals have sites on the Web. These sites range from pictures of someone's favorite dogs to entire retail businesses whose sole customer base is people buying products from its Web site. These Web sites have databases at the heart of their operation.

Users of a commercial Web site will connect to one or more databases during their online shopping experience. This connection is a remote database connection in a sense, but usually the person doing the shopping does not really connect to the database. The shopper sees only the result of queries run against the database according to the links and buttons clicked in the Web browser. The real connection to the database was made from the Web server computer to the database server computer. The Web server is the software using some type of client software to connect to the database.

 Web Database Connections are remote connections from the user, to the Web server computer, then to the database server computer on the Internet.

Direct Database Connections

You may hear people say that they have a direct connection to a database. A direct database connection occurs when there is no connection software between the client the user is working with and the actual database.

A direct connection to a database can be accomplished by using an Application Programming Interface (API) when writing the software used to access the database. This API knows the structure of the data and is able to bypass the traditional access of using SQL when accessing data.

 An *API* is a set of functions, procedures, and routines used by programmers to build software.

The advantage of using an API to access data in a database is that you have more control of actions on the data than you would if you used a high-level access method such as SQL. This control is limited to the way the program was written and how it uses these APIs. The access to the data can be much faster. The disadvantage of using this approach is the loss of flexibility when accessing data.

Some database client software allows the user to connect to the database directly or by using vendor-provided connection software.

Overview of Database Connection Software

As you have learned earlier in this hour, you can connect to a database in several ways. In this section, you will learn more about the actual software used to make those connections. You will also download, install, and set up an ODBC driver to connect to a MySQL database.

Database connection software comes in many forms, from the GUI front end that is specific to a database, to a piece of software that has the capability to connect to a database,

14

to a small bit of programming code used to do the actual "talking" between an application and a database.

Vendor-Provided Connection Software

Each vendor of database software must provide at least one way to connect to its database software. If you can't connect, you won't be able to use the database. At the minimum, a database vendor will provide a program that will connect to the database and give the user an interface to use SQL on the database. Table 14.1 lists each of the major database server packages, some of the major desktop databases, and the software the vendor provides to make a connection to its database. Each possible connection type will be listed along with the software name.

TABLE 14.1   Software and Connection Types

Client Software	Database Software	ODBC	JDBC	Native	Direct
Sql*Plus	Oracle	no	no	yes	yes
Sql Query Analyzer	Sql Server	no	no	yes	yes
QMF	DB2	yes	no	yes	yes
**Access	Access	yes	*yes	yes	yes
**Paradox	Paradox	yes	*yes	yes	yes

JDBC – ODBC bridge
** *Connectivity can be self-contained in the application*

Other Software with Database Connection Capability

Many commercial desktop software programs are available that serve today's computer user. Most business offices have a PC on every desk. Businesses today have huge amounts of data that need to be processed during a normal business day. A software program, or suite of programs, exists that will take care of almost any business need. These software programs must be able to utilize the data the business produces so that this data can be turned into useful information. This information is then used to make important decisions and keep the business on the right track. The following is a short list of available and popular desktop software applications that can connect to databases and be used to turn business data into meaningful information.

Spreadsheets

Following is a list of popular software used to create spreadsheets:

- Microsoft Excel
- Corel Quattro Pro
- Lotus 1-2-3

Desktop Databases

Following is a list of popular software for desktop database computing:

- Microsoft Access
- FoxPro
- Paradox

Word Processors

Following is a list of popular word processing software:

- Microsoft Word
- WordPerfect

Report and Query Tools

Following is a list of popular reporting tools:

- Brio Reports
- Crystal Reports
- Impromptu
- ReportSmith

ODBC

Most people who have used computer databases at work have heard about ODBC. ODBC stands for Open Database Connectivity. ODBC is an application programming interface (API) that is used to access databases. Programs using ODBC are able to access different databases using the same programming source code for each database.

NEW TERM *ODBC or Open Database Connectivity* is software that is used to connect to different databases while using the same programming source code for each database.

ODBC was created to fill a need. In the early days of corporate computing, most companies had only one or two large database systems. Each system had to have applications written specifically for it. This was expensive. As companies grew and systems became cheaper and faster, more databases from different vendors were available. With the advent of the personal computer and client/server computing, there needed to be a way to allow one application to connect to more than one type of database. ODBC is based on

14

the SQL Call Level Interface, which was developed by a group of software and hardware vendors called the SQL Access Group (SAG). Thus, Open Database Connectivity was born.

How Does ODBC Work?

ODBC has four components in its architecture:

- *Application*—The application that uses ODBC can be just about anything. There are spreadsheets, desktop databases, and word processors. Each application using ODBC will pass SQL statements to the next component of ODBC, the Driver Manager.

- *Driver Manager*—The ODBC Driver Administrator is installed on most Windows PCs today. This component of the ODBC architecture is the most visible to the end user. This is where the drivers are loaded for any application using ODBC. The Driver Manager is also where the end users set up a Data Source Name (DSN) to connect their applications to a database.

- *Driver*—The Driver is where all the magic happens. When an application sends a SQL statement to the Driver Manager, the Driver Manager hands it off to the driver for the database being queried. If needed, the driver will change the calls so they match the particular database's syntax. The SQL statement is then submitted to the database, and any return values are fed back to the application.

- *Data Source*—The Data Source is a combination of the database being used, the computer operating system, and—if the application and database are separated by a network—the network. Figure 14.2 illustrates the concept of ODBC database connections.

Setting Up an ODBC Connection

Now you are going to set up an ODBC connection to a MySQL database. Some preliminary steps must be taken before you can learn how to create and use an ODBC database connection. You should perform the following steps:

1. Ensure that the MySQL database is started and you are in the database you want to extract data from.

2. Download the MySQL ODBC driver from the MySQL Web site. Installing this will be explained in the next section, "Downloading MySQL ODBC Driver."

3. Install the MySQL ODBC driver onto a Windows computer. This is explained in the section, "Installing MySQL ODBC Driver."

4. Create a Data Source Name (DSN) to the MySQL database.

5. Connect an Excel spreadsheet to the database and query data from a table.

FIGURE 14.2

Simple ODBC connections.

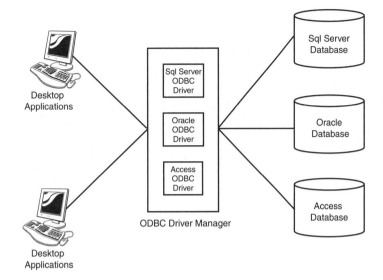

Downloading MySQL ODBC Driver

1. Go to `http://www.mysql.com`.

2. On the right side of the MySQL home page, you will see a box called Versions. Inside this box is a list called Production.

3. Click the link `MyOdbc 2.50 2.50.39`.

4. Scroll down on the Downloads for MyODBC 2.50 page until you reach the Windows downloads.

5. Click the download link (`Download`) for the full setup installation files for your operating system.

6. Choose MyODBC 2.50 for 95/98/Me full setup.

7. Choose MyODBC 2.50.39 for NT/2000/XP full setup.

8. On the next page, scroll down to North America and click the link HTTP next to a site that is closest to you. (This will help with download speed.)

9. When the file download dialog box appears, click the Save button.

10. Save the file in the Save As dialog box using the default name. You can save this file anywhere on your computer, but remember where it is.

11. When the download is complete, close the Download Complete dialog box.

Installing MySql ODBC Driver

1. Unzip the downloaded file into a directory of your choosing. If you are running Window XP on your computer, you should be able to double-click the .zip file, and all the files will show. You will then be able to do the next step.

14

2. After the files have been successfully extracted from the zip file, double-click the setup.exe file.

3. A window will appear on your screen called Microsoft ODBC Setup, as shown in Figure 14.3. Click the Continue button.

FIGURE 14.3
Microsoft ODBC window.

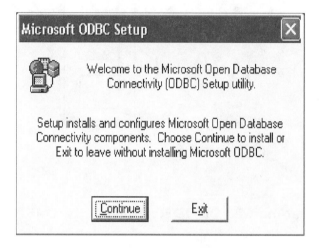

The Install Drivers window opens with a list of available ODBC drivers, as shown in Figure 14.4. Highlight MySQL by clicking it once, and then click the OK button.

FIGURE 14.4
Install Drivers window.

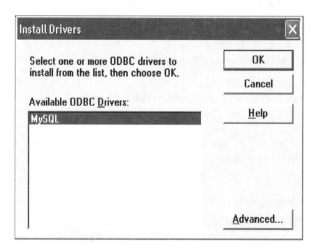

When the Data Sources window appears on your screen (see Figure 14.5), click the Close button. You will set up a data source later.

FIGURE 14.5
Data Sources window.

FIGURE 14.5
Data Sources window.

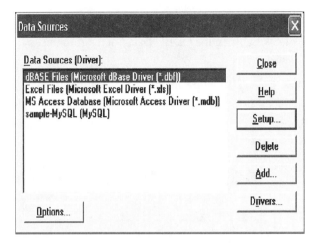

You will see a Success window like that in Figure 14.6. Click the OK button.

FIGURE 14.6
Successful Installation window.

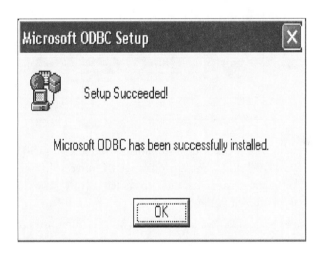

Congratulations! You have installed your first ODBC driver for MySQL. The next set of steps create a Data Source Name (DSN) in the Data Source Administrator.

NEW TERM A *Data Source Name*, or DSN, is the name you choose for the database connection you are creating when you use an ODBC driver. You will see the DSN when you set up software to use an ODBC data source, and you will see an example when you set up Excel to see your data via ODBC.

14

Creating a DSN to a MySQL Database

You create a DSN by using the ODBC Data Source Administrator. This is started from the Control Panel.

1. Open the Control Panel by clicking Start, Settings, Control Panel.

2. Inside the Control Panel, find the icon with the name Data Sources (ODBC). Double-click this icon to start the ODBC Data Source Administrator. You should see a dialog box like the one shown in Figure 14.7.

FIGURE 14.7

ODBC Data Source Administrator.

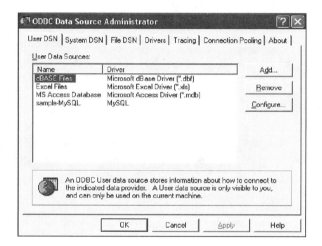

3. With the ODBC Data Source Administrator open, you will be able to see the MySQL ODBC driver and any other ODBC drivers that are installed on your system. To see the driver, click the Drivers tab. Scroll down the list until you see MySQL, as shown in Figure 14.8.

4. Click the System DSN tab in the Data Source Administrator. A System DSN is visible to anybody who uses this machine. To add a DSN, click the Add button on the right side of the DSN. The Create New Data Source window will pop up over the Manager window. Scroll down through the list of ODBC drivers until you find the MySQL driver, and then click it once to highlight it, as shown in Figure 14.9. Then click the Finish button.

5. In the MySQL Driver Default Configuration window, type in the values as shown in Table 14.2. When finished, it should look like Figure 14.10. Click the OK button.

FIGURE 14.8

ODBC Data Source Manager showing the MySQL driver in the Drivers tab.

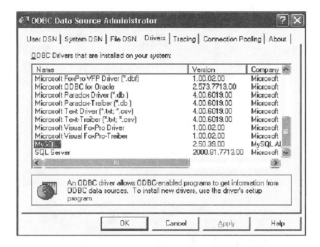

FIGURE 14.9

Create New Data Source window.

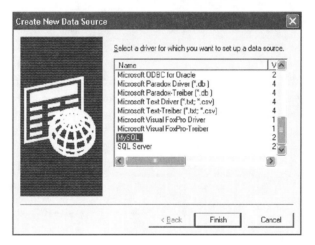

TABLE 14.2   MySQL Configuration

Name	Value
Windows DSN name:	testMYSQLodbc
MySQL host (name or IP):	localhost
MySQL database name:	test
User:	User
Password:	
Port (if not 3306):	
Sql command on connect:	

14

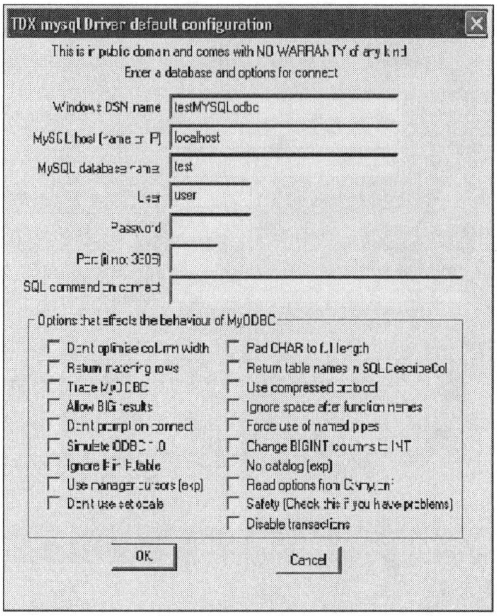

FIGURE 14.10

MySQL Driver Default Configuration window.

6. You will now be back to the ODBC Data Source Administrator, and the testMYSQLodbc system data source should be visible in the list of data sources. Click OK and you are done. The DSN will look like the one shown in Figure 14.11.

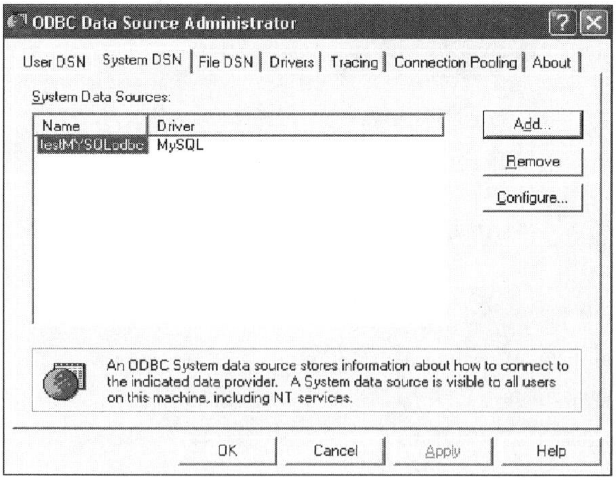

FIGURE 14.11

ODBC Data Source Administrator showing the DSN just created.

Putting the ODBC Driver to Use

Now that the MySQL ODBC driver has been installed and a Data Source Name has been created, you will go through the steps required to view some table data in Microsoft Excel.

1. Open Excel. Excel 2002 was used in this example. You will be able to do this in other versions of Excel, but the menu items could be named differently and located in different places.

2. Click the Data menu item, select the Import External Data item in the drop-down menu, and then click the New Database Query item in the pop-up menu. This will show the Choose Data Source dialog box, as shown in Figure 14.12.

FIGURE 14.12

Choose Data Source window.

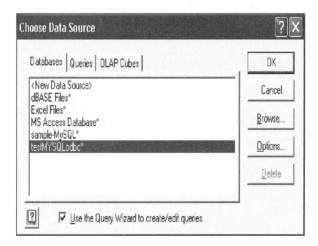

3. As you can see, the DSN you created earlier is in the window. Click the testMYSQLodbc DSN to highlight it, and then click the OK button. This connects you to the database you used when you created the DSN. After the connection is made, the Query Wizard-Choose Columns dialog box pops up. This dialog box shows you a list of all the tables you have access to in the database in the Available tables and columns section of the dialog box. Choose any table by clicking it once, and then click the button with the > on it. This moves all the table columns to the Columns in your query section of the dialog box, as shown in Figure 14.13.

4. To keep things simple, click the Next button until you get to the Query Wizard-Finish dialog box. Click the Finish button.

5. Click OK when the Import Data dialog box shown in Figure 14.14 appears. This dialog box enables you to tell Excel where you want to put the table data. The

14

default is the highlighted cell in Excel. You will see the column names and data in your Excel spreadsheet.

FIGURE 14.13

The Query Wizard-Choose Columns dialog box.

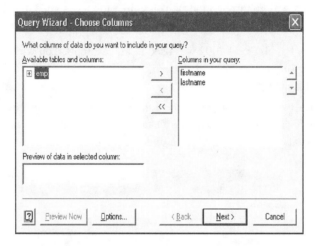

FIGURE 14.14

The Import Data dialog box.

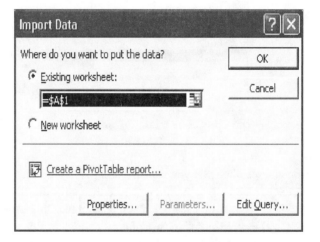

Spreadsheets and databases can be very powerful tools when used together. As you can see in Figure 14.15, it is simple to connect your Excel spreadsheet with any database when you have an ODBC driver. This same task can be accomplished with many other applications, so give them a try!

FIGURE 14.15

Data in an Excel spreadsheet.

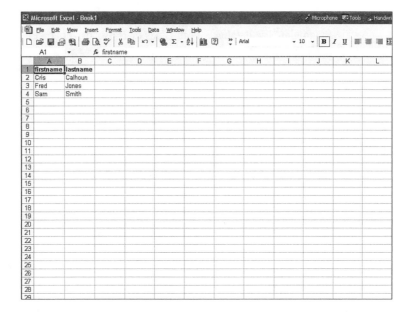

JDBC

Because you will be learning about Java Database Connectivity (JDBC), you need to know a little about the Java programming language. Java is a fairly new programming language that you probably have heard about if you spend time on the Internet. Java was developed by Sun Microsystems as a programming language that is portable, meaning that the code can be written once and run on a variety of software and hardware platforms.

JDBC is an API used to connect programs written in Java to many popular database platforms, spreadsheets, and flat files. Like ODBC, JDBC is based on the SQL Call Level Interface. It allows applications to send and receive requests to databases.

How Does JDBC Work?

JDBC is similar to ODBC in that it uses an API, a Driver Manager, and drivers to work with databases. You don't set up drivers and DSNs in a JDBC Driver Administrator like you did using ODBC in the previous section. The equivalent in JDBC connectivity is called the Driver Manager, and it is used from the Java program code. The Driver Manager loads the requested driver into memory so the program or Web page code can connect to the database. To sum it up:

- Java program uses the JDBC API to call the Driver Manager.
- A vendor-supplied database driver is loaded into memory by the Driver Manager.

14

- With the driver in memory, the program can use the JDBC API to access and manipulate the database. Four types of JDBC drivers can be used to connect to a database.

Types of JDBC Drivers

There are four types of JDBC drivers. The type of driver used in an application is dictated by environmental factors, such as network, database, middleware, and the programming language used. The end result is the same—a Java program sends requests and receives results with a database. The following list illustrates how each type of JDBC driver functions and why that particular type of driver would be used.

- *Type 1 JDBC Drivers*—These are called a JDBC–ODBC bridge. They allow you to connect to a database using ODBC from an application that is using the JDBC API. This type of driver is used when the need arises to connect to an ODBC-compliant piece of software.

- *Type 2 JDBC Drivers*—This driver is part Native API, part Java API. These drivers require that some native code be loaded onto the client machine.

- *Type 3 JDBC Drivers*—This driver uses a type of software called middleware. The JDBC calls are translated to the protocol the middleware uses. The middleware changes that to the correct protocol of the database being connected to.

- *Type 4 JDBC Drivers*—This driver converts the JDBC call to the protocol of the database being connected to. This is a good solution for company intranets.

NEW TERM   *Middleware* is software that sits on a server apart from the database server software. This software is used to hold and run code that is the business logic of an application or to control connectivity to other servers, software, and databases.

Summary

In this hour, you learned that to use a database you must be connected to it. You learned about connecting to a database remotely using native database connections, which involve using vendor-provided software. Next, you discovered the different types of client connection software, such as vendor-provided software, software that has database connectivity as a feature such as Microsoft Excel, and applications written for a specific purpose that use data in databases. Web-based and Telnet clients were also discussed as vehicles for connecting to a database. You learned about several types of software used to make database connections and some name brand software that has database connectivity as a feature. Then the discussion turned to ODBC drivers and their usage. You stepped through the process of downloading, installing, DSN creation, and using a MySQL ODBC driver. Last, you learned about JDBC and how it works.

Workshop

The following workshop consists of quiz questions and practical exercises. The quiz questions are designed to test your overall understanding of the current material. The practical exercises are intended to afford you the opportunity to apply the concepts discussed during the current hour, as well as build on the knowledge acquired in previous hours of study. Please take time to complete this workshop before continuing. You may refer to the answers at the end of the hour.

Quiz

1. Which JDBC driver could you use to connect to an Excel spreadsheet?
2. What does ODBC stand for?
3. What three components must be used to make a remote database connection?
4. What is the ODBC Driver Administrator used for?

Exercises

1. Set up a Data Source Name to a MySQL database.

Answers to Quiz

1. A Java application would need to use a Type 1 JDBC driver to connect to the Excel spreadsheet.
2. Open Database Connectivity
3. You must have client software, a database, and a network between them to have a remote connection.
4. The ODBC Driver Administrator is used to set up DSNs to existing data sources, to be used by programs that are ODBC enabled.

14

HOUR 15

Understanding the Standard Database Language: SQL

Structured Query Language, more commonly called SQL, is the standard language that is used to communicate with any relational database, and the relational database is the modern and most widely implemented database in today's information technology world.

The highlights of this hour include

- An introduction to and brief overview of SQL
- Understanding the basic components of SQL
- Understanding the difference between ANSI SQL and vendor implementations of SQL
- Using the MySQL database

Overview of SQL

As mentioned, SQL is the standard language used to communicate with a relational database. SQL is pronounced either S-Q-L or "sequel"; either pronunciation is acceptable. The SQL prototype was originally developed by IBM using Dr. E. F. Codd's paper ("A Relational Model of Data for Large Shared Data Banks") as a model. In 1979, not long after IBM's prototype, the first SQL product, Oracle, was released by Relational Software, Incorporated (it was later renamed to Oracle Corporation). Today, Oracle is one of the distinguished leaders in relational database technologies.

> SQL was briefly covered in previous hours to support important database concept coverage. This hour, as well as the next several, focus on how SQL is used to access relational databases.

SQL is a means of communication between a database user and a database server. A database server is simply vendor-provided software that stores data. A relational database server, also called a relational database management system (RDBMS), is software that stores data according to the relational model, as explained in Hour 6, "Understanding Relational Database Architecture." Database users who access the database using SQL range from DBAs to developers to end users.

Each implementation of SQL is based on a SQL standard. SQL standards are provided by the American National Standards Institute (ANSI) and by the International Standards Organization (ISO). Most implementations are compared to the ANSI standard. The following two sections deal with a background of the ANSI standard and how vendor implementations tend to follow the standard.

Understanding ANSI SQL

The American National Standards Institute (ANSI) is an organization that approves certain standards in many industries. SQL has been deemed the standard language in relational database communication, originally approved in 1986 based on IBM's implementation. In 1987, the ANSI SQL standard was accepted as the international standard by the ISO. The standard was revised again in 1992 and was called SQL-92. The newest standard is now called SQL-99 and is also referred to as SQL3. ANSI SQL is a standard, not a language itself. ANSI SQL provides standard guidelines for vendors to develop SQL-based databases (relational databases), such as Oracle, Sybase, and SQL Server.

NEW TERM *ANSI SQL* is the American National Standards Institute guidelines for the development of SQL-based databases.

Differentiating Between ANSI SQL and Vendor Implementations

15

ANSI SQL provides a standard for SQL-based database development. It is a guideline, not a requirement. Vendors can develop database software however they want, but there are definite advantages to adhering to the ANSI standard. By following the standard, an individual or organization familiar with SQL can more easily migrate between different implementations. This makes an ANSI-compliant implementation much more attractive to customers because less time is spent learning and more time is spent making productive use of the database. Having a standard for SQL makes code more portable as well. With a standard, vendors can be more competitive and must stay on their toes, ensuring that their software complies with the standard.

NEW TERM *Vendor Implementations* are specific adaptations of ANSI standard of SQL into their own product, adding functionality that is unique to their specific product, such as SQL*Plus.

The SQL standard offers proven features that are tested, and in many cases, already implemented by some vendors. However, the standard does not ensure that all vendors are 100% compliant. In fact, few implementations, if any, completely comply with the standard. Some vendors develop features that do not exist in the standard, and some of these features eventually become part of the standard. In addition, the standard offers suggestions for syntax structure. Many implementations vary, some dramatically, on the exact syntax of many SQL commands. So it is important to note that each implementation of SQL is unique, but most follow the standard and implement many of the same features.

Generally speaking, if you learn SQL in one implementation, your knowledge can be transferred to nearly any implementation of SQL with a minimal learning curve.

Understanding the Basic Components of SQL

The commands in the SQL language are divided into several logical components, or sets of commands, which allow for basic to advanced interaction with the database. This section provides an overview of the basic SQL components, and some of the most popular SQL operations and commands are discussed during the next two hours. Some of the fundamental activities supported by SQL include building database objects, manipulating objects, populating database tables with data, updating existing data in tables, deleting data, performing database queries, and controlling database access.

The following sections discuss the following components of the SQL language as defined in the ANSI standard and implemented by most relational database vendors:

- DDL (Data Definition Language)
- DML (Data Manipulation Language)
- DQL (Data Query Language)
- DCL (Data Control Language)
- Transactional control commands

Defining Database Structures Using DDL

Data Definition Language, or DDL, is the component of SQL that enables a database user to create and restructure database objects, such as the creation or the deletion of a table. DDL commands exist in the following three forms:

- CREATE
- ALTER
- DROP

 DDL or Data Definition Language is the component of SQL that creates, changes, and removes database objects.

CREATE commands allow database objects, such as tables, to be created. ALTER commands allow the structure of database objects to be modified. DROP commands allow database objects to be removed (deleted) from the database.

Popular CREATE commands include

- CREATE TABLE
- CREATE INDEX
- CREATE VIEW
- CREATE PROCEDURE

Popular ALTER commands include

- ALTER TABLE
- ALTER PROCEDURE
- ALTER VIEW
- ALTER TRIGGER

Popular DROP commands include

- DROP TABLE
- DROP INDEX

- DROP VIEW
- DROP PROCEDURE

Manipulating Data Using DML

Data Manipulation Language (DML) is the SQL component that allows a database user to affect data in the database. With DML, the user can populate tables with new data, update existing data in tables, and delete data from tables. Simple database queries can also be performed within a DML command.

NEW TERM *DML or Data Manipulation Language* is the component of SQL that allows you to record data, make changes to the data, and remove the data.

There are three basic DML commands in SQL:

- INSERT
- UPDATE
- DELETE

INSERT allows for creation of new data—insertion of new data into an existing table. UPDATE allows existing data to be changed. DELETE allows data to be deleted from database tables. DML commands are discussed in more detail in Hour 17, "Interacting with Databases to Manage and Retrieve Data."

Retrieving Data Using DQL

Data Query Language (DQL) is the component of SQL that allows the database user to query or request information from the database. A query is an inquiry into the database using the SELECT statement. A query is used to extract data from the database in a readable format according to the user's request. For instance, if you have an employee table, you might issue a SQL statement that returns the employee who is paid the most. This request to the database for usable employee information is a typical query that can be performed in a relational database.

NEW TERM *DQL or Data Query Language* is the component of SQL that allows the user to retrieve data from the database.

The SELECT statement, the command that represents DQL in SQL, is the statement used to construct database queries. The SELECT statement is not a standalone statement, which means that one or more additional clauses (elements) are required for a syntactically correct query. In addition to the required clauses, there are optional clauses that increase the overall functionality of the SELECT statement. The SELECT statement is by far one of the most powerful statements in SQL. The FROM clause is the mandatory clause and must always be used in conjunction with the SELECT statement.

A simple SQL query using the SELECT statement might appear as follows:

```
SELECT EMPLOYEE_NAME FROM EMPLOYEES;
```

This query would return a list of all employees' names as found in the EMPLOYEES table.

Though composed of only one command, DQL is the most concentrated focus of SQL for modern relational database users. This command, accompanied by many options and clauses, is used to compose queries against a relational database. Queries, from simple to complex, from vague to specific, can be easily created. The SELECT command is discussed in more detail in Hour 17, "Interacting with Databases to Manage and Retrieve Data."

Controlling Data Access Using DCL

Data control commands in SQL enable you to control access to data within the database. Control is provided not only for access into the database via user authentication, but for access to database objects through database privileges. These DCL commands are normally used to create objects related to user access and also control the distribution of privileges among users. Some common data control commands are as follows:

- ALTER PASSWORD
- GRANT
- REVOKE
- CREATE SYNONYM

 DCL or Data Control Language is the component of SQL that allows the user the ability to control the access to the database.

Controlling Transactions

In addition to the previously introduced categories of commands, commands exist that allow the user to manage database transactions. Database transactions are conducted using any combination of the DML commands (INSERT, UPDATE, DELETE). These are transactional control commands. Transactional control commands provide two basic benefits to the database user:

- The capability to finalize a transaction and save changes to the database
- The capability to undo a transaction

Transactional control commands exist in the following forms:

- COMMIT   Used to save database transactions
- ROLLBACK   Used to undo database transactions

15

- SAVEPOINT   Creates points within groups of transactions in which to ROLL-BACK, or undo work
- SET TRANSACTION   Used to label a set of DML commands as a single transaction

Transactional control commands are discussed in more detail in Hour 17.

 Transactional Control commands are the components of SQL that work in conjunction with DML commands.

Using SQL for Databases and Applications

As previously stated, SQL is used to communicate with a relational database. But what does this really mean to you as a database novice? SQL exists in many forms, has many uses, and is used by many users. The four main functions of SQL are

- Creating a database
- Populating the database with data
- Processing data
- Retrieving data

As discussed in Hour 4, "Relating to Modern Database Users," the types of SQL users range from end users to programmers to developers to database administrators. All SQL users use SQL in a variety of formats, ranging from command-line SQL execution to an extravagant application interface that makes calls to the database using embedded SQL.

Some of the different manifestations of SQL in the real world include

- Command-line execution of SQL code in a plain text format
- SQL code, such as Java and C++, that is embedded in computer programs
- Submission of SQL code via an application interface
- Calls to database-resident SQL code from the application interface (stored procedures)
- The execution of canned queries
- Using vendor-provided and third-party reporting tools that use SQL behind the scenes

Exploring an Open Source Solution: MySQL

MySQL is an open source database implementation that is molded mainly according to the relational (SQL) database model. MySQL does not comply to the ANSI SQL standard as well as some implementations, such as Oracle. It has its limitations, but those limitations balance out to provide a SQL database that is reliable, that performs well, and that is easy to use. MySQL is an excellent alternative to expensive SQL implementations for the thrifty database novice and for many modern organizations.

 MySQL is mentioned repeatedly throughout this book. It is not the leading database on the market, but it is an excellent database that can be utilized for many situations, particularly for the database novice.

Some of the advantages of MySQL are the following:

- It is free.
- It is easy to install.
- It is easy to use.

The following sections discuss MySQL to various degrees:

- "Using MySQL for Learning"
- "Using MySQL in the Real World"
- "Downloading and Installing MySQL for Microsoft Windows"
- "Downloading and Installing MySQL for Linux"

Using MySQL for Learning

MySQL is good for learning, mainly for two reasons: it is free and it is easy to use. Why invest hundreds or even thousands of dollars to learn basic SQL when this same objective can be achieved with open source software? Using MySQL for learning is quite appropriate in the following situations:

- Classroom training
- Individual training
- Individual hands-on practice
- Development and testing

Using MySQL in the Real World

MySQL is used in the real world by many organizations. Although MySQL lacks much of the functionality that most leading database implementations provide, it offers plenty of necessary SQL features that many organizations need in a database (and it is free, if we did not already mention that). In some cases, based on the use of MySQL, there may be a licensing fee that is nominal compared to the cost of most database software.

The following list identifies many of the scenarios that the MySQL database can be used to support:

- Many small to mid-sized applications
- An organization seeking an open source solution
- A multiuser environment that is expected to perform well
- Organizations that rely on Linux-based systems

> The current stable version of MySQL is 3.23. MySQL is free for most situations. One example in which a license must be purchased is if you are linking another program to MySQL that works only with MySQL. Check www.mysql.com for current software licensing details.

Downloading and Installing MySQL for Microsoft Windows

Use the following instructions if you will be installing MySQL on a computer with Microsoft Windows. Note that steps 1–6 may vary according to the layout of www.mysql.com.

1. Go to www.mysql.com to download MySQL.
2. Select Downloads from the main menu.
3. Select the latest stable version, MySQL 3.23.
4. Review the provided information about version 3.23.
5. Find the appropriate Windows download for your system and then click the Download selection.
6. Select a mirror site for download that is close to your location. Save the file to your computer.
7. Create a folder under C:\ called "mysql."
8. Double-click the zip file that was downloaded, and then extract all files to your mysql folder.
9. Go to your mysql folder, and then double-click the file "setup.exe."
10. Follow the instructions to install MySQL on your computer.
11. After MySQL is successfully installed, test the software installation by executing mysql.exe under C:\mysql\bin.

12. You should get a mysql> prompt. At the mysql> prompt, type **help**. You should see a list of commands.

13. If all the preceding steps were successful, you are ready to use MySQL for exercises in this book.

If you experience problems during the installation, repeat steps 1–13. If you are still unable to obtain or install MySQL, contact MySQL for support.

Downloading and Installing MySQL for Linux

Use the following instructions if you will be installing MySQL on a computer with Linux. Note that steps 1–6 may vary according to the layout of www.mysql.com.

 If you have Red Hat Linux 7.1, MySQL should already be included.

1. Go to www.mysql.com to download MySQL.

2. Select Downloads from the main menu.

3. Select the latest stable version, MySQL 3.23.

4. Review the provided information about version 3.23.

5. Find the appropriate Linux download for your system, and then click the Download selection. More than likely, you will need to download and install the following file: MySQL-client-VERSION.i386.rpm.

6. Select a mirror site for download that is close to your location. Save the file to your computer.

7. Copy the file MySQL-client-VERSION.i386.rpm to your Linux computer.

8. Execute the following command as root to install MySQL. This is the standard minimal installation.

   shell> rpm -i MySQL-VERSION.i386.rpm MySQL-client-VERSION.i386.rpm

9. After installation, MySQL data will be located in /var/lib/mysql.

10. After MySQL is successfully installed, test the software installation by following the instructions in the post-installation portion of the online documentation.

11. If all the preceding steps were successful, you are ready to use MySQL for exercises in this book.

If you experience problems during the installation, repeat the previous steps. If you are still unable to obtain or install MySQL, contact MySQL for support.

MySQL is also available for Mac OS and most other versions of Unix.

Summary

During this hour, you learned about some of the basic fundamentals of the preferred, and standard, relational database language, SQL. SQL stands for Structured Query Language and is used by all sorts of database users to communicate with a relational database. There are many vendors that provide SQL database implementations. Most of these vendors charge a premium for their software, and some offer their software for a nominal fee, or even for free. MySQL is an open source SQL database solution that is generally free; it is used by many individuals and organizations that seek a cost-effective alternative to expensive database software.

By now, you should understand the basic components of the SQL language—not details, just basic concepts. You should understand that SQL is used to create database objects, insert data into the database, manipulate and manage data, and retrieve data using queries and reporting tools. SQL is not only easy to understand, it is a mandatory ingredient to the knowledge base of any person serious about learning more about modern databases. Now that you know what SQL is, the following hours will go into a bit more detail about popular features of the SQL language and show some examples of how SQL is used to manage and retrieve data.

Workshop

The following workshop is composed of quiz questions and practical exercises. The quiz questions are designed to test your overall understanding of the current material. The practical exercises are intended to afford you the opportunity to apply the concepts discussed during the current hour, as well as build on the knowledge acquired in previous hours of study. Please take time to complete this workshop before continuing. You can refer to the answers at the end of this hour.

Quiz

1. What does SQL stand for?
2. What type of database model uses SQL?
3. Identify a few users of SQL.
4. What are the three categories of commands that data definition language (DDL) comprises?

5. What three commands compose data manipulation language (DML)?

6. What is the primary SQL command used to query a database?

7. What are two benefits of using MySQL?

8. What are two drawbacks of using MySQL?

9. Is ANSI SQL an actual language?

Exercises

1. Download MySQL.

2. Create a MySQL database.

Answers to Quiz

1. SQL stands for Structured Query Language.

2. The relational database model uses SQL.

3. Some users of SQL include end users, developers, programmers, and database administrators.

4. CREATE, ALTER, and DROP.

5. INSERT, UPDATE, and DELETE.

6. SELECT is the primary SQL command used to query a database.

7. MySQL is free; it is easy to install and easy to use.

8. MySQL does not comply with the ANSI standards nearly as much as most SQL implementations do, and it lacks many features that most implementations provide.

9. ANSI SQL is not an actual language. It is a standard, or set of guidelines, for a vendor to develop SQL-based database software.

Hour **16**

Creating Databases and Database Objects

During the previous hour, you learned about the basic components of SQL, the standard language that is used to communicate with relational databases. This hour focuses on the use of SQL to create databases and database objects. The creation of database objects is also referred to as *data definition*, and it uses the component of SQL called data definition language (DDL).

After this hour, you should understand

- Basic concepts related to database creation
- Data definition and data types
- The basics of table creation and management using DDL
- The basics of index creation and management using DDL

Creating a Database

Before any database objects or data can be defined, the database itself must be created. When speaking of database creation, two ideas may come to mind depending on your background. To some individuals, the database corresponds to the database software and background structure that hosts the environment for database objects and data. To others, the database corresponds to the actual database objects and data itself. Both descriptions accurately compose a database. In the following sections, you will explore

- The creation of the database environment, which refers to the database software and background structure that is used to host database objects and data
- The creation of objects that compose a database, referring to elements such as tables, indexes, and data

Creating the Database Environment

The creation of the database environment typically includes the following steps:

1. Configuration of the database server
2. Installation of the database software
3. Creation of the database
4. Establishment of database users to create database objects

The configuration of the database server includes tasks such as the selection of a computer, selection of an operating system environment, determination of required storage, and the allocation of system resources for databases and other software that will run on the server. The most common operating system environments for relational databases are Unix, Windows NT/2000, Novel, and Linux. Determination of required storage involves projecting data storage needs for various applications that will run on the server and selecting brand, type, speed, and quantity of data storage. Usually, data storage is accomplished through the use of both internal and external disk drives. The allocation of system resources often includes making available ample disk space for data and the assignment of CPU and memory usage for the database.

After the database server is ready to go, you must install database software. After you select and purchase the desired database product, you install the database software in most cases by using a vendor-provided CD-ROM. Database software installation, as well as server configuration, may not require SQL usage. Oracle, however, requires SQL scripts to be executed that build internal database objects that are important to the operation of the database.

Creating the database may include some SQL but is always vendor specific. Each vendor has its own version of SQL, and the process of creating a database varies widely between implementations. Many vendors provide a CREATE DATABASE command for the creation of the database. Others make database creation as simple as the click of a button.

A database structure exists—that is, the database—but database objects must be created before data can be stored. Database objects are created by users; therefore, database users must be created. You create database users by using the ANSI-standard CREATE USER command. In some cases, scripts or applications may be available to assist in user creation. Establishing database users enables the creation of database objects.

Creating Objects That Compose a Database

In the previous section, the implication was that little SQL is used to install database software and create the actual database. When you create database objects, a full utilization of SQL is involved. More specifically, DDL, the component of the SQL language that is used to create and manage database objects, is used to manage database objects in the following ways:

- CREATE   This command is used to create or define database objects.
- ALTER   This command is used to alter the structure or definition of database objects.
- DROP   This command is used to delete database objects.

The following list identifies the most common database objects that are created and managed using SQL's DDL:

- Tables
- Indexes
- Views
- Stored procedures
- Constraints

NEW TERM   *Tables* are the basic storage objects for data in a relational database. *Indexes* provide pointers to data in tables for speedy data access. *Views* are virtual tables, that represent different perspectives of data. *Stored procedures* are computer programs that are actually stored in the database as data. *Constraints* are objects that are associated with tables that provide rules for how data is stored.

Understanding Data Definition

Before proceeding to the actual creation of database objects, it is important to have a firm grasp on data definition itself. Data is a collection of information stored in a database as one of several data types. Data includes names, numbers, dollar amounts, text, graphics, decimals, figures, calculations, summarization, and just about anything else you can possibly imagine. Data can be stored in uppercase, lowercase, or mixed case letters. Data can be manipulated or changed; most data does not remain static for its lifetime.

DDL is used to define data and implement the assignment of data types, which enables the storage of data.

The following sections discuss

- Understanding data types
- Creating and managing tables
- Creating and managing indexes

Understanding Data Types

Data types are used to provide parameters and rules for all data stored in the database. A data type determines the way values are stored in a column insofar as the length allocated for the date and whether values such as alphanumeric, numeric, and date and time data are allowed. A data type exists for every possible bit or combination of data that can be stored in a particular database. Data types are characteristics of the data itself, whose attributes are placed on fields within a table.

| NEW TERM | *Data Types* are characteristics of data. |

The very basic data types, as with most other languages, handle the following:

- Character (alphanumeric) values
- Numeric values
- Date and time values
- Null values
- Boolean values

Each implementation of SQL has its own set of data types. The use of implementation-specific data types is necessary to support the philosophy of each implementation on how to handle the data storage. However, the basics are the same among all implementations. For instance, all implementations allow for the storage of character, numeric, and date and time values.

Defining Character Values

Character values are the most common data stored in most databases. Character values include letters of the alphabet, numbers, spaces, and special characters. Special characters that are allowed are vendor-implementation specific. There are basically two types of character values:

- Constant-length character strings
- Variable-length character strings

16

Constant characters—those strings that always have the same length—are stored using a fixed-length data type. An example of constant length data is a state abbreviation, because all state abbreviations are two characters. The most common constant-length data type is CHAR. Again, a data type is simply an identifier that tells the database what type of data can exist in a particular table's field or column.

NEW TERM *CHAR (pronounced CAR)* is a character based data type that is of a fixed length.

Spaces are usually used to fill extra spots when using a fixed-length data type. If a field's length was set to 10 and the data entered filled only 5 places, the remaining 5 spaces are recorded as spaces.

Variable-length data values are values that vary in length, such as an individual's name or address. Common data types for variable-length character values are the VARCHAR and VARCHAR2 data types. VARCHAR is the ANSI standard, which Microsoft SQL Server and MySQL use. Both VARCHAR and VARCHAR2 are used by Oracle. The data stored in a character-defined column can be alphanumeric, which means that the data value may contain numeric characters.

NEW TERM *VARCHAR/VARCHAR2 (pronounced VAR-CAR/VAR-CAR2)* is a character based data type that is of variable length.

 Later in this hour, you will see how to apply your knowledge of data types when defining tables.

Defining Numeric Values

Numeric values are those that include only numbers (0–9) and the period, which represents a decimal place. Sample numeric data values with which most individuals are familiar include a person's salary, a person's height in inches, the cost of a product, an invoice amount, and so forth. Numeric values are stored in fields that are defined as some type of number, typically referred to as NUMBER, INTEGER, REAL, DECIMAL, and so on.

NEW TERM   The data types *Number, Integer, Real, and Decimal* are numeric data types and are used to store numbers along with the period in order to denote positions to the right of the decimal.

A common numeric data type in SQL implementations is NUMBER, which accommodates the direction for numeric values provided by ANSI. Numeric values can be stored as zero, positive, negative, fixed, and floating-point numbers. The following is an example of a NUMBER definition:

`NUMBER(5)`

This example defines a numeric value that can have a maximum length of 5. The minimum value would be –99999 and the maximum value would be 99999.

The following are the standards for SQL numeric values:

BIT(n)

BIT VARYING(n)

DECIMAL(p,s)

INTEGER

SMALLINT

FLOAT(p)

REAL(s)

DOUBLE PRECISION(P)

Decimal values are numeric values that include the use of a decimal point. The standard for a decimal in SQL follows, where the p is the precision and the s is the decimal's scale:

`DECIMAL(p,s)`

p represents a number identifying the allocated, or maximum length, of the particular field for each appropriate definition.

s is a number to the right of the decimal point, such as `34.ss`.

The precision is the total length of the numeric value. In a numeric defined DECIMAL(4,2), the precision is 4, which is the total length allocated for a numeric value.

The scale is the number of digits to the right of the decimal point. The scale is 2 in the previous DECIMAL(4,2) example.

If a numeric value was defined as the following data type, the maximum value allowed would be 99.99:

`DECIMAL(4,2)`

Allowed values for a column defined as DECIMAL(4,2) include the following:

12

12.4

12.44

12.449

The last numeric value, 12.449, is rounded off to 12.45 upon input into the column.

Defining Date and Time

Date and time data values are used to keep track of information concerning dates and time. Standard SQL supports what are called DATETIME data types, which include the following specific data types:

DATE

TIME

INTERVAL

TIMESTAMP

The elements of a DATETIME data type consist of the following:

YEAR

MONTH

DAY

HOUR

MINUTE

SECOND

> Each implementation of SQL tends to have its own customized data type for dates and times. The previous data types and elements are standards to which each SQL vendor should adhere, but be advised that most implementations have their own data type for date values, varying both in appearance and the way date information is actually stored internally.

 New Term *Datetime* data types are used to store date values.

NULL Values

A NULL value is an unknown or missing value. A NULL value is different from a zero and different from a space. A NULL value refers to a field in a database table in which no data has been entered. NULL values are used in nearly all parts of SQL, including the creation of tables, search conditions for queries, and even in literal strings.

 Null denotes an unknown or missing value, a field where no data has been input.

The following are two methods for referencing a NULL value:

- NULL (the keyword NULL itself)
- ''(single quotation marks with nothing in between)

BOOLEAN Values

A BOOLEAN value is a value of either TRUE, FALSE, or NULL. BOOLEAN values are used to make data comparisons. For example, when criteria are specified for a query, each condition evaluates to either TRUE, FALSE, or NULL. If the BOOLEAN value of TRUE is returned by all conditions in a query, data is returned. If a BOOLEAN value of FALSE or NULL is returned, data may not be returned.

 Boolean Values are results of conditions or comparisons such as are found in the WHERE clause of an SQL statement. The results are TRUE, FALSE, or Null.

Consider the following example:

```
WHERE NAME = 'SMITH'
```

This line might be a condition found in a query. The condition is evaluated for every row of data in the table that is being queried. If the value of NAME is SMITH for a row of data in the table, the condition returns the value TRUE, thereby returning the data associated with that record.

Creating and Managing Tables

The table is the primary storage object for data in a relational database. A table is a logical collection of data. For instance, you might have an EMPLOYEES table, a PRODUCTS table, and a CUSTOMERS table. Each table represents a logical and distinguished set of data. A table consists of rows and columns (also known as fields), both of which hold data.

Using SQL, tables are created and managed throughout the life of the database. Table creation commands exist within the DDL subset of SQL commands. The DDL commands that you use to create and manage tables are

CREATE TABLE

ALTER TABLE

DROP TABLE

The CREATE TABLE statement in SQL is used to create a table.

The basic syntax to create a table is as follows:

SYNTAX

```
CREATE TABLE TABLE_NAME
( FIELD1  DATA TYPE  [ NOT NULL ],
  FIELD2  DATA TYPE  [ NOT NULL ],
  FIELD3  DATA TYPE  [ NOT NULL ],
  FIELD4  DATA TYPE  [ NOT NULL ],
  FIELD5  DATA TYPE  [ NOT NULL ] );
```

Each column has been assigned a specific data type and length and by using the NULL/NOT NULL constraint, you have specified which columns require values for every row of data in the table.

NULL is a default attribute for a column; therefore, it does not have to be entered in the CREATE TABLE statement. NOT NULL must always be specified.

Some form of a STORAGE clause is available in many relational database implementations of SQL. The STORAGE clause in a CREATE TABLE statement is used for initial table sizing and is usually done at table creation. The syntax of a STORAGE clause as used in one implementation is shown in the following example:

```
CREATE TABLE EMPLOYEE_TBL
(EMP_ID        CHAR(9)        NOT NULL,
 EMP_NAME      VARCHAR(40)    NOT NULL,
 EMP_ST_ADDR   VARCHAR(20)    NOT NULL,
 EMP_CITY      VARCHAR(15)    NOT NULL,
 EMP_ST        CHAR(2)        NOT NULL,
 EMP_ZIP       NUMBER(5)      NOT NULL,
 EMP_PHONE     NUMBER(10)     NULL,
 EMP_PAGER     NUMBER(10)     NULL)
STORAGE
    (INITIAL    3K
     NEXT       2K );
```

When you select names for objects, specifically tables and columns, the name should reflect the data that is to be stored. For example, the name for a table pertaining to employee information could be named EMPLOYEE_TBL. Names for columns should follow the same logic. When storing an employee's phone number, an obvious name for that column would be PHONE_NUMBER.

A table can be modified through the use of the ALTER TABLE command after that table's creation.

The standard syntax for the ALTER TABLE command follows:

```
ALTER TABLE TABLE_NAME [MODIFY] [COLUMN COLUMN_NAME][DATATYPE|NULL NOT NULL]
[RESTRICT|CASCADE]
                      [DROP]   [CONSTRAINT CONSTRAINT_NAME]
                      [ADD]    [COLUMN] COLUMN DEFINITION
```

Dropping a table is actually one of the easiest things to do.

```
DROP TABLE TABLE_NAME [ RESTRICT|CASCADE ]
```

> Whenever dropping a table, be sure to specify the schema name or owner of the table before submitting your command. You could drop the incorrect table. If you have access to multiple user accounts, ensure that you are connected to the database through the correct user account before dropping tables.

Creating and Managing Indexes

Simply put, an index is a pointer to data in a table. An index in a database is very similar to an index in the back of a book. In a book, for example, if you want to reference all pages that discuss a certain topic, you first refer to the index, which lists all topics alphabetically; you are then referred to one or more specific page numbers. An index in a database works the same way in that a query is pointed to the exact physical location of data in a table. You are actually being directed to the data's location in an underlying file of the database, but as far as you are concerned, you are referring to a table.

An index is stored separately from the table for which the index was created. An index's main purpose is to improve the performance of data retrieval. Indexes can be created or dropped with no effect on the data. However, once dropped, performance of data retrieval may be slowed. An index does take up physical space and often grows larger than the table itself.

As with tables, indexes are managed using SQL commands—again, commands from the DDL subset of SQL. The basic commands used to create and manage indexes are

CREATE INDEX

DROP INDEX

The structure of an index is altered by dropping the index and re-creating it.

The basic syntax to create an index is as follows:

SYNTAX

```
CREATE INDEX INDEX_NAME ON TABLE_NAME (COLUMN1, COLUMN2, ...);
```

16

Following is an example of an index creation on the previously discussed EMPLOYEE_TBL:

```
CREATE INDEX EMPLOYEE_IDX ON EMPLOYEE_TBL (EMP_ID, EMP_NAME);
```

The basic syntax to drop an index is as follows:

SYNTAX

```
DROP INDEX INDEX_NAME;
```

For example:

```
DROP INDEX EMPLOYEE_IDX;
```

An index is usually automatically dropped when its referenced table is dropped, because the index cannot really exist without the table itself.

Indexes can be very good for performance, but in some cases may actually hurt performance. Refrain from creating indexes on columns that will contain few unique values, such as sex, state of residence, and so on.

Creating a MySQL Database

The purpose of this section is to show an example of creating a MySQL database using the built-in WinMySQLAdmin tool. Creating a database in MySQL is easy to accomplish. Part of the installation process automatically creates two databases for you. They are TEST and MYSQL. The MYSQL database contains tables that store system data. The TEST database is a workspace that is provided for your use.

As part of the MySQL installation, you are provided with an executable file called winmysqladmin.exe; its location is in the mysql\bin directory. Execution of this file starts up MySQL and enables you to connect to the database. When MySQL successfully starts, you will see the MySQL admin tool flash momentarily on your monitor, and then it will minimize to a traffic light icon on your taskbar, as shown in Figure 16.1.

FIGURE 16.1

MySQL traffic light icon in the Windows taskbar.

MySQL traffic light

Click the icon and then select SHOW ME.

Figure 16.2 is a screenshot of the WinMySQLadmin tool.

FIGURE 16.2

Illustration of the WinMySQLadmin tool.

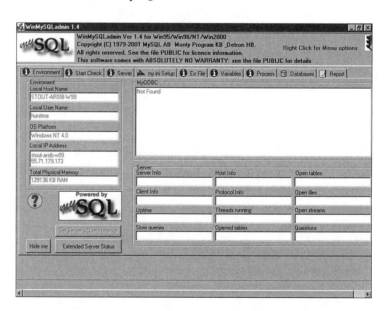

Locate and click the Databases tab to view information on MYSQL and TEST databases, as shown in Figure 16.3.

This example contains more than just the MYSQL and TEST database, but you get the idea.

FIGURE 16.3

Databases tab in MySQLadmin tool.

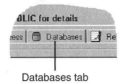

Databases tab

By clicking the mysql database name and then clicking a table within the database, you can now view table and index information as seen in Figure 16.4.

FIGURE 16.4

Viewing database information in the MySQLadmin tool.

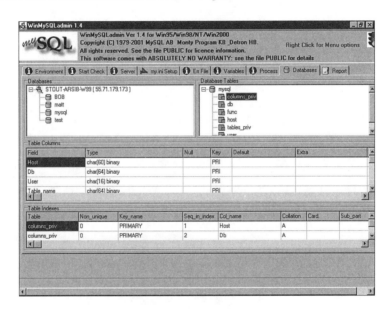

Locate and invoke the MySQL.exe file. It is located in the mysql\bin directory (see Figure 16.5).

Type the following command at the mysql> prompt to see all available databases:

```
mysql> show databases;
```

To use or go into another database you would type the following:

```
mysql> use mysql;
```

To create a new database, you could type the following, replacing the [database name] with an actual database name:

```
mysql> create database [database name];
```

FIGURE 16.5

Obtaining the mysql>
prompt using
mysql.exe.

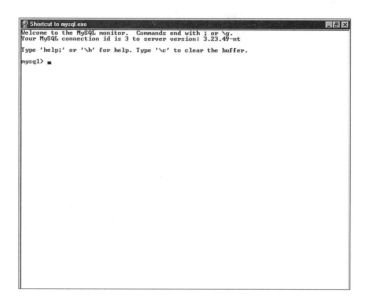

You can also create a database, among other things, using the MySQLadmin tool.

If you right-click the machine name under the Databases tab, you are presented with several options, as shown in Figure 16.6.

FIGURE 16.6

Database related tasks
available when you
right-click.

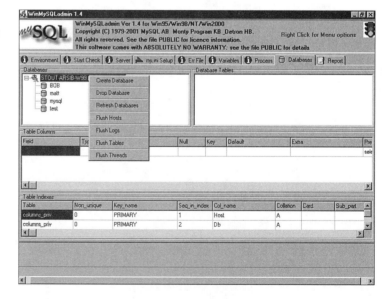

> Refer to the MySQL online documentation for information relating to specific MySQL issues that you may encounter during software installation. After your database has been created in MySQL, you can use SQL to create tables, insert and manage data, and retrieve data. SQL commands are submitted at the mysql> prompt.

16

Using MySQL for Database and Object Creation

The purpose of this section is to show a few examples of DDL commands using MySQL at the command prompt. If you have installed MySQL on your computer, feel free to follow along with the following examples. To follow along, locate and execute the mysql.exe file from the "bin" folder of your MySQL installation folder.

Figure 16.7 illustrates the creation and designation of a new MySQL database called "hour16":

FIGURE 16.7

Creating and designating the new database.

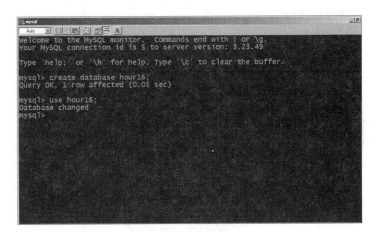

Figure 16.8 illustrates the creation of the PRODUCTS table:

FIGURE 16.8

Creating the new table.

Figure 16.9 illustrates a modification to the structure of the PRODUCTS table using the ALTER TABLE command:

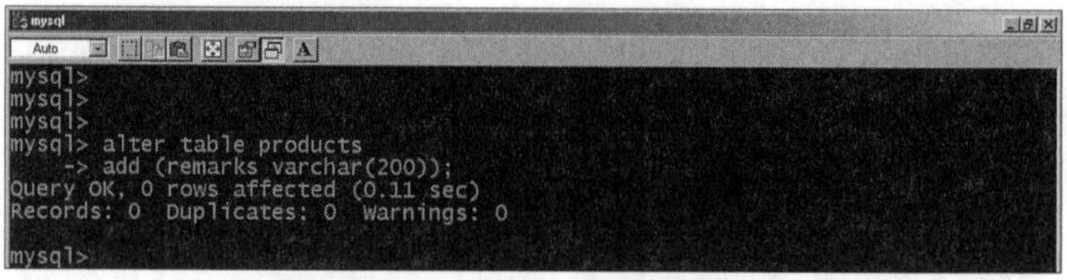

FIGURE 16.9
Using ALTER TABLE to modify the table structure.

Figure 16.10 illustrates the deletion of the PRODUCTS table using the DROP TABLE command:

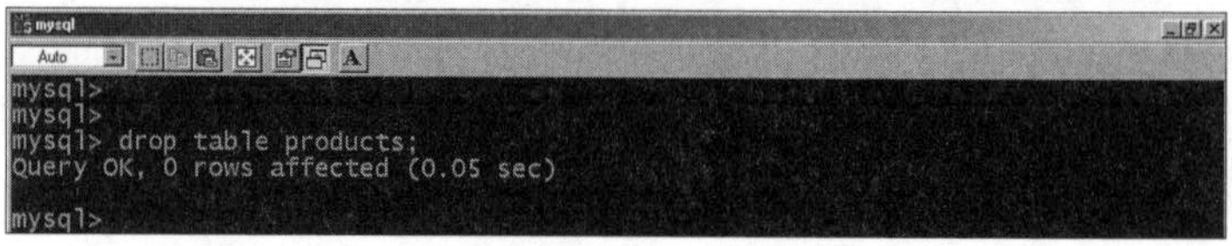

FIGURE 16.10
Using DROP TABLE to delete a table.

Summary

During this hour, you have learned the very basics of creating a database and creating objects within your database. A database is created using database software provided by a vendor such as Oracle, Microsoft, or MySQL. In this hour, you followed an example of creating a database using MySQL. MySQL is a limited tool, but good for learning about databases and the standard database language, SQL. After the database has been created, you can use SQL to create database objects such as tables. Tables hold data with which users need to interact, serving the purpose of a database. In following hours, you will learn more about interacting with data using SQL.

Workshop

The following workshop is composed of quiz questions and practical exercises. The quiz questions are designed to test your overall understanding of the current material. The practical exercises are intended to afford you the opportunity to apply the concepts discussed during the current hour, as well as build on the knowledge acquired in previous hours of study. Please take time to complete this workshop before continuing.

Quiz

1. What is information called that is stored in a database?
2. What do data types accomplish?

3. What are the three basic types of data that might be found in a database?

4. What is the main purpose of an index?

5. What does DDL stand for?

6. What are the three basic categories of DDL commands?

7. What three DDL commands are used to manage tables?

Exercises

1. Invoke the MySQL database software.

2. Create a new MySQL database using the following command:

```
CREATE DATABASE HOUR16;
```

3. Point to your new database using the following command:

```
USE HOUR16;
```

4. Create a table in your new database as follows:

```
CREATE TABLE CUSTOMERS
(CUST_ID     INTEGER(9)   NOT NULL,
 LAST_NAME   VARCHAR(25)  NOT NULL,
 FIRST_NAME  VARCHAR(25)  NOT NULL,
 ADDRESS     VARCHAR(30)  NOT NULL,
 CITY        VARCHAR(30)  NOT NULL,
 STATE       CHAR(2)      NOT NULL,
 ZIP         VARCHAR(5)   NOT NULL,
 PHONE       VARCHAR(10)  NULL);
```

5. Alter your table using the following command:

```
ALTER TABLE CUSTOMERS
ADD (PAGER VARCHAR(10) NULL);
```

6. Drop your table using the following command:

```
DROP TABLE CUSTOMERS;
```

7. Try creating and managing some tables on your own.

Answers to Quiz

1. Data.

2. Data types enable you to define the data that is stored in a database.

3. Character values, numeric values, and date/time values.

4. An index speeds up access to data in a table.

5. DDL = data definition language.

6. CREATE, ALTER, and DROP.

7. CREATE TABLE, ALTER TABLE, and DROP TABLE.

16

Hour **17**

Interacting with Databases to Manage and Retrieve Data

During Hour 16, "Creating Databases and Database Objects," you learned about the creation of databases and database objects. Databases and database objects are created using the relational database language SQL. SQL is also used to manage and retrieve data. In this hour, you will learn how SQL is used to input data into a database, manage data, and retrieve data.

The highlights of this hour include

- An overview of data manipulation
- An overview of data retrieval
- Inserting data using SQL
- Updating data using SQL
- Deleting data using SQL
- Retrieving data using SQL

Overview of Data Manipulation

Data manipulation involves updating, deleting, and adding data to a database. Data Manipulation Language (DML) is the part of SQL that allows a database user to actually propagate changes to data in a relational database. With DML, the user can populate tables with new data, update existing data in tables, and delete data from tables.

There are three basic DML commands in SQL:

- INSERT
- UPDATE
- DELETE

Each of these commands is discussed in the following sections, along with examples.

NEW TERM   *DML or Data Manipulation Language* is the SQL syntax that allows one to put data into tables (INSERT), make changes to that data (UPDATE), and remove data from the tables (DELETE).

Inserting Data with the INSERT Command

After a database table is created, data must be entered into the table for the table to be useful. You use the INSERT statement to insert new data into a table. The basic syntax of the INSERT statement is as follows:

```
INSERT INTO TABLE_NAME (COLUMN1, COLUMN2, ETC.)
VALUES ('VALUE1', 'VALUE2', ETC. );
```

Suppose that you had a table called COLORS and you wanted to insert some new colors (rows of data) into the table. Your INSERT statements might appear as follows:

INPUT
```
INSERT INTO COLORS (COLOR_NAME)
VALUES ('RED');
INSERT INTO COLORS (COLOR_NAME)
VALUES ('BLUE');
INSERT INTO COLORS (COLOR_NAME)
VALUES ('GREEN');
```

As another example, suppose you wanted to insert new product data into a table called PRODUCTS. Your INSERT statement might appear as follows:

INPUT
```
INSERT INTO PRODUCTS (PROD_ID, PROD_NAME, COST)
VALUES ('1','PENCIL','.59');
```

These examples make the INSERT command appear simple because it is simple. In fact, all DML commands are very simple because they perform simple operations.

In many situations, an end user does not insert data by typing an INSERT command. Typically, the end user has a user-friendly point–and-click application that allows the user to easily manipulate data without having knowledge of SQL. The user application would have embedded SQL in it that executes the DML commands discussed during this hour.

> The column list in the INSERT statement does not have to reflect the same order of columns as in the definition of the associated table, but the list of values must be in the order of the associated columns in the column list.

17

Updating Data with the UPDATE Command

After data is loaded into the database, you may need to modify or update it. Existing data is modified using the DML command UPDATE. The UPDATE command does not add new records to a table, nor does it remove records—UPDATE simply updates existing data. Again, there is nothing difficult about it.

The simplest form of the UPDATE statement is its use to update a single column in a table. Multiple columns may also be updated with the same UPDATE statement. The basic syntax of the UPDATE statement is as follows:

SYNTAX

```
UPDATE TABLE_NAME
SET COLUMN1 = 'VALUE',
  [COLUMN2 = 'VALUE',]
  [COLUMN3 = 'VALUE']
[WHERE CONDITION];
```

Following is a simple example of an update statement:

INPUT

```
UPDATE COLORS
SET COLOR_NAME = 'BLUE';
```

This statement would change the column value of COLOR_NAME to 'BLUE' for all rows of data in the COLORS table.

Let's say you had a misentered color called 'BLEW'. You might issue an UPDATE command as follows to make the correction:

INPUT

```
UPDATE COLORS
SET COLOR_NAME = 'BLUE'
WHERE COLOR_NAME = 'BLEW';
```

As a more practical example, suppose an employee received a pay increase. You may issue an UPDATE command similar to the following:

```
UPDATE EMPLOYEES
SET SALARY = 50000
WHERE LAST_NAME = 'SMITH'
 AND FIRST_NAME = 'JOHN';
```

Suppose you wanted to update multiple columns:

```
UPDATE EMPLOYEES
SET SALARY = 50000,
   BONUS = 1000
WHERE LAST_NAME = 'SMITH'
 AND FIRST_NAME = 'JOHN';
```

Notice the use of the SET in this syntax—there is only one SET, but multiple columns and each column is separated by a comma. You should start to see a trend in SQL. The comma is usually used to separate different types of arguments in SQL statements.

> Extreme caution must be used when using the UPDATE statement without a WHERE clause. The target column is updated for all rows of data in the table if conditions are not designated using the WHERE clause.

Deleting Data with the DELETE Command

The DELETE command is used to remove entire rows of data from a table. The DELETE command is not used to remove values from specific columns; a full record, including all columns, is removed. The DELETE statement must be used with caution because if not used carefully, all data can be erroneously removed from a table.

To delete a single record or selected records from a table, the DELETE statement must be used with the following syntax:

SYNTAX

```
DELETE FROM TABLE_NAME
[WHERE CONDITION];
```

Notice the use of the WHERE clause. The WHERE clause is an essential part of the DELETE statement if you are attempting to remove selected rows of data from a table. You rarely issue a DELETE statement without the use of the WHERE clause.

The following example would remove all rows of data from the COLORS table:

INPUT
```
DELETE FROM COLORS;
```

Sometimes the DELETE is useful without a WHERE clause, but most often, you will probably require a WHERE clause. Study the following example:

INPUT
```
DELETE FROM EMPLOYEES
WHERE LAST_NAME = 'SMITH'
  AND FIRST_NAME = 'JOHN';
```

> If the WHERE clause is omitted from the DELETE statement, all rows of data are deleted from the table. As a general rule, plan to use a WHERE clause with the DELETE statement.

As with the INSERT command, UPDATE and DELETE commands are typically embedded within a user application and executed by the application without the requirement of the end user possessing a knowledge of SQL.

Overview of Data Retrieval

Data retrieval refers to the process of mining your database for useful data. You have created database objects, inserted data, updated data, and deleted data. Using DML, you can easily and effectively manage data in a database. Now that the data has been loaded, you probably will need to retrieve the data for a variety of purposes.

Data is typically retrieved from the database for the following reasons:

- To create a report
- For quality assurance
- For decision making
- To study trends
- To answer a question
- To perform calculations
- To summarize data

Data is retrieved using Data Query Language (DQL). DQL consists of a single command, called SELECT. The SELECT is coupled with what is known as the FROM clause. All DQL must at least have a SELECT clause and a FROM clause. This tells the database "give me data from the tables that I specify". The SELECT statement is fairly simple but has many options that provide great flexibility when querying a database.

The following sections discuss data retrieval to the following magnitudes:

- Basic data retrieval with the SELECT command
- Retrieving data with criteria
- Selecting data from multiple tables
- Molding retrieved data with functions

Basic Data Retrieval with the SELECT Command

A query is an inquiry into the database using the SELECT statement. A query is used to extract data from the database in a readable format according to the user's request. As previously mentioned, the SELECT statement, the command that represents DQL in SQL, is the statement used to construct database queries.

The basic syntax of the SELECT statement is as follows:

```
SELECT [ * | ALL | DISTINCT COLUMN1, COLUMN2 ]
FROM TABLE1 [ , TABLE2 ];
```

The simplest form of the select statement is as follows:

INPUT
```
SELECT * FROM COLORS;
```

OUTPUT
```
COLOR_NAME
==========
RED
BLUE
GREEN
```

Multiple columns can be selected as follows:

INPUT
```
SELECT FIRST_NAME, LAST_NAME
FROM EMPLOYEES;
```

OUTPUT
```
FIRST_NAME      LAST_NAME
============== ================
JOHN        SMITH
MARY        HIGGINS
STEVE       WILLIAMS
```

The SELECT statement is used in conjunction with the FROM clause to extract data from the database in an organized, readable format.

The FROM clause must always be used in conjunction with the SELECT statement. The FROM clause's purpose is to tell the database what table(s) to access to retrieve the desired data for the query. The FROM clause may contain one or more tables. The FROM clause must always list at least one table.

Commas are used to separate arguments in a list in SQL statements. Some common lists include lists of columns in a query, lists of tables to be selected from in a query, values to be inserted into a table, and values grouped as a condition in a query's WHERE clause.

Retrieving Data with Criteria

A condition is part of a query that is used to display selective information as specified by the user. The value of a condition is either TRUE or FALSE, thereby limiting the data retrieved by the query. As with the UPDATE and DELETE commands, the WHERE clause is used to place conditions on a query by eliminating rows that would normally be returned by a query without conditions.

There can be more than one condition in the WHERE clause. If there is more than one condition, they are connected by the AND and OR operators. An operator is a character or keyword in SQL that is used to combine elements in an SQL statement.

The basic syntax of the SELECT command with the WHERE clause is as follows:

```
The syntax for the WHERE clause is as follows:
SELECT [ ALL | * | DISTINCT COLUMN1, COLUMN2 ]
FROM TABLE1 [ , TABLE2 ]
WHERE [ CONDITION1 | EXPRESSION1 ]
[ AND CONDITION2 | EXPRESSION2 ]
```

Following is a simple example of a SELECT command with a WHERE clause:

INPUT
```
SELECT *
FROM COLORS
WHERE COLOR_NAME = 'BLUE';
```

OUTPUT
```
COLOR_NAME
===========
BLUE
```

Following is a more practical example:

INPUT
```
SELECT FIRST_NAME, LAST_NAME, SALARY
FROM EMPLOYEES
WHERE SALARY > 40000;
```

OUTPUT
```
FIRST_NAME       LAST_NAME        SALARY
==============   ==============   ========
JOHN             SMITH            41000
MARY             HIGGINS          55000
```

Following is a simple query with multiple conditions:

INPUT
```
SELECT FIRST_NAME, LAST_NAME, SALARY
FROM EMPLOYEES
WHERE SALARY > 40000
   AND SALARY < 50000;
```

OUTPUT
```
FIRST_NAME      LAST_NAME      SALARY
==============  =============  ========
JOHN            SMITH          41000
```

Following is another example with multiple conditions:

INPUT
```
SELECT PRODUCT_CATEGORY, PRODUCT_NAME, COST
FROM PRODUCTS2
WHERE PRODUCT_CATEGORY = 'PEN'
   AND COST > .99;
```

OUTPUT
```
PRODUCT_CATEGORY     PRODUCT_NAME          COST
===================  ====================  =========
PEN                  FELT PEN              1.49
PEN                  FINE POINT PEN        1.99
PEN                  BALL POINT PEN        1.09
```

Selecting Data from Multiple Tables

Having the capability to select data from multiple tables is one of SQL's most powerful features. Without this capability, the entire relational database concept would not be feasible. Single-table queries are sometimes quite informative, but in the real world, the most practical queries are those whose data is acquired from multiple tables within the database. A JOIN is an operation in SQL that combines two or more tables to retrieve data from multiple tables.

Suppose you have the two following tables:

PRODUCTS Table:

PRODUCT_ID	PRODUCT	COST
==============	===============	=======
1	PENCIL	.39
2	PEN	.99
3	ERASER	.59

INVENTORY Table:

PRODUCT_ID	QUANTITY
===============	=========
1	9878
2	7864
3	8769

If you were ask how many pencils were in stock, you would identify the PRODUCT_ID for PENCIL and then find the QUANTITY of that PRODUCT_ID in the INVENTORY table. This is exactly how SQL works.

The SQL query would appear as follows:

```
SELECT QUANTITY
FROM PRODUCTS, INVENTORY
WHERE PRODUCTS.PRODUCT_ID = INVENTORY.PRODUCT_ID
   AND PRODUCT = 'PENCIL';
```

The output would appear as follows:

```
QUANTITY
========
9878
```

Molding Retrieved Data with Functions

When you retrieve data from the database, you may want it to appear slightly different from how it is stored in the database.

For example, you might specify JOHN SMITH'S name to appear in mixed case, as follows, by using the INITCAP function:

New Term   *INITCAP* is a function that is performed on a CHAR or VARCHAR column, making the first letter of a column appear in upper case, and subsequent letters in the column appear in lower case. This altering of appearance is only for the SQL script that is being processed, it does not affect the state of the data as it is stored.

```
SELECT INITCAP(FIRST_NAME), INITCAP(LAST_NAME)
FROM EMPLOYEES
WHERE FIRST_NAME = 'JOHN'
 AND LAST_NAME = 'SMITH';
```

```
INITCAP(FIRST_NAME)   INITCAP(LAST_NAME)
==================  ==================
John                Smith
```

Maybe you want to find the length of each employee's last name:

INPUT
```
SELECT LAST_NAME, LENGTH(LAST_NAME)
FROM EMPLOYEES;
```

OUTPUT
```
LAST_NAME       LENGTH(LAST_NAME)
==============  =================
SMITH           5
HIGGINS         7
WILLIAMS        8
```

NEW TERM   When the function *Length* is performed on a column, the result is the numeric length of each value in the column.

Finally, you may want to represent each color by its initial:

INPUT
```
SELECT SUBSTR(COLOR_NAME,1,1)
FROM COLORS;
```

OUTPUT
```
SUBSTR(COLOR_NAME,1,1)
======================
R
B
G
```

NEW TERM   *Substr* is an abbreviation for substring. The function *substr* returns a specified portion of a column or *sub of the string*. The function starts at a designated position in the string, continues for a specified amount of characters, and returns the value.

These are just a very few examples of the functions in SQL that you can use to mold the appearance of retrieved data. The point is that there is much flexibility as to how data is displayed.

Summary

During this hour you have learned the very basics of data management, data manipulation, and data retrieval using SQL. You learned how data can be manipulated using the INSERT, UPDATE, and DELETE commands, and the possible dangers of performing DML operations without the use of a WHERE clause. You also learned how to retrieve data (query the database) using the SELECT command. The commands shown in this hour were simple. The SELECT command can get much more involved, but for the most part, SQL is a relatively simple language to learn and use to manage data in a relational database.

Workshop

The following workshop is composed of quiz questions and practical exercises. The quiz questions are designed to test your overall understanding of the current material. The practical exercises are intended to afford you the opportunity to apply the concepts discussed during the current hour, as well as build on the knowledge acquired in previous hours of study. Please take time to complete this workshop before continuing. You can refer to the answers at the end of the hour.

Quiz

1. What does DML allow a user to do?

2. What are the three basic DML commands?

3. What allows you to merge data from multiple tables?

4. What would happen if you wanted to delete a specific row of data but you neglected to use the WHERE clause in your DELETE statement?

Exercises

1. Invoke MySQL and create a database using the following command:

   ```
   CREATE DATABASE HOUR17;
   ```

2. Point to your new database using the following command:

   ```
   USE HOUR17;
   ```

3. Create a new table using the following command:

   ```
   CREATE TABLE PRODUCTS
   (PROD_ID  VARCHAR(2),
    PRODUCT  VARCHAR(10),
    COST     DECIMAL(4,2));
   ```

4. Insert data into your table with the following commands:

   ```
   INSERT INTO PRODUCTS VALUES ('1','PENCIL','.39');
   INSERT INTO PRODUCTS VALUES ('2','PEN','.99');
   INSERT INTO PRODUCTS VALUES ('3','ERASER','.59');
   ```

5. Query your table as follows:

   ```
   SELECT * FROM PRODUCTS;
   ```

6. Update your data as follows:

   ```
   UPDATE PRODUCTS
   SET COST = '.89'
   WHERE PRODUCT = 'PEN';
   ```

17

7. Query your table to view the changes to your data:

```
SELECT * FROM PRODUCTS;
```

8. Delete some data as follows:

```
DELETE FROM PRODUCTS
WHERE PRODUCT = 'ERASER';
```

9. Query your table to view the changes to your data:

```
SELECT * FROM PRODUCTS;
```

10. Perform the following query:

```
SELECT PRODUCT, COST
FROM PRODUCTS
WHERE COST > .40;
```

Answers to Quiz

1. What does DML allow a user to do?

   Data Manipulation Language (DML) is the part of SQL that allows a database user to actually propagate changes to a relational database.

2. What are the three basic DML commands?

   The three basic DML commands are INSERT, UPDATE, and DELETE

3. What allows you to merge data from multiple tables?

   A JOIN combines two or more tables to retrieve data from multiple tables.

4. What would happen if you wanted to delete a specific row of data but you neglected to use the WHERE clause in your delete statement?

   Not only would you succeed in removing the specific row you wanted to remove, but all the rest of the rows in the table would be deleted. Probably not a good thing!

HOUR **18**

Effective Reporting and Data Usage

Welcome to Hour 18. Now that you have a better understanding of how to create a database and store your data within it, in this hour, you will explore some methods of retrieving the data from the database. Data that is stored within the tables of your database is just that, data. It is not until the data is retrieved in a meaningful way that it becomes information.

The process of *normalization*, storing your data in several smaller, specific tables that relate to each other, is fundamental to relational database design. If your database is properly normalized, you would seldom, if ever, be able to report meaningful, detailed information from just one table. Whether providing reports or applications for customers and users or retrieving system information to monitor the state of operation of the database, IT professionals have many needs for reporting data.

The highlights of this hour include

- A discussion of database reporting
- An overview of effective data usage

- A discussion of reporting considerations
- An overview of some popular reporting tools

What Is Database Reporting?

Database reporting is the process by which data is selected from tables in a database and then presented for a specific use. The data that is selected comes from specific columns from a table, and depending on the needs of the report, can be sorted, grouped, or summarized, and then displayed in a specific order. After the report has been completed and is verified to be correct, it can then be distributed for use.

Good communication skills and patience are absolutely vital when you're preparing to do any type of database reporting. Requests that come to you can and will be in almost any format imaginable. Meetings might be held in person or by teleconference to determine requirements. Requests may come to you in writing or by email. You may find a sticky note attached to your monitor when you come back from lunch, cryptically asking for figures from the sales department. Often, the request will come from your boss, who suddenly appears over the top of your cubicle, breathlessly demanding to know where the shipping numbers are. Regardless of how the request comes to you, it is important and vital, and you can be assured that the requestor needs *you*.

 NEW TERM **Database Reporting** is the process by which data is selected from relational database tables and is presented for a specific use.

 It would not be practical to provide examples of all SQL implementation syntax in this text. The examples and exercises in this hour will focus on using MySQL.

Tables and Insert Statements Used in This Hour

The disk that comes with this book contains SQL statements for creating tables and inserting data into the tables in a MySQL database. The following are select statements in a MySQL environment so you can have a look at your data.

The select * from [table_name] syntax enables you to select all rows from the specified table name.

```
mysql> select * from comp;
+-----------+--------+--------+
| emp_id    | salary | hourly |
+-----------+--------+--------+
| 333445555 | 120000 |   NULL |
| 111223333 |  70000 |   NULL |
| 222334444 |  70000 |   NULL |
| 444556666 |   NULL |  15.75 |
| 555667777 |   NULL |  25.32 |
| 666778888 |   NULL |   9.25 |
| 777889990 |  40000 |   NULL |
| 888991111 |  32000 |   NULL |
| 999112222 |  42750 |   NULL |
| 333224444 |  38752 |   NULL |
+-----------+--------+--------+
10 rows in set (0.12 sec)
mysql> select * from dept;
+---------+--------------------+
| dept_id | description        |
+---------+--------------------+
| 1000    | PRESIDENT          |
| 1010    | VICE PRESIDENT CEO |
| 1011    | VICE PRESIDENT     |
| 2000    | OFFICE MGR         |
| 2020    | OFFICE SALES COORD |
| 2003    | OFFICE RECEPTIONIST|
| 3000    | SALES MGR          |
| 3001    | SALES REP          |
| 3002    | SALES REP          |
| 3003    | SALES TRAVEL COORD |
| 3020    | SALES AST COORD    |
| 3021    | SALES AST COORD    |
+---------+--------------------+
12 rows in set (0.06 sec)
mysql> select * from emp;
+-----------+---------+------------+----------+----------+----------+-------------+
| emp_id    |dept_id| hire_dt    | lname    | fname    | mname    | city        |
+-----------+---------+------------+----------+----------+----------+-------------+
| 111223333 | 1010    | 2001-06-25 | HURST    | KAY      | YVONNE   | SOUTHPORT   |
| 222334444 | 1011    | 2001-06-26 | JUSTESS  | HEATHER  | JANE     | HOMECROFT   |
| 333445555 | 1000    | 2001-06-01 | CHAUCER  | GEOFFERY | PENN     | SOUTHPORT   |
| 444556666 | 2000    | 2001-07-02 | ST LOUIS | WARNER   | MARSHALL | SOUTHPORT   |
| 555667777 | 2020    | 2001-06-18 | WINSTON  | JENNY    | LEE      | INDIANAPOLIS|
| 666778888 | 2003    | 2001-06-18 | WALTERS  | TANYA    | JEAN     | INDIANAPOLIS|
| 777889990 | 3000    | 2001-06-01 | TULL     | JETHRO   | PIPER    | FRANKLIN    |
| 888991111 | 3001    | 2001-06-01 | BROWN    | CLARENCE | NULL     | GREENWOOD   |
| 999112222 | 3020    | 2001-06-01 | JESSE    | BETTY    | LEW      | GREENWOOD   |
| 333224444 | 3021    | 2001-06-01 | SLATTERY | DAVID    | LOU      | CAMBY       |
+-----------+---------+------------+----------+----------+----------+-------------+
10 rows in set (0.00 sec)
mysql> select * from products;
```

18

```
+———+————+———————————+
| prod_id | price  | description           |
+———+————+———————————+
| 1111    |   3.95 | SPY GLASSES           |
| 2222    | 195.95 | MP3 PLAYER            |
| 3333    |  59.95 | DIGITAL RECORDER      |
| 4441    |   5.00 | FAKE DOGGIE DOO       |
| 5551    |   3.95 | SNAKE IN A CAN        |
| 6661    |   1.95 | PEPPER GUM            |
| 5552    |   4.75 | WOOPIE CUSHON         |
| 5554    |   6.00 | DRIBBLE GLASS         |
| 7777    |  49.95 | WATCH WINDER          |
| 6662    |   4.50 | XRAY SPECS            |
| 4442    |   3.95 | FAKE VOMIT            |
| 5553    |   4.25 | LOADED DICE           |
| 9991    |  29.95 | MAGICIANS KIT         |
| 999A    | 200.00 | TOP HAT WITHOUT RABBIT |
| 999B    | 500.00 | TOP HAT WITH RABBIT   |
| 4443    |   4.35 | FLY IN OINTMENT       |
+———+————+———————————+
16 rows in set (0.04 sec)
mysql> select * from sales;
+———————+————+————+————————+————————————————+
| emp_id    | prod_id | amount | ship_date  | destination             |
+———————+————+————+————————+————————————————+
| 333224444 | 7777    |      2 | 2001-09-03 | YE OLD CLOCK SHOP       |
| 333224444 | 2222    |      7 | 2001-09-07 | SHOCKING ELECTRONICS    |
| 333224444 | 2222    |      6 | 2001-09-02 | SHOCKING ELECTRONICS    |
| 333224444 | 3333    |     14 | 2001-09-27 | SPYS R US               |
| 999112222 | 5552    |     16 | 2001-09-27 | FANCY PRANKS            |
| 999112222 | 6661    |     45 | 2001-09-27 | FANCY PRANKS            |
| 999112222 | 6662    |     32 | 2001-09-27 | FANCY PRANKS            |
| 999112222 | 5553    |     20 | 2001-09-27 | FANCY PRANKS            |
| 999112222 | 5551    |     25 | 2001-09-27 | FANCY PRANKS            |
| 999112222 | 4443    |     40 | 2001-09-27 | FANCY PRANKS            |
| 888991111 | 1111    |     72 | 2001-10-25 | R PRANKS R FANCIER      |
| 888991111 | 999A    |      1 | 2001-11-01 | TUX RENTAL              |
| 888991111 | 9991    |      4 | 2001-11-03 | BLACKSTONES READING ROOM |
| 888991111 | 999B    |      1 | 2001-11-15 | BLACKSTONES READING ROOM |
| 777889990 | 4441    |     10 | 2001-09-15 | SELF                    |
| 777889990 | 5551    |      5 | 2001-09-20 | SELF                    |
| 777889990 | 4442    |      8 | 2001-09-30 | SELF                    |
| 333445555 | 999B    |      4 | 2001-10-01 | BUGSYS FORMAL DINER     |
| 333445555 | 5554    |     72 | 2001-10-01 | SIGMA ALPHA PLEW        |
| 333445555 | 1111    |     67 | 2001-10-09 | SIGMA ALPHA PLEW        |
| 333445555 | 5551    |     47 | 2001-10-12 | SIGMA ALPHA PLEW        |
| 333445555 | 4441    |     50 | 2001-10-17 | SIGMA ALPHA PLEW        |
| 333445555 | 5552    |     87 | 2001-10-28 | SIGMA ALPHA PLEW        |
| 333445555 | 4442    |     60 | 2001-10-30 | SIGMA ALPHA PLEW        |
+———————+————+————+————————+————————————————+
24 rows in set (0.06 sec)
```

Using Data Effectively

The Create Table and Insert statements that are in this hour are found on the accompanying disk. They can be loaded at the MySQL prompt as indicated below.

```
mysql> source a:\chp18wkshp.sql;
```

You can also copy and paste the statements at the MySQL prompt.

Now, let's take a few moments to discuss the data. The tables and data that you have just created are representative of a business system. It contains data on the employees, how they are paid, and at what rate. It also contains data on what duties each employee performs and a record of business that is conducted. Granted, this is a scaled-down representation that should work well for the purposes of this hour.

Because you are the one who created these tables, you are said to be the owner. This command you will see allows you to see your tables if you are using a MySQL database.

▼ SYNTAX

```
mysql> show tables;
+---------------+
| Tables_in_matt |
+---------------+
| comp          |
| dept          |
| emp           |
| products      |
| sales         |
+---------------+
5 rows in set (0.01 sec)
```

The describe command enables you to view the structure of the columns in each table.

```
desc dept;
```

Note the column names in your tables that end with _id. By viewing the data in these tables, you should be able to identify the tables where these columns contain unique values and the tables where values may repeat. This is part of table relationships. However, in a real-world database environment, such a technique most likely would be of no use. It's not unheard of for a small-to-medium database to contain several hundred tables, so visual inspection would not be practical.

The use of ID in the column-name naming convention can be a good indicator of what column is being used to relate to another table. Entity Relationship Diagrams (ERDs), like the one found in Figure 18.1, show a clear-cut picture of how the relationships exist.

18

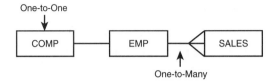

FIGURE 18.1.
An Entity Relationship diagram.

As Figure 18.1 shows, there should be one and only one COMP record for each record in the EMP table. This is based on the values of the EMP_ID column being equal in both tables. This is known as a one-to-one relationship. In the figure, notice the relationship between the EMP table and the SALES table. The line branches into three points as it connects to the SALES table. This convention is used to indicate that for every row in the EMP table, there could be many rows in the SALES table. This is known as a one-to-many relationship.

When retrieving data from your tables for reports, you must have an understanding of how the tables relate to each other in order to report accurate information. You'll see more of this later. You must also know how the data is stored.

Data stored in tables should be in either all uppercase or all lowercase. It should never be in mixed case, and punctuation should never be stored. Generally, some human is adding or updating rows in the table via an input screen. If the data is stored in mixed case, it is nearly impossible to standardize the way that data is input. Some implementations of SQL are case sensitive with regard to how data is referenced in a select statement. For example, if an Oracle database contains the table CITYS that has the value of Indianapolis, a select statement searching for the value INDIANAPOLIS would return no rows.

SYNTAX

```
SQL> create table citys
  2 (city  varchar2(27));
SQL> insert into citys values ('Indianapolis');
SQL> select * from citys where city = 'INDIANAPOLIS';
no rows selected
```

Understanding Reporting Needs

When users come to you requesting a report, it's because they have a need for the information. You may or may not be in a position to determine if the need is "real" or just a "want," but you do have a certain obligation to try to understand the difference. The following sections discuss some considerations that are associated with understanding reporting needs (using the tables and data you created earlier as a guide):

Does the Data Exist and Do You Have Access to It?

The tables to which you have access deal with employee and sales data. A request for reports that deal with MARKETING would be outside your capability to provide because you do not have access to that data. Possible fixes to this would be to request access to the MARKETING tables or to send the requestor to another department.

What Are the Time Constraints?

In a perfect world, each request comes 7 to 10 days before the requestor has to have a finished product (this is known as a "drop dead" date). How does the request fit into your already busy schedule? Do you need to get authorization from your boss to set your current assignment aside for this request?

How Specific Is the Request?

Never be afraid to make the requestor take the time to consider exactly what they are requesting. Sometimes the requestor doesn't really know exactly what they want to see and how they want to see it. By taking a few minutes to communicate openly and professionally, you can save much time and effort. There is nothing worse than presenting a finished product only to hear "Gee, that's neat, but what I really wanted was..."

Is This Request Similar to Any Request You've Fulfilled in the Past?

After a time you will begin to build a catalog of reports that you have created. Sometimes you can take a similar pre-existing report, copy it, make a few revisions to the copy, and use the result as your finished product. This can be a tremendous time-saver.

Does the Requestor Have a Legitimate Need for the Information?

This is not to suggest that anyone in your organization would knowingly attempt to gain access to information they shouldn't have, but there may be times when requestors ask for such data. A good solution to this might be establishing a set of standards and guidelines that detail what information is released to whom.

Although it may seem reasonable for the sales manager to request statistics on the sales staff, it may not be appropriate for them to request comparisons in salary for those outside of the sales department. The intent of the request may be innocent, but allowing employees access to each other's pay data could cause problems within the company.

18

Is This a One-Time Request, or Will the Requestor Require This Report on a Continuing Basis?

If the information that is being requested needs to be periodically updated and redistributed, how might this be done? Does your situation require that a schedule be accomplished? Some operations systems allow for processes to be run at regularly scheduled times.

Communicating with the Requestor

Understanding the importance of communicating with the requestor of a report is one of the keys of generating an accurate and useful report from the database. It is important to understand the viewpoint and language of the requestor and convert the requestor's needs into a useful report. The following sections discuss both verbal and written requests.

Verbal Requests

In many situations, this can be the most common form of request that you will receive, and depending on the expertise of the person making the request, it could have the most risk. Questions such as, "Can you get me a listing of products?" sounds simple enough, if that's all the requestor really wants.

SYNTAX

```
mysql> select description from products;
+----------------------+
| description          |
+----------------------+
| SPY GLASSES          |
| MP3 PLAYER           |
| DIGITAL RECORDER     |
| FAKE DOGGIE DOO      |
| SNAKE IN A CAN       |
| PEPPER GUM           |
| WOOPIE CUSHON        |
| DRIBBLE GLASS        |
| WATCH WINDER         |
| XRAY SPECS           |
| FAKE VOMIT           |
| LOADED DICE          |
| MAGICIANS KIT        |
| TOP HAT WITHOUT RABBIT |
| TOP HAT WITH RABBIT  |
| FLY IN OINTMENT      |
+----------------------+
16 rows in set (0.00 sec)
```

Imagine that you proudly take this finished product to the boss, only to hear, "Why are you giving me this? I want sales totals *for* the products." This is not to suggest that the boss would intentionally mislead you, but rather, misunderstandings do occur.

It is always good to take notes and to ask questions. An example of discussion on the previous example might be:

BOSS: Fred, get me a listing of the products.

YOU: Right, just the products. Do you want to know how many we have?

BOSS: No, no. Just the number sold.

YOU: Of each? For what period of time? Do you need to know who sold what?

BOSS: Hmmmm…I see your point. Just get me the totals for the month of September. That's good thinking on your part, Fred. Put yourself in for a raise.

Okay, so maybe that last part is a little far-fetched. The idea here is that by engaging the requestor in conversation, you greatly increase your chances of providing the right information the first time.

Written Requests

Usually, written requests for reports are the best. Causing the persons making the request to sit down and put into words exactly what their needs are helps them to better understand what they actually want to see. If they are certain of what they need to see, it is easier for you to provide it for them.

The written request can be

- A standardized form in which they respond to questions.
- An electronic form in which the answers to the questions are sent to you.

In any case, keep in mind that a written request will not eliminate all misunderstandings, but it should help reduce the number of them.

How to Give Productive Recommendations

It is important to remember that when someone comes to you asking for information it is because *you* are the "expert." Any recommendations that you provide need to be from the point of view of helping the requestors fulfill their requirements as much as possible, without sacrificing the integrity of the data or its security. The requestor may not have your specific technical knowledge, so you should speak to them in terms they understand and are comfortable with. Communication should always be professional and relaxed. The person making the request is the customer. Never traumatize the customers by speaking "down" to them or by allowing your frustration to show. If you are honest, open, and professional, chances are they will be, too.

18

Reporting Methods

There are many methods of creating reports today, with more being developed all the time. Keep in mind that when working within a relational database, SQL is at the base of all of them.

Report Tools

Reporting tools are Graphical User Interface (GUI) applications that connect to your database and can assist with creating queries to select your data or make use of pre-existing queries (or both). They then take that data and present it in a format that you specify.

> **NEW TERM** *GUI or Graphical User Interface*, as it is referred to in this section is software that assists the user in creating reports by intuitively guiding the user through the report building process.

Reporting tools are very complex in nature, but are generally designed to be somewhat intuitive. That is to say, the software helps you make decisions on how to build your report. In some cases, the software will make decisions for you without asking you. Because of the overall nature of reporting tools and the fact that so many are in existence, the following sections discuss just a few. We do not intend to endorse or recommend any specified reporting tool over any other. Rather, we will discuss the overall qualities each possesses.

Crystal Reports and Oracle Developer

Both of these tools are designed to connect to an outside data source and provide tools for creating queries (the foundation of the report) or for utilizing pre-existing queries. They can also be used to create a report based on the contents of an entire table. *Outside data source* means that the database does not reside within Crystal Reports or Oracle Developer, but at another location. This location may be somewhere else on your machine, such as a Microsoft Access database, an Oracle database, or at another physical location across a network.

As the name implies, Oracle Developer is designed to connect specifically with an Oracle database, but it can also function with other databases when configured to do so. Crystal Reports is also designed to connect to different database types, such as MS Access, Oracle, DB2, MS Excel, FoxPro, SQL Server, and Powersoft.

Both contain utilities to assist in creating queries, storing the queries, and generating reports. Both have tools for creating your own reports, storing reports either locally or externally, and granting permissions for others to execute reports.

Microsoft Access and MS Excel

Like Crystal Reports and Oracle Developer, Access and Excel have the capability to connect to external data sources; they also have the added feature of being able to store data within the application.

Excel is, simply stated, a spreadsheet with a lot of add-ons. It contains the capability to query data in its cells or to query data from another source outside of Excel.

Access is a database that contains, among other things, tools to enable you to create a report within the database. As explained previously, Access enables you to use its tools to create a report or it can provide you with the capability to create your own.

Mission-Specific Reporting Tools

Some GUI reporting tools are designed with a specific business or mission in mind. Software developers have taken standards and practices of a given industry and have incorporated them into reporting software that is marketed directly to that industry. Software is designed specifically for the medical profession, veterinarians, hospital administration, wineries, and almost any profession you can imagine.

So How Do I Find All These Reporting Tools?

Obviously there are the industry standards that you can go to: Microsoft, Oracle, Seagate Software, for example. But you should keep in mind that for a majority of the wonderful, intuitive, GUI software out there, there is probably a cost. By doing searches on the Internet, however, you might be able to find software that is free or at a minimal cost. But remember that in some cases, you get what you pay for.

Report Tools Can Make Assumptions on Your Data

It is important to remember that query-designing applications can make assumptions on your data. Most query tools have the option to have the program establish relationships, or joins, between your tables for you. This can be useful, but you should remember that the decisions the program makes on joining your tables may not be the decisions you want.

Professional Results from All of These

Probably the greatest strength of report tools is their capability to present information in various ways. The intuitive nature of the software allows users to create detailed reports that can include graphics, links to other documents, picture files, and sound files. The software can help you format the results based on your specifications as well as guide you through distributing your report. All these capabilities are provided in a point-and-click environment so that even novice users are able to present high-quality reports without extended amounts of training on the software.

18

Verifying Report Completeness

There's more than one way to skin a "SQL cat."

Using MySQL and the tables found on the Web site for this book at www.samspublishing. com, you are going to create tables, insert data, then learn how to do some command-line select statements. After putting the disk into the A: drive on your computer, you can load the tables and data by issuing the following command from the MySQL prompt:

NEW TERM *Source:* Different implementations of SQL have different key or reserved words. If you were working from the SQL> prompt in an Oracle database, you would issue the command 'start' and then provide the path to the file that you wanted to execute. MySQL, on the other hand uses the key word 'source' instead of start.

SYNTAX
```
mysql> source a:\mysql_tbls.txt;
```

Table Joins

As discussed earlier, you seldom will be able to access all your data from just one table. Joining enables you to retrieve data from two or more tables based on some sort of relationship between the data in the tables. This book assumes that you have a certain amount of experience with SQL, so we will not be going into the same detail as we might for a SQL book.

▼ SYNTAX
```
mysql> select e.fname, e.lname, c.salary
    -> from emp e, comp c
    -> where e.emp_id = c.emp_id
    -> and c.hourly is null;
+----------+----------+--------+
| fname    | lname    | salary |
+----------+----------+--------+
| GEOFFERY | CHAUCER  | 120000 |
| KAY      | HURST    | 70000  |
| HEATHER  | JUSTESS  | 70000  |
| JETHRO   | TULL     | 40000  |
| CLARENCE | BROWN    | 32000  |
| BETTY    | JESSE    | 42750  |
| DAVID    | SLATTERY | 38752  |
+----------+----------+--------+
```
▲ 7 rows in set (0.03 sec)

The previous example consists of selected columns from two tables where equality exists based on the value for emp_id being equal in both tables. But what happens if you leave out the join?

```
mysql> select e.fname, e.lname, c.salary
    -> from emp e, comp c
    -> where c.hourly is null;
```

The result, which is too lengthy to display here, is known as a CARTESIAN PRODUCT. This occurs when tables are incorrectly joined or not joined at all. When the database tries to execute your query, it cannot return the proper rows because it has no idea how the tables relate to each other (the JOIN). Subsequently, it attempts to join every row from the first table to every row in the other tables in the FROM clause.

The EMP table should contain 10 rows. The COMP table should also contain 10 rows. So if this is true, shouldn't the CARTESIAN PRODUCT return 100 rows? No. The reason is found in the WHERE clause of both SQL statements. You limited the number of rows that can be returned by placing a condition in the WHERE clause. This limits eligible rows to those that contain a null value in the HOURLY column.

Computations

Very often, requirements are such that you will need to take data as it is currently stored, perform some sort of computation or function on that data, and display the results for someone to use. Suppose you have a request for information on what the hourly employees currently make, and then to determine what a 10% increase would be.

▼ SYNTAX

```
mysql> select e.lname,
    ->     c.hourly,
    ->     c.hourly*.1,
    ->     c.hourly+c.hourly*.1
    -> from emp e, comp c
    -> where e.emp_id = c.emp_id;
+----------+--------+------------+----------------------+
| lname    | hourly | c.hourly*.1 | c.hourly+c.hourly*.1 |
+----------+--------+------------+----------------------+
| CHAUCER  |  NULL  |    NULL    |         NULL         |
| HURST    |  NULL  |    NULL    |         NULL         |
| JUSTESS  |  NULL  |    NULL    |         NULL         |
| ST LOUIS | 15.75  |    1.58    |        17.32         |
| WINSTON  | 25.32  |    2.53    |        27.85         |
| WALTERS  |  9.25  |    0.93    |        10.18         |
| TULL     |  NULL  |    NULL    |         NULL         |
| BROWN    |  NULL  |    NULL    |         NULL         |
| JESSE    |  NULL  |    NULL    |         NULL         |
| SLATTERY |  NULL  |    NULL    |         NULL         |
+----------+--------+------------+----------------------+
```

▲ 10 rows in set (0.00 sec)

Here is an example of joining three tables to get the total hourly wages by department. Notice that there is no direct relationship between the DEPT and COMP tables. The EMP table was used because it has a direct relationship to both of the other tables.

18

▼ SYNTAX

```
mysql> select d.description, sum(c.hourly)
    -> from emp e, dept d, comp c
    -> where e.emp_id = c.emp_id
    ->  and e.dept_id = d.dept_id
    ->  and c.salary is null
    -> group by description;
+--------------------+--------------+
| description        | sum(c.hourly) |
+--------------------+--------------+
| OFFICE MGR         |        15.75 |
| OFFICE RECEPTIONIST |         9.25 |
| OFFICE SALES COORD |        25.32 |
+--------------------+--------------+
3 rows in set (0.00 sec)
```

In both of these examples, you can provide useful information in the form of a perfectly good report. However, by taking a few extra steps, you can make your output even more presentable.

Formatting the Report

Formatting a report allows ease of readability and should make the information more understandable. Report tools, discussed earlier, are applications that contain many options for how you can arrange the information on your report. Different RDBMSs contain different options for creating command-line reports. It is important that you search your documentation thoroughly to determine what is available for use.

Remember that at the heart of all RDBMSs, there is SQL. Although the exact syntax may vary from implementation to implementation, the concept is the same. Rather than focusing too much on implementation-specific SQL syntax, you can take the previous example and reformat it in a way that is general to most implementations.

▼ SYNTAX

```
mysql> select e.lname Name,
    ->     c.hourly "Hourly Wage",
    ->     c.hourly*.1 ".1 Increase",
    ->     c.hourly+c.hourly*.1 "New Wage"
    -> from emp e, comp c
    -> where e.emp_id = c.emp_id
    -> and hourly is not null
    -> order by 3;
+--------+-------------+-------------+----------+
| Name   | Hourly Wage | .1 Increase | New Wage |
+--------+-------------+-------------+----------+
| WALTERS |        9.25 |        0.93 |    10.18 |
| ST LOUIS |      15.75 |        1.58 |    17.33 |
| WINSTON |       25.32 |        2.53 |    27.85 |
+--------+-------------+-------------+----------+
3 rows in set (0.01 sec)
```

In this example, you have added a restriction to your WHERE clause so that you eliminate rows that do not pertain to the information that you require. Column headings are renamed or given an alias so that they are more descriptive of the data they contain. Finally, by adding the ORDER BY clause, you can see your results in order of the lowest amount of increase to the highest.

Distributing the Report

After you create the report and determine that it does in fact represent valid information, you need to deliver it. Printing and handing the report to the requestor like it was a baton in a track-and-field meet is the good old-fashioned method. You get the product out of your immediate responsibility and you're able to quickly go on to the next project. But keep in mind that the person you hand the baton to may track you down for further adjustments. It might be better to stay a minute or two in case there are questions.

Sending the report via the postal or local mail distribution system does still happen in this day and age. If the report is new to the requestor, you may want to do some follow-up to ensure that they understand what they have received. Putting a copy of their written request with the report is generally a good idea in all cases.

Using email or posting reports in a Web environment can be a bit risky if you are reporting sensitive information or if you need to pinpoint exactly who sees the report. If you are working in a secure network environment, it may be perfectly acceptable to post reports in a network folder and direct users to its location. Restrictions can be placed on that folder so that only the intended users have access.

18

> Security consideration: In all cases, you should take a moment to consider the information that you are providing and what impact it could have should it get to the wrong recipient.

Summary

Keep in mind that although some of the questions are theoretical, "what would you do in this case?" questions, they are based on real-world work environment situations. The answers are not intended to be the only resolution to the situation, but rather to promote ideas and show that options may exist.

Now you have a good basic knowledge of database reporting. You learned that data stored in a RDBMS doesn't become information until it is presented in a meaningful way. You learned how to look at a list of your tables, how to view their contents, and how the data should be stored within the tables. You also know that there are many issues that need to be considered when fulfilling a request for a report. Communication is vital when you receive a request for a report, and although several wonderful tools are out there to assist in creating reports, it is always best to have a sound, working knowledge of the SQL that is working behind the scenes in these tools.

Q&A

Q Is it necessary to know how to write a SQL statement manually when I am using a reporting tool?

A No, but knowing your data, tables, and how to manually write SQL is a big plus in retrieving accurate and complete data on your report.

Q Why is communication important between a requestor of information and the person retrieving the information?

A There are many reasons for good communication. When do you need the report? What information should be contained in the report? Who will be reading the report? Will there be any Privacy Act data on the report? Do you need hard copy or electronic copy? Will this report be requested again?

Workshop

The following workshop consists of quiz questions and practical exercises. The quiz questions are designed to test your overall understanding of the current material. The practical exercises are intended to afford you the opportunity to apply the concepts discussed during the current hour, as well as build on the knowledge acquired in previous hours of study. Please take time to complete this workshop before continuing. You may refer to the answers at the end of the hour.

Quiz

1. What is database reporting?

2. What command enables you to view the structure of the columns of a table.

3. What are Report Tools?

4. What does formatting a report attempt to accomplish?

5. What are probably the most important aspects to consider when writing a report and the distribution of the report?

Exercises

1. Imagine that you are working at your desk in your cubicle, and suddenly a face appears from over the wall. It's your boss frantically needing sales figures to distribute at the teleconference. You've had requests like this before, so using MySQL and the tables provided, construct a report that tells the boss the name of each product sold, who sold it, who it was sold to, and the price and the cost of the item.

2. Now that you've gotten the report finished, how do you get it to the boss?

3. Your boss has taken a couple of moments to calm down now that he has the report. You hear him mutter things like "Yes" and "Good." For a brief moment you're the hero, until he tells you that the column headings are all wrong and that nobody will understand them. "Why is there an LNAME column? I didn't ask for that!" he says. As he hands you back the report, he say, "Look, I have to leave in seven minutes. Just give me totals on everything sold to whom; put the good news first."

4. Your company has an item called "Woopie Cushion," but when you try to do a select on the item no rows are returned. Upon investigation you discover that when the item was initially loaded, it was misspelled as "Woopie Cushon." How can this be corrected and are there any steps that can be taken to ensure this doesn't happen again?

Answers to Quiz

1. Database reporting is the process by which data is selected from tables in a database and then presented for a specific use.

2. The describe command enables you to view the structure of the columns in each table.

3. Report tools are Graphical User Interface (GUI) applications that connect to your database.

4. Formatting a report allows ease of readability and should make the information more understandable.

5. Security concerns and Privacy Act data.

Answers to Exercises

1.
```
select e.lname,
       p.price,
       s.amount,
       p.description,
       s.destination
```

```
from emp e,
    products p,
    sales s
where e.emp_id = s.emp_id
  and s.prod_id = p.prod_id;
```

2. In this case, because of how vague and urgent the request is, it may be best to hand-carry the report to the requestor. That way, you can receive instant feedback and effect adjustments in the shortest time possible.

3.

```
select Sum(p.price*s.amount) Income,
       p.description Product,
       s.destination Customer
from emp e,
    products p,
    sales s
where e.emp_id = s.emp_id
  and s.prod_id = p.prod_id
group by e.lname,
         p.description,
         s.destination
order by 1 desc;
```

4. If you refer to the section in Chapter 17 on DML, Data Manipulation Language, you can issue the following command:

```
update products
```

```
set description = 'WOOPIE CUSHION'
```

```
where description = 'WOOPIE CUSHON';
```

Also, constraints on your tables and quality assurance procedures will assist in maintaining data integrity. Open and productive communication between departments in a company is also helpful in having these types of errors brought to your attention.

PART V

Practical Database Integration with Business

Hour

HOUR 19

Using Databases to Process and Manage Data

Congratulations! If you have reached this point in the book by reading straight through, you have already completed 75% of the material. The last 25% of the book will bring into focus the use of different databases to manage a company's data, how the data is used to monitor and improve the company, how the database market is evolving and then, finally, you'll take a look at ways that you can become a part of the database world.

You started out by looking at the concepts of what a database is and the historical changes that database technology has undergone. Then you looked at examples where you and I are exposed to databases as users throughout our normal daily activities. You also looked at all the different roles that are involved in the development, implementation, and support of the databases.

After that groundwork was completed, you spent several hours studying the mechanics of building the database itself, creating tables and indexes, and connecting to the database. Several hours were dedicated to using SQL to actually get data into your tables, to update or edit the data, or to delete the data. The last hour discussed how to use the data in your database to generate useful and meaningful reports.

This hour explains how the database is used within the context of a business from an "insiders" perspective rather than as a user. By the end of the hour, you should have a good understanding of the concept of "data processing" in a general sense and begin to understand the differences in databases used to conduct business transactions and databases used to analyze the business. You will also look at different database environments—from mainframe to client/server to Web based.

During this hour, you will be introduced to

- An overview of data processing
- Online transactional processing databases
- Issues related to transactional databases
- Variations of transactional databases

Overview of Data Processing

Before you begin looking at how the database is used within a business to process data, let's spend a few minutes looking at data processing in very general terms.

Let's start by defining what a data processing system is in its most basic form:

> The main focus of this chapter is to illustrate how modern organizations use databases for data processing. Keep in mind that SQL is the primary method for processing data in a relational database. Each of the situations described in this hour imply the use of SQL for database creation, data loading, data manipulation, and data retrieval.

 A **Data Processing System** is a set of procedures and methods used to collect, store, and maintain data by electronic means.

Figure 19.1 shows a classic data processing system.

The Input symbol represents the source data that is entered into the system via punched card, magnetic tape, bar-code scan, or more commonly, by keyboard or mouse entry.

The Process symbol represents the manipulation of the data that must take place. This could take the form of arithmetic or logic operations, parsing, sorting, retrieving, recording, and updating of data within the system.

FIGURE 19.1

Looking at a sample data processing system diagram.

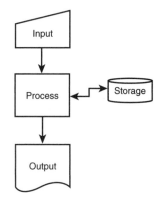

The Storage symbol is indicative of some type of electronic storage of data for future reference. The media involved predominantly represents disk devices or DASD (Direct Access Storage Devices) and magnetic tape, but it could also represent more portable technological media, such as disks or CD-ROMs.

The Output symbol represents the desired outcome from the system. Printed reports, magnetic tape, hard disk, CD-ROM, disk and terminal output are all included as different media types of outputs the system could produce.

To this day, every interaction with a computer system follows this primary model—although some interactions are considerably more complex. These interactions fall into one of two categories: transaction processing or batch processing.

Batch Processing

Batch processing occurs when a group, or batch, of inputs to a process is stored and then executes a "process" one step at one time. Batch jobs are usually scheduled during off-hours and require no user interaction. The generation of credit card bills is a common example of a batch processing job. The unit of work to be completed in a batch process is referred to as a "job" and typically consists of several processing steps. Depending on data volumes and the system resources that are available, a batch job could take several hours to complete. Figure 19.2 shows a process diagram for a batch material requirements planning (MRP) job that would be executed several times a week in a manufacturing environment.

NEW TERM *Batch Processing* is a group of inputs to a process that are stored and then executed one process at a time during 'off-hours'.

19

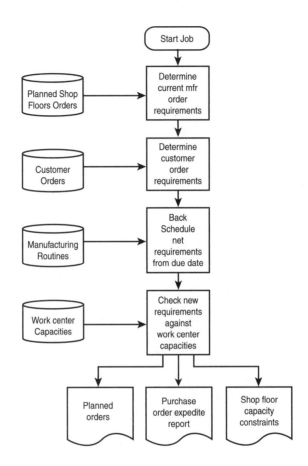

FIGURE **19.2**

Viewing a sample batch job process diagram.

Interactive Processing

Some interactions, even though they follow the same pattern, occur while the user awaits a reply. These types of interactions are called *transactions*. The ATM example presented in Hour 3, "Relating to Modern Databases," is a familiar example of transaction processing.

NEW TERM   *Interactive Processing* is a transactional process where actions are initiated by a user or group of users, where users are prompted periodically for further actions to take, until the entire process has completed, or the transaction is rejected.

Transactions, in contrast to batch processing, are ideally completed in subsecond response time. The types of transactions available in an interactive setting are predefined and consist of short, often-repeated steps and are usually executed by many users concurrently within the system. Figure 19.3 shows an ATM funds transfer transaction process.

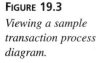

FIGURE 19.3
Viewing a sample transaction process diagram.

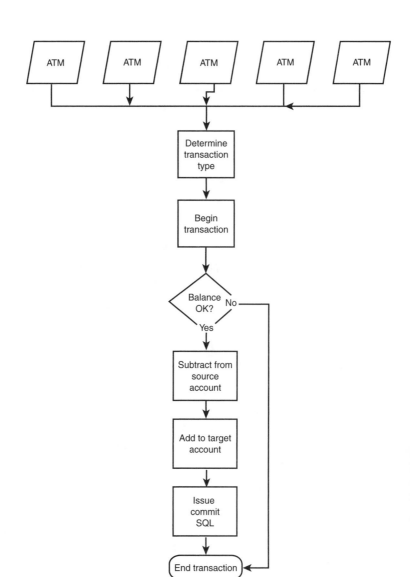

19

Explanation of OLTP Databases

Now that you've reviewed the basis of all data processing interactions in both interactive and batch modes, it's time to discuss where all this data will end up. All the data, which ends up residing on some disk unit, can be classified into one of two types of databases: OLAP and OLTP.

OLAP

OLAP, or Online Analytical Processing, databases are covered here only briefly; the next hour will explain OLAP in more detail so that you can spend more time looking in detail at OLTP databases. Suffice it to say that OLAP is built, used, and managed differently than OLTP databases are.

OLTP

OLTP, or Online Transaction Processing, databases are made up of data from high-volume, repetitive business processes that users perform online or interactively. As previously mentioned, this unit of work is simply referred to as a transaction. You probably use OLTP systems and databases every day. The examples from Hour 3 of using an ATM, getting a prescription filled, and getting your items scanned at a checkout all use OLTP databases. Other common activities, such as making hotel or airline reservations or getting a credit card authorization are other good examples of OLTP databases in use.

In the following sections, you will look at four consistent characteristics of OLTP databases in more detail: online processing, high availability, response time, and low cost/transaction.

Online

The user, needs to have a client device, a workstation, or a terminal with a connection to the database system to be online. Physically, the connection can be local, through a LAN or WAN or via the Web. The logical connection is more complicated because usually several layers come into play for a user to actually retrieve and update the data. Figure 19.4 shows some common layers that are involved in an OLTP database system.

High Availability

Most, OLTP databases, being at the strategic core of a business's activity, have availability requirements that approach 99.99% during a 24/7 workload. These systems need to be built with combinations of hardware, software, and application components that minimize downtime occurring because of system failures or recovery problems.

Response Time

In typical, OLTP databases—for example, those in use by bank tellers—employees and users (at the ATM) are using the system repeatedly as a normal part of their work routines as you, the customer, wait for the work to be completed. Minimizing response time, to subsecond response, is critical to the effective use of the database.

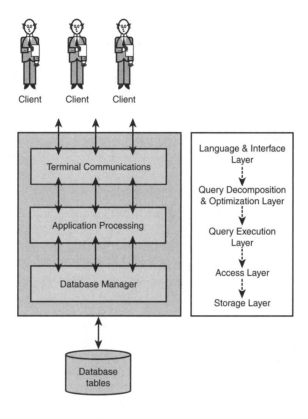

FIGURE 19.4
Understanding logical connection layers.

Low Cost/Transaction

As, you've already seen, in OLTP systems, the transactions being completed are a core component of their business and are repeated hundreds of time throughout the normal course of business. Response time is critical operationally, but the total cost of the transaction is critical financially. The total cost must take into consideration the cost of hardware, software, and support staff required to build, support, and operate the entire OLTP system and database.

Issues with OLTP Databases

OLTP transactions, by their nature, make up a critical piece of a company's database. The OLTP database is used to track the current status of the business: the current balance, current inventory levels, current customers, and current orders. Each of these OLTP transactions must have certain properties for the OLTP database to be effective, called ACID properties, which stands for Atomicity, Consistency, Isolation, and Durability.

19

First, the transaction must be *atomic*. Atomic means the pieces of the transaction cannot be separated; if, for any reason, the transaction fails—all of the transaction must be undone. Each transaction in an OLTP database system has a logical transaction beginning, and at the completion of the process, the *entire* transaction is either committed or rolled back. SQL has specific statements for these two options: COMMIT and ROLLBACK.

The atomic nature of the transaction, with the logical completion resulting in either a COMMIT or ROLLBACK, ensures that the database will have *consistency*. You can imagine the problems if, in your ATM transaction, the transfer amount was subtracted from your savings account but the addition to your checking account failed!

The third property is *isolation*. Data that is available to all users to view must appear as if each user is operating in a single-user system. Most RDBMSs use a pessimistic concurrency control feature to effect this property. Pessimistic concurrency will put a lock on data before reading or writing, assuming that other users will be trying to access the same data. A lock prevents other transactions from accessing the same data and forces the second transaction to wait for the lock to be released at the completion of the first transaction.

The final property is *durability*. This means that the committed transactions are permanently stored in the database and the OLTP database has built-in, failure-resistant features to safeguard against data loss.

As you have already seen, OLTP databases have thousands of transactions every day—sometimes every hour! At a certain point, the number of transactions that are maintained in the OLTP database begin to act as a constraint on the performance. OLTP data is purged periodically at the end of some cycle—maybe at the end of a month or at the end of a quarter. But where does this data go? Now we are back to the OLAP database. The OLAP database, a data warehouse, is built for a different user and for different processing requirements. The purpose of the data warehouse is to keep these historical transactions for analytical processing. Figure 19.5 highlights some of the significant differences between OLTP and OLAP databases.

FIGURE 19.5

Analyzing OLTP versus OLAP attributes.

	OLTP	OLAP
Typical user	Clerical	Management
Type of usage	Normal business functions	Analysis of historical data
Normal processing	Select, update, delete	Read
Type of queries	Predefined	Ad hoc
Unit of work	Transactions	Query
Level of isolation required	High	Low
Number of rows accessed	< 100	> 500,000
Number of concurrent users	< 1000	< 100
Business objective	Date entered and/or modified	Summary of data
Data normalized	Yes	No

OLTP Database Variations

When you look at all the OLTP databases in use today, you have to remember that the availability, capability, and cost of technology have had a huge impact on the way the systems were configured and built.

19

The following subsections deal with data processing considerations of common database environments that were discussed during earlier hours.

Mainframe Databases

Thirty years ago when the early OLTP-type databases were being built, the only real choice that you had were mainframe systems. Although there is a plethora of technological choices today, mainframe systems are still in use. This can be attributed to the maturity of the hardware and software components, and with the software management tools available, the reliability and stability of mainframe systems allow IT shops to surpass the 99.9% system availability desired for so many OLTP systems.

Another advantage to the mainframe system is that the sophisticated transaction-processing monitors can ably handle concurrent users numbered in the thousands. Even with this kind of workload, the Transaction Processing Performance Council (TPPC) benchmarks demonstrate that mainframe systems can reliably provide subsecond response time.

Several disadvantages exist, though, to a mainframe solution to your OLTP database needs. The cost of ownership, with the initial capital costs of the equipment and software, are considered to be high. The costs associated with support staff, administrative staff, and development staff can be greater in a larger installation with a mainframe system to support.

Client/Server Databases

After mainframe systems, proprietary minicomputers such as the IBM AS/400, the Hewlett Packard HP3000, and the DEC VAX systems became popular. These systems enjoyed their niche, but they soon gave way to an even smaller system—the PC.

PC-based servers quickly gained market share and with the availability of functionally rich packaged software and systems, they soon became a viable option to deploy OLTP systems. Figure 19.6 shows a typical three-tier client/server architecture.

FIGURE 19.6

Understanding the three-tier client/server architecture.

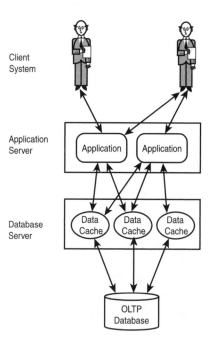

A constant balancing of price/performance versus system reliability issues push implementation choices one way or the other. You don't often have to reboot your mainframe because it "just locks up" or because you get some type of GPF error! However, you can't argue with the price/performance of PC-based servers and the scalability they provide.

Other considerations must be taken into account with client/server systems with regard to the maintenance and support they require. A substantial amount of support and management is required to ensure that 1,000-plus PC clients are configured properly to access the OLTP database. Software changes and new software distribution can also become a daunting task.

Web-Based Databases

The final variation you are going to look at is the architecture that is generating the most publicity these days—the Web-based systems and databases.

The World Wide Web (WWW) has some significant features that position it as an attractive platform choice for your OLTP database application, but it also has some serious disadvantages that must be taken into consideration as well.

The graphical user interface (GUI) that the popular Web browsers support make the Web more user friendly than the typical user interface available in a mainframe environment. As an additional advantage, the Web, like a mainframe solution, provides for a centralized repository of your application software and your data. One of the significant disadvantages we looked at with client/server was the problem of trying to manage and support hundreds, or possibly thousands, of PC systems throughout an organization. With a Web-based system, a simple modification to a Java program or stored procedure added to your server can mean that all your users will immediately have access to the new versions of your database system.

Although the Web provides some nice improvements over a client/server system, for a couple of significant reasons it has a long way to go to be the architecture of choice for high-volume mission-critical OLTP database systems.

First, there is the need for an OLTP database to be available 99.9% of the time or better. Anyone who has used the Web has experienced times when a connection could not be established at all, or maybe worse, the connection dropped in the middle of your session. Other times, even though the connection doesn't drop, users experience noticeable response-time differences. Mission-critical OLTP databases require response times that are both quick and consistently achieved.

When a session is dropped, transaction consistency is an issue. Remember from the discussion regarding the properties of OLTP databases, each transaction has a logical starting point; at the completion of the transaction, either a commit or a rollback must occur

19

to provide the consistency and atomicity of the system. When sessions are dropping in the middle of a transaction, both of these properties could be compromised.

The second issue is one of security. Hacking and the unauthorized use of sensitive information that OLTP database may be dealing with are concerns that many users have in conducting their transactions across the Web. Electronic commerce has made enormous gains in the marketplace, but security weaknesses, perceived or real, have throttled the growth of the segment as a whole.

Summary

Data processing transforms input data into the desired output form. The process is composed of a combination of factors that include hardware, software, data, people, and procedures.

All data processing systems have three major components: input, processing, and output. The output can be something as simple as a printed report, or as an integral part of the OLTP database, or output will be to a disk device.

Data processing work falls into one of two categories: batch or transaction processing. Batch saves its input into a group, or batch, and completes the actual processing at a later time. The printing of payroll checks once a week is a good example of batch processing. Batch work is referred to as a job and is completed without any interaction from the user. Transaction processing, on the other hand, is completed while the user waits for the transaction to complete. The posting of your payroll check deposit at the bank is a good example of transaction processing.

The collection of mission-critical, transaction-based processing output is called an OLTP database. Historical data from an OLTP database is purged, filtered, and cleansed and is used as input into an associated OLAP database.

OLTP databases provide access on-line, with high availability, with subsecond response time, and with a low cost/transaction. OLTP databases must also provide certain properties—ACID properties. Atomicity, consistency, isolation, and durability are properties that the OLTP database system must provide to be effective and useful as a mission-critical database system.

OLTP databases constitute the backbone of almost all businesses in today's marketplace. OLTP databases have been successfully implemented on a variety of information system architectures, including mainframe, client/server, and Web based. Each has strengths and weaknesses that must be evaluated before deciding which strategic direction a company should follow.

Workshop

The following workshop is composed of quiz questions and practical exercises. The quiz questions are designed to test your overall understanding of the current material. The practical exercises are intended to afford you the opportunity to apply the concepts discussed during the current hour, as well as build on the knowledge acquired in previous hours of study. Please take time to complete this workshop before continuing. You can refer to the answers at the end of the hour.

Quiz

1. Which of the following make up the basic building blocks of all data processing systems? Select all that apply.

    a. Output devices

    b. Network protocols

    c. Processing

    d. Password authentication

    e. Input devices

    f. Record locking

2. Batch and transaction processing both require the same level of interaction with the user (True or False).

3. Which of the following attributes highlight the differences between OLTP and OLAP databases? Select all that apply.

    a. Number of rows processed

    b. Number of concurrent users

    c. Amount of CPU memory required

    d. Volume of network traffic

    e. Data normalization requirements

    f. Implementation costs

4. The OLTP properties that compose the ACID acronym are made up of which of the following attributes?

    a. Available

    b. Atomic

    c. Archived

    d. Consistency

    e. Characters

19

    f. Continuity

    g. Instance

    h. Internal

    i. Isolation

    j. Developed

    k. Durability

    l. Dependency

5. An OLTP database can be implemented successfully only on a mainframe system (True or False).

Exercise

1. Identify five business segments using OLTP databases that are extensively used on a daily basis.

Answers to Quiz

1. a, c, e. The other component that was discussed as part of OLTP databases, by definition, would be storage on some electronic media—in most cases, disk devices.

2. False. Batch jobs are processed at the end of some business cycle—the end of day, the end of week, the end of month, and so on; they don't require the interaction of the user. Transaction processing occurs interactively while the user awaits the reply or an indication that the transaction has been completed.

3. a, b, e. The number of rows in an OLTP is much smaller than in OLAP database instances. The number of concurrent users in an OLTP system can number in the thousands, whereas the number of concurrent users conducting analysis of the historical data within an OLAP database might be far fewer than 100.

4. b, d, i, k. The ACID acronym stands for atomicity, consistency, isolation, and durability.

5. False. OLTP databases have been implemented successfully on mainframe, midrange, client/server, and Web-based systems. Each system has distinct advantages and disadvantages, but each has its place in the complexity of today's business environment to support OLTP databases.

Answers to Exercise

1. Your answer may vary significantly with the answers provided here, but that is just a result of the pervasive use of OLTP databases in activities and business transactions that we commonly complete in our daily lives.

   a. Banking transactions: ATM, deposits, balance transfers, withdrawals, and so on.

   b. Airline reservations: booking flights, either over the phone or online via a Web application.

   c. Credit card processing: credit card authorizations, processing purchases, cash advances, checking credit limit balances, and so on.

   d. Web retail purchases: checking inventory availability and entering orders at retailers such as Amazon.com, L. L. Bean, and Lands' End.

   e. Web auction services: entering items for sale, entering a bid, and so on.

   f. Securities and exchange services: checking current stock values, P/E ratios, entering sell orders, entering buy orders, and so on.

19

HOUR 20

Using Databases for Business Analysis

Databases play a key role in today's business analysis needs. To make critical business decisions, more and more businesses are relying on information gathered in a variety of areas or purchased from other information providers. Whether the goal is to increase sales, to reduce costs, or to plan for future trends, some type of data has to be gathered, stored, and analyzed before making any business decisions.

Databases are important not only in the financial field, but also in areas such as government, health care, industry, and manufacturing.

In this hour, you will learn

- How databases play a key role in today's business decision-making processes
- Some common ways data is retrieved from databases and the tools available in the market to facilitate data retrieval.
- How the data is used in business decision-making processes

Overview of Data Analysis

Organizations rely heavily on data; many cannot function without it. Organizations and individuals use data in different ways. One of the most powerful uses for data is retrieval and analysis. It is important not only to understand the best approach for storing data, but how the data should be used after it is stored in the database. There are six key steps to the basic storage of data that leads to data analysis:

1. Formulate a question or a series of questions that need to be answered by the data analyst.

2. Select and use the appropriate statistical methods to analyze the data.

3. Collect the necessary data. The data must be gathered in an organized manner and should be relevant to the goal associated with the data analysis.

4. Validate the data for accuracy and timeliness.

5. Identify a database structure and create the database. This means creating tables, indexes, and other database objects.

6. Enter the data into the database for evaluation. This can be done in a variety of ways and is dictated by the product vendor.

At this point, the data is ready to be transformed according to your business rules and business needs. This involves using your selected statistical method identified in step 2 or writing customized reports. You would write one or many select statements against the database that processes the information. Figure 20.1 illustrates the flow of data from creation to analysis.

 Data Analysis is the process by which data is examined and interpreted by decision makers.

How Is the Data Stored?

A question you might ask is, "How does data storage have anything to do with business analysis?" The answer is this: the key to business analysis is data and the availability of that data. Physical storage devices are the main source in keeping that data available. Data is stored in a variety of ways in the database and is based on the type of database application being developed.

Some of the commonly used devices that physically store the data are discussed in the sections that follow.

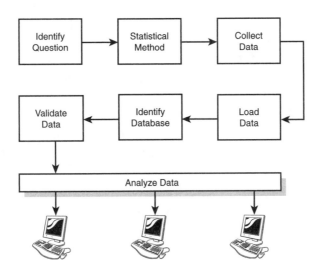

FIGURE 20.1
From data creation to analysis.

Disk Drives

Disks are the most common data storage devices used by the databases. Disks are usually internal devices in a database server (they can also be stored externally from the computer). These disk drives, besides having some advanced features, are not any different from the disk drives on your personal computers.

Using RAID

Disk drives are also the most used and most fragile piece of hardware on a database server, thus increasing the chances of failure. To increase performance and to reduce the down time of an application because of drive failures, it is very common to have RAID, or a redundant array of independent disks.

NEW TERM *RAID* is a redundant array of independent disks whose purpose is to store your data across the available disk space and to provide for maximum security in case of failure.

There are basically six types of RAID levels.

- *RAID Level 0 (Disk Striping without parity)*—In RAID 0 several disks are used and data is spread across all the disks in the array. This is ideal for environments in which performance is more important. Although it has very fast read-and-write access, any drive failure in the disk array will cause total loss of all stored data.

- *RAID Level 1 (disk mirroring)*—RAID Level 1 provides a total redundancy of storage for data security. Typically this is accomplished by "mirroring" data on two disk drives. Basically, two identical disks are written with the same information.

20

Although this provides complete protection for all your data, your overhead costs are doubled. In case of failure, the good disk takes over for the bad disk, which is known as *breaking the mirror*.

- *RAID Level 2*—This is similar to RAID Level 3, but it is not commonly used because it requires special disk features.

- *RAID Level 3 (disk striping with parity)*—RAID Level 3 writes redundant information in the form of parity to a parallel striped disk, allowing regeneration and rebuilding in the event of a disk failure. RAID Level 3 provides better performance and high availability at a lower cost than mirroring.

- *RAID Level 4 (disk striping with parity)*—Like RAID Level 3, RAID Level 4 writes redundant information in the form of parity to a single disk.

- *RAID Level 5 (disk striping with parity)*—At least three drives are required for a RAID 5. Data and parity information are striped across all the drives in an array. Parity information is distributed across all the disks. By distributing the parity information across all the disks, RAID Level 5 reduces the write bottleneck associated with RAID Level 4 for writing to a single disk.

The most commonly used RAID environments are RAID Level 1, RAID Level 5, and a combination of RAID Level 0 + 1, where disks are striped and mirrored at the same time.

Tape Drives

Another commonly used device for database backups is the tape drive. The market today has several varieties of tape drives, such as single drives or multiple drives. The multiple drives have tape libraries. These autoloading devices are also known as jukeboxes. The term "juke" can be applied not only to the tape drives but also to CD-ROM autoloading devices. These devices, sometimes called *optical drives*, can also store files for the databases in case the original files are lost as a result of disaster or failure.

SAN (Storage Area Network) Devices

A SAN (storage area network) is a specialized high-speed system consisting of cache memory and multiple disk arrays of RAID sets. It is designed to handle high-traffic loads between the server and this storage device while maintaining no single point of failure. Today's technology demands fast and reliable access to large amounts of data. The introduction of SAN devices offers high performance and redundancy for today's business needs.

NEW TERM *SAN Devices* are storage area network devices that combine cache memory and RAID to ensure speed, availability, and the security of redundancy.

How Is Data Retrieved?

After a business creates the database, the users need a way to retrieve the data from its database. There are several ways of doing this. The method selected will depend on how the database is going to be used. If the purpose of the database is to provide quick results or to make instant updates to the database, an interface needs to be created, also known as a front end. A graphical user interface (GUI) can be designed with tools available on the market. For instance, Oracle Forms, Visual Basic, Java, and so on are possible front-end GUIs. If the purpose for the database is to create hard-copy reports, similar tools are available to do so. The following sections take some of these tools and discuss them in some detail.

Tools to Create Forms-Based Applications

You can use many techniques to create form-based applications. Some application developers prefer to code directly using programming languages C and Java. Other developers rely on the use of tools, which generate much of the program code. Three of the most common tools that are briefly discussed in the following sections are Visual Basic .NET, Oracle Forms, and Java Forms.

Visual Basic .NET

Visual Basic .NET enables you to create rich applications for Microsoft Windows in less time. This program enables you to incorporate data access from a wide range of database scenarios with minimum code. It enables developers to create GUI screens and forms for the Windows operating system. A key feature of Visual Basic .NET is rapid deployment of the application. Visual Basic .NET offers flexible and simple data access and supports full object-oriented programming to create reusable code. One of the new features in Visual Basic .NET is Web Forms Designer. It enables developers to create Web-based applications in Visual Basic .NET. Visual Basic developers can apply the skills they have today to build true thin-client Web-based applications.

Oracle Forms

Oracle Forms is part of the Oracle Developer tool set. It is a GUI application tool that assists the development of GUI client applications. It enables users to easily access a database. The tool uses helpful wizards, help menus, and it supports Open Database Connectivity (ODBC) to also connect to non-Oracle databases. The generated application can be run on a variety of operating systems such as Sun Solaris, HP-UX, or the Windows operating system environment.

20

Java Forms

Java is such a multidimensional language that it can also be used to write forms. Writing Java-based forms requires a very good understanding of the Java language. It also requires a Java Runtime Environment to be installed on the client.

Another twist to a graphical interface is the Web-based interface—an application interface available via an Internet browser. This enables the application to be operating-system independent because the application interface can be accessed anywhere a browser is available, whether it is running on Unix, Linux, or a Windows-based operating system. This gives the application portability or independence from the operating system on the client PC.

Tools Used to Create Web-Based Applications

As with form-based applications, many techniques exist for creating Web-based applications. Some application developers code directly using language such as HTML and Java. Other developers rely on the use of tools that generate much of the program code. Two of the most common tools, ColdFusion and Oracle PL/SQL, are discussed in the following sections.

ColdFusion

ColdFusion allows for the creation of dynamic, database-powered Web applications. ColdFusion also includes support for SQL and ODBC by allowing connectivity to multiple database vendors. ColdFusion's visual tools and high-level interfaces allow rapid deployment of applications. Instead of programming in languages such as Java and C++, developers can use the ColdFusion Markup Language (CFML) that has syntax very similar to HTML and XML. The software also includes visual debugging and administration tools. Scalability is a key feature of ColdFusion. The application can be configured to use and divide the work among multiple servers. For high-traffic, very dynamic environments, this provides a great benefit. There are some limitations, however, and the code is proprietary. It requires a ColdFusion interpreter to use the application.

Oracle PL/SQL

PL/SQL is an Oracle proprietary procedural language. PL/SQL Web applications are designed to pass HTML or XML code back to the Web browser. It allows the developer to create dynamic Web-based applications that are stored and then called within the database.

A module called mod_plsql enables the output from the stored procedures or packages to be automatically sent to the client's browser. Because the PL/SQL is an Oracle proprietary language, the application is limited to an Oracle database and Oracle application servers. Because the application code is stored and executed in the database, this increases the application performance tremendously.

If the users require a printed copy of the data, a reporting tool is utilized. These tools allow the users to create customized and canned reports. These reports can be created by the database developer or created on-the-fly by the database user.

Tools to Create Reports

Business survival in today's economy requires flexible and powerful reporting capabilities. To assist businesses in their markets, they require the understanding of customers and business trends. Business administrators demand dynamic reports during real-time work. The reporting tools discussed next allow businesses to create enterprise-level reports rapidly and keep up with rapidly changing information at a reasonable cost.

Crystal Reports

Crystal Reports is a reporting tool that allows end users or developers to transform data into powerful, interactive reports. It also gives end users the capability to modify the data. The software is capable of integrating a variety of data sources into one powerful reporting application.

By sharing and reusing existing reports, businesses can save a considerable amount of time. These reports can be viewed via the Web, wireless devices, and other text-viewing applications. Such flexibility allows the decision-maker to quickly analyze the data and make informed decisions. The end users can create and customize reports using Report Design Wizards and other easy-to-use formatting tools integrated into the Crystal Reports.

Oracle Reports

Oracle Reports Developer, like Crystal Reports, is a reporting tool used to build reports that dynamically retrieve, format, and distribute data being stored in the database. Reports Developer enables businesses to publish reports on the Web while allowing unlimited data-formatting capabilities. The tool supports Design Wizards, which allow easy report creation. Using this tool, users can create reports in a variety of formats, including HTML and PDF format.

20

Flat Files

If the business needs to retrieve data for use by other types of databases or tools, the data is retrieved in the form of a flat file. The flat file is nothing more than a text file. However, it has a format that enables it to be loaded into other databases using a variety of tools. These files can be comma delimited or custom-character delimited. This means that either a comma or special character separates every column in the text file. Most modern database come with some type of utility that gives the databases the capability to read and load a comma-delimited or tab-delimited flat file into the database.

Figures 20.2 and 20.3 show samples from both comma-delimited and tab-delimited flat files. Refer back to Hour 2, "History and Evolution of Databases," for more information on flat files and how they are used.

FIGURE 20.2

A sample comma-delimited flat file.

```
1, "Michael", "Smith", 2212, "My Street", "Indianapolis", "IN", 46241
2, "David", "Collins", 2345, "My Street", "Indianapolis", "IN", 46241
3, "Sandy", "White", 4563, "My Street", "Indianapolis", "IN", 46241
4, "David", "Smith", 4578, "My Street", "Indianapolis", "IN", 46241
5, "Chris", "Thomas", 9917, "My Street", "Indianapolis", "IN", 46241
6, "David", "Adrews", 3345, "My Street", "Indianapolis", "IN", 46241
7, "Michael", "Angelo", 6678, "My Street", "Indianapolis", "IN, 46241
8, "Sherri", "Callis", 2367, "My Street", "Indianapolis", "IN", 46241
```

FIGURE 20.3

A sample tab-delimited flat file.

1	Michael	Smith	2212	My	Street	Indianapolis	IN	46241
2	David	Collins	2345	My	Street	Indianapolis	IN	46241
3	Sandy	White	4563	My	Street	Indianapolis	IN	46241
4	David	Smith	4578	My	Street	Indianapolis	IN	46241
5	Chris	Thomas	9917	My	Street	Indianapolis	IN	46241
6	David	Adrews	3345	My	Street	Indianapolis	IN	46241
7	Michael	Angelo	6678	My	Street	Indianapolis	IN	46241
8	Sherri	Callis	2367	My	Street	Indianapolis	IN	46241

How Is Data Used?

Databases are being used in everyday life. There are so many types and varieties of databases on the market, which an average person cannot even tell if he or she has accessed a database or provided information that is entered into a database.

Let's discuss for a few minutes how databases have become a part of everyday life.

It is time to go home. You receive a call from your spouse to pick up some items from the grocery store on your way home. You realize that you do not have enough cash on hand, so you decide to stop at the ATM inside the grocery store to get some cash. After you have the cash in your hand, you pick up the items that you were asked to get. You bring these items to the cashier. The cashier asks you if you have any coupons. You just happen to have a coupon for the name-brand crackers that you are purchasing. The cashier also asks you for your discount card (a key chain bar code tag). She says that if you have that, she can give you an additional discount on certain selected items. You are that lucky person with a discount card. The cashier scans it in and gives you the appropriate discount. You pay for the items and the cashier gives you the receipt and some other coupons that were printed specially on the receipt for future use.

Without even realizing it, you just accessed and updated two databases and contributed information to three other databases.

Let's take each of the preceding transactions and see how databases came into play.

- When you withdrew cash from the ATM machine, you accessed the bank's database. The ATM verified with your bank that you had enough money for the transaction. The ATM gives you the cash and then updates your account with the withdrawal information. This update does not include only the amount of money taken out, but also includes the date, time, and location of the withdrawal plus a service charge of $2.00. The automatic camera at the ATM was also activated when you put in the ATM card. Your photo was taken and saved in the accessing bank's database for security reasons.

- When you provided the coupon to the cashier, you provided input for the coupon manufacturer's database about your buying habits, such as where you got the coupon, how long you had the coupon before you used it, and the geographic location in which you used it. The bar code on the coupon gave the manufacturer all the information it needed. This information goes into huge databases holding similar information. Based on this information, businesses can plan better marketing strategies. For example, they can review which newspaper or magazine to use and what item to market better.

- When the cashier scanned your key chain tag, you also provided information about your purchase habits. For example, it tells businesses when you like to shop and what combination of items you like to purchase. Based on this information, the grocery store can create a better marketing plan or analyze market trends. The transaction is so quick that, based on the items you purchased, the grocery store can provide to you coupons from other competitors for your future purchases.

Examples of these types of database updates are common and numerous. Someone is looking at any information that you so knowingly provide. Businesses are establishing market trends and making major decisions based on these databases.

All across the world, businesses gather data on consumers. As consumers, some of these processes are even unknown to us. For example, every time a person goes online to a Web site, software is available to keep track of their mouse-clicking habits. Where do you click first? How long do you stay at a Web site? What type of information are you looking up? Someone is looking at everything you do on the Web and decisions are being made based on this information.

The government has thousands of databases holding information about taxpayers. The IRS, the Department of Health and Human Services, and the welfare department are just some examples of these types of databases. Databases also play an important role in law

20

enforcement. Police agencies all across the country keep local databases of criminal activity and wanted suspects in their neighborhood. This information is uploaded to large databases such as IDACS (Indiana Data and Communication Service) or NCIC (National Crime and Information Center), where the information is available to other law enforcement agencies. There are numerous specialized databases not commonly known to the public. Within the government arena, there are databases kept by the courts for records on criminal and civil proceedings.

Let's look at some of the other areas databases being used.

Best Practices

Another common use for databases is having a database for best practices. This is a database in which time-tested and results-oriented ideas are stored. For example, pharmaceutical salespeople access a database of best practices in which they store information about the different drugs and information about the doctors. One salesperson used a brochure to introduce a new drug to the doctors on his or her route. The results were outstanding, so the salesperson decided to put this information on the best practice database for the other salespeople to use. Another salesperson used an organized golf outing for all the doctors on his route to introduce a series of new drugs coming to the market. This was a huge success and resulted in high sales figures. This salesperson also decided to share his idea in the best practice database. The third salesperson was just assigned a new drug to market. He researches the database to come up with some ideas on how to market this drug. The search resulted in the ideas mentioned previously. He decides to implement the golf outing idea and adds a twist to it by giving some free movie tickets. This idea results in major sales for him and he also decides to contribute this idea to the database. This is how the database keeps getting built for the new incoming sales staff to improve their sales by using these time-tested practices.

Examples of applications using databases are numerous. Best practice can be used anywhere, from sales to manufacturing to industry. The application of this type of database is unlimited.

Data Mining

Data mining is the process of gathering data, analyzing the data from a different perspective, and finding a correlation between the data in the database and other outside variables. Managers use the results to make decisions about reducing costs, increasing sales, or conducting targeted marketing. Data mining allows companies like the grocery store in the example to use data mining software to analyze customers' buying habits. Based on analyzing the results, the store can plan and predict future sales, increase sales, and dispense on-the-spot coupons for future purchases.

NEW TERM *Data Mining* is the process of gathering data, analyzing that data with the objective of determining correlations between the data in the database and outside data. The goal is to find trends and make decisions based upon the comparisons.

Businesses can also use data mining to categorize the data in a variety of ways and correlate it to other data. For example, an online mortgage broker may have data mining software to capture various information every time a person comes to the company's Web site. The business can use this data and correlate it to the job market to develop a marketing strategy. It allows his business to see how the Web site attracts more people if the job market is good or when the interest rates are low.

Decision Support System, aka Business Intelligence

Decision support systems help businesses increase efficiency, productivity, and profitability by identifying market trends. Processing mounds of raw data develops these trends. Decision support systems are being used in a variety of businesses. For example, in the health care industry, health care administrators use a decision support system to fully identify which type of treatment, medication, and physician combination provides the most cost-effective solutions for their organization and for the insurance companies.

OLAP (Online Analytical Processing)

This database is uniquely designed to handle a high transaction volume. The customer usually wants an immediate response back from the database. OLAP databases are usually available 24 hours a day, 7 days a week. Because of high availability requirements, this database has very little downtime allowed. All the backups are conducted without shutting down the database. If the database needs to be shut down for maintenance or to perform an offline backup, it is usually done during odd hours when the database is least used. Key issues for this database are to process a high number of transactions with performance and availability.

Data Warehouse

20

 NEW TERM A *Data Warehouse* is defined as a centralized location for a high volume of data.

The database is specifically designed for querying, reporting, and data analyses. The data is usually updated in off-hours via large batch processes. Applications are written to select data and analyze it for historical and archival business requirements.

A Real-World Example of Using Data for Business Analysis

Amazon.com is a classic example of a company that uses consumer information to determine purchasing habits. Every time a consumer goes to its Web site, Amazon.com recognizes the consumer; if the customer has previously purchased anything from the store, Amazon.com creates a customized Web page with all the new books that have come on the market related to the customer's previous purchases. If you sign up for email notification, Amazon.com will also send you emails about the arrival of new books on your choice of topics, plus a discount coupon. All this information is stored in the company's database. Furthermore, a process is in place that identifies the last time you made a purchase; if it has been too long, the process dispatches an email or coupon to invite you to visit its Web site again. To accomplish this, a common method is using cookies within the Web browser.

Frequently traveled Web browsers are classic examples of data mining applications. These businesses keeps track of all the mouse clicks you make on their browser. Every link on their Web site holds a key position based on previous data gathered on consumers. They have identified that every time a person comes on their site, they look at certain areas—for example, the right margin. Because the right margin is the first place someone looks, they charge more money for placing advertisement in that area compared to the other areas. Some browsers have even identified an average of how long a consumer stays at a site. So if there is something that they want you to look at, they have that amount of time to get your attention.

Summary

Databases play a key role in our everyday life. Like it or not, information about anything you do is being recorded in some database. New marketing strategies are being developed to get the consumer's attention. Before the data can be analyzed, it has to be collected in an organized manner. The data has to be relevant and timely. The data is then inserted into the database. Based on the use of the database, the proper database design structure must be created.

Workshop

The following workshop is composed of quiz questions and practical exercises. The quiz questions are designed to test your overall understanding of the current material. The practical exercises are intended to afford you the opportunity to apply the concepts discussed during the current hour, as well as build on the knowledge acquired in previous hours of study. Please take time to complete this workshop before continuing. You can refer to the answers at the end of the hour.

Quiz

1. Name three types of storage devises commonly used to store data or backup the data in a database.

2. Name forms application development tools discussed in this hour.

3. Name six steps to data analysis.

Exercises

1. Using the following six key steps, analyze the business that you are currently in or have extensive experience with and knowledge about. You may refer back to the section at the beginning of this hour for reference.

   A. Formulate a question or a series of questions that need to be answered by the data analyst.

   B. Select and use the appropriate statistical methods to analyze the data.

   C. Collect the necessary data. The data must be gathered in an organized manner and should be relevant to the goal associated with the data analysis.

   D. Validate the data for accuracy and timeliness.

   E. Identify a database structure and create the database. This means creating tables, indexes, and other database objects.

   F. Enter the data into the database for evaluation. This can be done in a variety of ways and is dictated by the product vendor.

2. Identify five database applications that you may have used in your daily business activity.

3. Identify three Internet Web sites where you have noticed data mining to develop business trends.

20

Answers to Quiz

1. Disk Drives

   Tape Drives

   SAN (storage area network)

2. Visual Basic .NET

   Oracle Forms

3. 1. Formulate a question.

   2. Select and use appropriate statistical methods.

   3. Collect the necessary data.

   4. Validate the data.

   5. Identify a database structure.

   6. Enter the data into the database for evaluation.

HOUR 21

Building Applications That Use Databases

You have been introduced throughout the book to an abundance of database jargon, fundamentals, and theory. Without discounting any material up to now, the point should be made that databases are not really useful as standalone entities. In fact, databases are rarely used on a standalone basis. The utility of databases becomes apparent when databases are integrated with applications. Applications and databases compose useful systems.

It is time to show the big picture and demonstrate how the concepts of this book are applied and used in environments to create useful systems. In this hour you will see how databases and applications are developed and integrated to do this very thing.

The highlights of this hour include

- Traditional approaches to data storage
- An overview of the database-enabled application
- Creating the database application
- Connecting to a database from an application

Traditional Approaches to Data Storage

The first thing you will learn about in this hour is the alternative to storing data in a database. Recall from Hour 2, "History and Evolution of Databases," that the alternative to storing information in a database is for applications to store data in their own proprietary format, called flat files.

Before database technology became popular, applications were commonly written to store data in proprietary flat files. The format of flat files was chosen by the programmer at development time. Data stored from one application was not necessarily compatible with data stored in another application. Figure 21.1 demonstrates how different applications could use different data files.

FIGURE 21.1

Traditional application file storage.

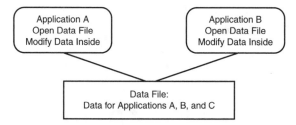

This application data storage model just discussed is problematic. For one thing, files are managed by the operating system. The operating system is designed to manage files efficiently; it is not concerned with file security, data integrity, data reliability, and so on. A database management system, however, is concerned with these issues.

Consider this point, which was discussed briefly in Hour 2; different applications cannot easily share data when the data is stored in a file. In large enterprise environments, hundreds or thousands of different applications might exist, each storing data in its own unique proprietary format. This is a data management nightmare! Imagine how difficult it would be to update a customer record correctly if the record is distributed among even three or four applications.

Another problem with this data storage model is data security. Consider how difficult it would be to control data access among different users and different user types. Security could be implemented; however, it would have to be implemented from within the application and would require additional logic. On many operating systems, users could copy the entire data files to floppy disks and walk out. Operating systems are not, in general, designed with security of files in mind.

Overview of the Database-Enabled Application

Many benefits occur when you use a database as a central data repository for different applications. One great benefit is that data exists in a central location; the data is not scattered throughout the enterprise—some here, some there. This greatly decreases data management complexity and increases data reliability and data consistency. Database storage also allows definition and enforcement of representation standards for data items. Figure 21.2 demonstrates the simplicity of this architecture.

NEW TERM   The term *Enterprise* may be defined in this context as the automated system that represents the business or activity.

FIGURE 21.2

Applications sharing a database.

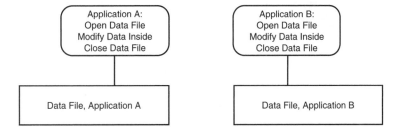

Another benefit is concurrent access to data. Many applications can read the same data at the same time. Only one application is allowed to change data at any given time, however.

Still another benefit with using a central database is the possibility of data security. Users and user roles with privileges/permissions can define access to subsets of data held within the database.

Now that you have learned about the benefits of using a database with an enterprise application, you can take a look at the details of how a database is actually used with an enterprise application. The next sections discuss canned queries, front-end applications, and Web-based applications.

Canned Queries

A canned query is simply a prewritten piece of code that is designed to access the database in a certain way. Examples where canned queries are commonly used include bank teller systems, insurance sales representative systems, inventory control systems, and point-of-sale systems. Each of these systems uses a prewritten query or set of queries to access data in a certain manner in a database.

21

A *Canned Query* is one that is specific in nature, has been analyzed by the database, and can be processed numerous times.

A canned query is designed to limit a certain user to a certain specific set of actions. For example, an insurance sales representative should have the capability to enter customer data into the system to obtain a quote. The insurance sales representative does not have access to modify rates per vehicle. Someone at the corporate office has this type of access to the system and would be trusted with entering new data as new cars are produced, or correcting/updating existing data. For security reasons, the insurance sales representative is not allowed to change a company's rate for a certain vehicle. The insurance sales representative is limited in functionality by the canned transactions present in his or her software. Refer to Figure 21.3 for an example of a canned transaction. This example demonstrates a company's hour entry system. The employee can enter his or her hours for the week, but is not allowed to modify the pay rate or any other information in the database.

FIGURE 21.3

Canned transaction.

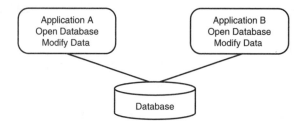

Canned transactions may differ in functionality between different types of users. For example, consider the banking environment. The bank teller needs only simple functionality and limited access to the database. The bank manager needs more complex access to the database. These two user types would have very different canned transactions available.

 Canned Transactions are those that are specific to the function of the user or group of users.

Multitiered Systems

Multitiered systems, as discussed in Hour 5, "Understanding Modern Database Architectures and Environments," consist of user layer applications (tier 1), middle layer applications (tier 2), and the data layer (tier 3). Each layer or tier provides channels or paths to the next layer. To access the data layer from tier 1, channels in tier 2 should be used. It is bad programming practice—a security violation—to allow direct access to the data layer from tier 1.

Tier 1 consists of applications with user interfaces or external interfaces. Any time a user is allowed to enter data into the system, the user does so in tier 1. The data entered into tier 1 applications is sent to tier 2 functions or methods. Tier 2 consists of applications that validate the data from above and execute canned queries to the data layer. Tier 3 consists of the database. One of the benefits of the multitiered system is that each layer is implemented separately from the preceding layer. The application layer does not need to know what kind of database is used in the data layer.

Web Applications

Web applications are multitiered systems. Web application tier 1, the user interface, consists of the Web browser and associated files on the Web server. The application layer and data layer for Web-based software is similar to the application layer previously discussed. Additional security is involved for Web applications, but security will not be discussed in this context.

Web application architecture was discussed in Hour 5; therefore, this section does not go into great detail. You will be given the opportunity at the end of this hour to examine the architecture of the Web application described previously in the book and determine the separate tiers involved.

Creating the Database Application

Now that you have learned about general application architecture, you will look at the general processes involved in creating an application and associated database. The application life cycle and the database life cycle occur somewhat concurrently.

The application life cycle, which is covered in this hour, consists of six separate phases: The requirements phase, the specification phase, the design phase, the implementation phase, the integration phase, and the maintenance phase. The database life cycle also consists of six separate phases: The requirements phase, the analysis phase, the conceptual design phase, the logical design phase, the physical design phase, and the implementation phase.

The application life cycle and database life cycle can be blended into an overall development process—the database application life cycle. The following sections briefly discuss the phases of the database application life cycle.

DB Application Life Cycle: Phase 1, Requirements

During the requirements phase of the database application life cycle, one single team might be working to discern the requirements of both the application and the database at

21

the same time. As the process continues into later stages, however, the database team and the application programming team will divide and conquer the project.

During the requirements phase, various aspects of the database application and data storage needs are detailed. These aspects might include interface details, necessary tasks to perform, security requirements, or performance requirements. It is important during this phase to represent the requirements, constraints, and expectations of the application. Time spent identifying valid, detailed requirements saves money and coding time in the long run.

These requirements are used extensively in the next stage of application development—the specification phase. The deliverable for the requirements phase is a document describing each of the valid application requirements. An optional deliverable for this phase is a nonfunctional prototype that demonstrates the appearance of any user interfaces of the application.

DB Application Life Cycle: Phase 2, Specifications

The specification phase can prove to be a tedious part of the database application life cycle because of the amount of detail involved. During the specification phase, the functionality of the application is planned in a concrete, detailed manner. The database conceptual schema is created in a high-level manner that will demonstrate the data storage needs of the system. The results of this planning are recorded in a specification document. Each specification listed in the specification document relates to a requirement listed in the requirements document.

The functionality described in the specification document includes inputs and required results. If extraneous information will be needed for the application, such as pay rates, garbage collection times, employee job function codes, and so on, this information should be taken into consideration and included in the specification document.

In a commercial software development environment, the specification document provides a signed contract for a client and developer. The signed specification document provides a legal basis for functionality, which will be included in the application. If functionality is not included in the specification, the development company is not responsible for including this functionality in the end application. On the flip side, if the specification document lists a certain behavior for a given set of inputs, this behavior should be included in the finished application.

Note that the details of application implementation have not been mentioned to this point. No code is written or even discussed until the specification document is created and processed. After the specification document has been written, examined, reviewed, revised, accepted, and signed, the design process can begin.

DB Application Life Cycle: Phase 3, Design

The design phase is where the database application and database are designed in detail. The term *design* when used in this phase, however, does not mean that the application is coded in a programming language. Rather, design means that the application is broken into functional segments or modules.

The functionality of each module in the design is decided along with the general logic necessary to make the module work correctly (as described in the specification document). Communication paths between modules should be laid out and recorded in detail.

When specifying communication paths between modules, it is important to record details such as what data types are passed, the order in which passed data should be arranged, and what data types are returned.

Take a look at an example where the communication path is not clearly defined. Two modules in some project have been designed to work together. The designers specify that a certain function in a module needs an integer and two strings. This function will take this integer and two strings, do work, and return a string. The designers neglect to specify whether the function takes the values as (string, integer, string) or (integer, string, string) or (string, string, integer).

This is the kind of ambiguity that must be addressed in the design phase. If this ambiguity exists in the next phase, implementation, it will introduce unnecessary complexity.

During this phase the database is designed in detail, including transactions. A database management system is chosen in this phase, if is has not been decided on already. The logical and physical database designs can both be created during this phase.

The deliverable in this phase is a document containing the details of the database application and database designs. This document should be written with sufficient detail so that programmers can pick it up and write the code. The design document should relate directly to the specification document. The design document is commonly reviewed before approval. Upon approval, the implementation process begins.

DB Application Life Cycle: Phase 4, Implementation

Implementation is the phase where the database application begins to come into existence, and the database is put into place. The database should be implemented early in this stage of the life cycle so that the application can be properly developed and tested.

The accepted database application design document is passed to a programming team (perhaps the programming team developed the design document) to implement.

21

The application modules identified in the design document are created in code by the programming team and tested. A team of programmers will work concurrently on the development of different modules.

Programmers tend to test their modules as they write the code, but the application level testing will occur in the integration phase after the application is assembled. Because programmers tend to test their modules as they write, the database, or a test database, should be in place by this time—with test data—to permit this. If a test database is used, other database development processes, such as migration of existing or legacy data—a time-consuming process—can continue in a concurrent manner. There is no need for database completion, such as data migration, and so on until the end of the next phase.

Application modules and the database developed in this phase will be reflections of those described in the design document. The deliverable for the implementation phase includes commented source code for each module and relevant information regarding the database, such as user account information, diagrams, and so on.

DB Application Life Cycle: Phase 5, Integration

After the code for each module is complete, the modules are integrated into one package, the database application. The database application is checked thoroughly against the specifications. The customer will judge the quality of the application by how well the application satisfies the behaviors set forth in the specification document.

The final testing, verification, and so forth usually is done by a group other than the developers. It is more productive for a third party to examine the application and give a critical evaluation. The original programmers might overlook bugs or flaws in the application.

This point of the database application life cycle is where database tuning might begin. Performance of the database is important, and therefore should be watched closely early in the process. Improvements in the performance of the database will most likely be seen throughout the entire application.

The deliverables of the integration phase include a completed database application, manuals, and source code.

DB Application Life Cycle: Phase 6, Maintenance

The maintenance phase lasts for the duration of the database application life. Maintenance in the form of bug fixes, renovations in functionality or appearance, performance tuning, and the like are done on a continuing basis.

When modifications are made to the application or database, changes should be well documented and tested. Care needs to be taken not to introduce new faults with any changes.

Connecting to a Database from an Application

The purpose of the previous section was to demonstrate the process by which a database application is developed. In this section, you will examine the procedure of connecting to a database from an application, at the code level. Even though this is an introductory text, it is beneficial to include a code-level explanation of this process. If you are not a programmer and have no interest in ever writing code, you might want to skip this portion.

The code in this section is written in Java. The JDBC functionality provided in the Java environment allows connections to be made easily to databases. It is important to realize that the steps described here are not exhaustive. There are many ways to connect to databases. You may have heard of Open Database Connectivity (ODBC). ODBC provides a means for programming database connections from Visual Basic, C++, and other languages. Although ODBC and JDBC are very different, the basic steps, and end result, are the same (data is brought from a database and used in an application). Java provides a much simpler and better-designed database programming interface—JDBC.

JDBC Connection Requirements

To access a database from Java, you will need valid database user account information (username and password), a JDBC driver for the brand of database used, and the URL of the database, including the port number.

 JDBC is Java Database Connectivity.

Database User Account Information

The valid database user account information will come from the system or database administrator. Validate the username and password by logging in to the database normally before attempting to create a database connection from an application. Bad user account info can leave a programmer with unnecessary connection errors!

JDBC Driver

The JDBC driver is a piece of software that usually comes with the database. The driver software tells the Java programming environment exactly how to communicate with the

21

certain database. Different databases have different JDBC drivers, but every JDBC driver has to provide a certain set of functions to the programmer.

Database URL

Databases have URLs just like Web servers do. The URL of the database can be as simple as the IP address of the server where the database resides, or it can be an address, such as `database69.sams.net`.

The database will use a specific port. Refer to your specific database documentation for this port information. If the database server has the IP address 192.168.0.230 and the database uses port 1521 (Oracle), the server URL you need to use is 192.168.0.230:1521. The port is specified in the URL by appending it to the IP address following a colon.

Using JDBC

Five main processes are involved in accessing a database from a programming language. These five processes are fairly standard in other programming languages, but will be done differently in many cases. The specific processes for JDBC connections are

1. The database driver for the database management system is loaded and registered.
2. A connection to the database is established.
3. Queries or updates are sent to the database.
4. Results are returned from the database.
5. The database connection is closed.

The following sections show what the Java code looks like for each of these steps.

Step 1: Loading and Registering the Database Driver

The driver for the database management system is loaded and registered in one step by calling the method

```
Class.forName()
```

If the JDBC driver is called oracle.jdbc.driver.OracleDriver, the following method call will register and load this JDBC driver, assuming that the Java Development Environment variables, specifically the $CLASSPATH and $PATH, are correctly configured. Configuration of these variables is beyond the scope of this book.

```
Class.forName("oracle.jdbc.driver.OracleDriver");
```

Step 2: Establishing a Database Connection

After the JDBC driver is loaded and registered, a specific connection must be established to the database. To establish a connection to the database, you need the full URL, valid username, and valid password for an account on the database. The database URL should be constructed as follows:

```
String dburl = "jdbc:oracle:thin:@192.168.0.230:1521:dbname"
```

The text `"jdbc:oracle:thin"` specifies the type of JDBC driver in use. This information is obtained in the database documentation. The thin driver specified here is conservative of network bandwidth.

The database connection is established as follows:

```
String username = "jmusacha";
String password = "1irateguy";
Connection C = DriverManager.getConnection(dburl, username, password);
```

Note that the database username and password are included directly in the code. This is a good reason to put this code in tier 2 in the multitiered and Web environments.

Step 3: Sending Transactions to the Database

Now that the connection is established, transactions can be sent to the database. SQL commands are sent to the database with the execute(), executeUpdate(), or executeQuery() methods of the Statement class. The execute() method will execute any transaction (CREATE SCHEMA, CREATE TABLE, DROP TABLE, and so on). The executeUpdate()method is used solely for SQL update statements (UPDATE, INSERT, and so on). The executeQuery()method is used for SQL queries (SELECT statement).

Here's how to select the last names (LNAME column) and employee numbers (EMP_NUM column) of all members of an employee table named EMPLOYEES.

```
Statement S = C.createStatement();
S.execute("SELECT lname, eMP_num from employees order by lname");
```

The Connection object is used to create a statement. A connection can be used to create many statements. The execute call causes the line of SQL code to be sent to the database. Note that the preceding code directly accesses the database. This type of code should be part of tier 2 only in the multitiered model. A well-written enterprise application should never call the database directly from tier 1. The application should call stored procedures in tier 2 (PL-SQL, Java, or some other type of routine). These stored procedures will allow certain canned transactions, like this one, to be processed by the database.

Step 4: Retrieving Results from the Database

The next step of the transaction process is to view the results of the query. When a database is queried in Java, a ResultSet object is returned. This ResultSet stores the results of the last query. The contents of the query executed previously could be printed to the

21

command line by parsing through the ResultSet line by line using the ResultSet next() method as follows:

```
ResultSet R = S.getResultSet(); // S is the Statement Object
while (R.next()) {
  long ssn = R.getLong("SSN");
  String ln = R.getString("LAST_NAME");
  String fn = R.getString("FIRST_NAME");
  String mi = R.getString("MIDDLE_NAME");
  System.out.println(ssn + " " + ln + " " + fn + " " + mi);
}
```

Step 5: Closing the Database Connection

When finished with a database connection, any statements and the connection should be closed. Closing the database statements and connection frees the resources that were involved on the client and the database server. The database statements and connection are closed as follows:

```
S.close();
C.close();
```

Performing Additional Queries

Often, you'll need to store data within a database. The procedure for storing or updating data in a database is similar to the preceding code, except that no ResultSet object will be involved. Instead, there will be a count of the number of rows of data that were affected. The following example demonstrates how to search for an employee number of "123456" and change the last name to "Jones." Perhaps the employee was recently married.

```
Statement S = C.createStatement();
S.execute("UPDATE EMPLOYEE SET LNAME=JONES WHERE ENUM=123456");
Int lines = s.getUpdateCount();
System.out.println(lines + " rows were modified.");
```

This query might raise a few eyebrows. It would seem that the simplest way to get the task done would be to go directly to the database and change it. It's only one update to one person—perhaps this could be done by the database administrator. What happens when the company has 25,000 employees? Taking changes like this to the database administrator is a good way *not* to make a friend! The database application should be written to allow such changes to be made without the intervention or assistance of administrative authority. This functionality would allow these changes to be made by data entry personnel.

Summary

This hour discussed the development of applications that use databases. First, you learned about some of the drawbacks associated with using operating system files to store data, such as lack of data sharing, data security, and data reliability. This was followed by the benefits of using a database management system to manage enterprise data, which results in secure, reliable, centralized data storage. The concept of a canned query was introduced and then applied to the multitiered application architecture. The three-tiered architecture (user interface layer, application layer, database layer) was laid out as applicable to in-house and Web applications. Then you learned about the database application life cycle and looked at an example of how an application connects to a database.

Q&A

Q Are there instances when it is better to store application data in a file rather than in a database?

A Of course! Consider files that store application settings, for example. It wouldn't make sense in most cases to put this data within a database.

Q Can I use a database for real-time processing?

A This would be inadvisable. Databases add a certain amount of delay to systems. Real-time processing usually introduces serious time constraints on the performance of the system. To ensure that the system continuously meets these time constraints, store real-time data in some other manner.

Q The database application life cycle described in this hour is different from others I have seen. What is correct for my company?

A The database application life cycle described in this hour is intended to be a loosely organized outline of the process. It is by no means the only way of developing a database application. Many companies spend thousands to millions of research dollars developing a cost-effective development process. If the process is proven to give good results, go with it.

Workshop

The following workshop is composed of quiz questions and practical exercises. The quiz questions are designed to test your overall understanding of the current material. The practical exercises are intended to afford you the opportunity to apply the concepts discussed during the current hour, as well as build on the knowledge acquired in previous

21

hours of study. Please take time to complete this workshop before continuing. You can refer to the answers at the end of this hour.

Quiz

1. What are some benefits of storing data in a database versus storing the data in a file?

2. What other options are available for data storage if a database is not used?

3. What are the general phases of the database application life cycle?

4. What deliverables are produced upon the completion of each phase?

5. What steps are involved when connecting to a database from a Java application?

Exercises

1. A company has a need for a database application. It wants to consolidate its existing data in one central location. Currently the data is stored on six smaller databases located on various servers. The company wants to retain the functionality provided by existing applications, but wants to redesign the enterprise applications to be more efficient and robust. Outline a development process for this company using the database application life cycle described in this hour.

2. Take the following information and construct Java that will query the Oracle database described next and return the pay rates and employee ID numbers for employees located in the engineering department. The query reads as follows:

```
SELECT PAY_RATE, EMP_ID from EMPLOYEES E, DEPARTMENT D
WHERE E.DEPT_CODE = D.DEPT_CODE
AND D.DEPT_NAME = 'Engineering'
```

Database Server	192.168.0.43
Database Port	1521
Database Name	Employee_DB
UserName	standard
Password	3MRF%?D

Answers to Quiz

1. Data exists in a central location, the data can be accessed concurrently, the data is stored securely, and the data storage is reliable and robust.

2. If a database is not going to be used, data can be stored in a file or in memory, depending on the requirements of the application and the constraints of the system.

3. Phases: Requirements, Specification, Design, Implementation, Integration, and Maintenance.

4. Deliverables per phase include the requirements phase: requirements document; specification phase: specification document (signed contract between developer and client); design phase: design document; implementation phase: source code; integration phase: source code, user manuals test cases; maintenance phase: modification records, test cases.

5. 1) The database driver for the database management system is loaded—and registered, in the case of Java; 2) a connection to the database is established; 3) queries or updates are sent to the database; 4) results are returned from the database; 5) the database connection is closed.

21

HOUR 22

Popular Database Software and Third-Party Tools

Many database-related software products are on the market. It is a monumental task to decide what database software you want to spend your budget money on when there are so many choices. Each of the major database vendor products has many features in common, but each of them has unique features, or features that *seem* unique. When you put together features, platforms, price, and licensing, there is bound to be a fit for your needs.

After you have chosen the database software, you must decide if you will use the native database management software, a third-party database administration package, or maybe a combination of both. There are fewer third-party database administration packages available than there are database vendors, so the choice is not as difficult.

If you are doing any in-house development, you might consider a software/database development package. There are many to choose from.

What you pick will depend on what it is you are developing. A database front end can be created by just about any programming language, a desktop database, or an HTML page with embedded code. If data mining is what you will be doing, several applications can be used for data mining, which would be your interface into the database.

This hour will attempt to ease the burden of buying and researching the different database-related software by giving you an overview of each package and some of its features. You will learn about

- Commercial database software
- Open source database software
- Desktop database software
- Third-party database administration software
- Data-mining software
- Development software

Commercial Database Servers

The first type of database software you will examine is commercial database server software. This is the software that is used to manage data in the corporate environment. The basic functionality of commercial database server software includes the capability to create databases, manage transactional environments, manage data-mining environments, interact with the database using queries or data manipulation, provide tools and utilities to ease database administration, and so forth. Some of the most popular commercial database servers are examined here, including

- Oracle 9i
- Sybase ASE
- Informix Dynamix Server
- DB2 UDB
- SQL Server 2000

Oracle 9i

Oracle 9i is the latest version of database server software provided by Oracle Corporation. The following sections discuss its manageability, data integration capabilities, performance and scalability, security, business intelligence, and development.

Manageability

Oracle 9i can be managed in several ways. The easiest is by using Oracle Enterprise Manager (OEM). With OEM, you have almost all the standard DBA functions right at your fingertips. Database configuration, job scheduling, event alerts, replication, space management, security, and more can be accomplished with this client-side or Web GUI. Another tool available to DBA's and users alike is SQL*Plus. This tool is a SQL reporting tool where SQL can be input and formatted, and all the database management commands can be run from it.

Data Integration

The main information-sharing technology in Oracle 9i is Streams. Streams can be used to load changed data into data warehouses, replicate data between databases, and even send notifications of database events. Two other important data integration features of Oracle 9i are Advanced Replication and Advanced Queuing.

Performance and Scalability

Oracle 9i can be scaled from a single processor server to an SMP or MPP mainframe. Oracle 9i Real Application Clusters (RAC) allows for unlimited scalability by allowing clustering of low-cost hardware that works together as one system.

Security

Oracle Advanced Security supports PKI (Public Key Infrastructure) through Public Key Certificate Standard (PKCS) #12 wallets. Oracle PKI integrates with Oracle Wallets, Entrust Profile, and Microsoft Certificate Store. Business rules that implement data visibility can be implemented by using Oracle Virtual Private Database. Oracle supports data encryption at the column level via programming, and Oracle also supports LDAP technology called Internet Directory.

Business Intelligence

A data warehouse is key to business intelligence. With the vast amounts of data in a data warehouse, it is getting more difficult to manage. Oracle offers the capability to divide tables into smaller parts called partitions. This speeds access to the important data that decisions are made with. Oracle also has integrated an OLAP engine right into the database and has included a suite of extraction, transformation, and load capabilities into the database.

Development

Oracle development capabilities start with standard SQL and Oracle's Procedural Language PL/SQL. These are the core of Oracle application development. Oracle is XML enabled. XML documents can be stored in the database and retrieved via SQL. The results of any SQL query can be converted to XML. Oracle is Java enabled and has the capability to use JSP; SQL code can be embedded into Java applications via SQLJ, and Oracle provides all types of JDBC drivers.

Sybase ASE

Sybase ASE is the database server software provided by Sybase Corporation. The following sections discuss its manageability, data integration capabilities, performance and scalability, security, business intelligence, and development.

Manageability

DBA's can manage Sybase ASE 12.5 by using Sybase Central. Sybase Central is a Java-based application GUI loaded on by default during installation. This application is a shell for plug-ins that can be used to manage your database.

Data Integration

Sybase ASE offers support for XML, Java EJB's (Enterprise Java Beans), Unicode data, and Java classes and objects. Sybase ASE has an XML query engine that understands all XML documents. EJB's can be run successfully and be deployed inside the database engine.

Performance and Scalability

Sybase ASE features dynamic tuning to help keep up with the always changing workload. Because of these on-the-fly tuning capabilities, it is a good DBMS for use with transaction processing/query database environments. CPU level, resource limitations, and index caching can be changed without rebooting the server. CPU and system allocations can be changed without restarting the database server.

Security

Row-level storage security allows the DBA to set up each user or group to see only the rows of data that are allowed for that user. This is done using login triggers and the Application Context Facility. Clients are authenticated using login/passwords, and other servers can be authenticated using SSL with the option of also using digital certificates for server authentication.

Business Intelligence

Sybase has two separate core products to support business intelligence. The first, Industry Warehouse Studio (IWS), is an infrastructure that helps build business intelligence applications. The second, Adaptive Server IQ Multiplex, is a relational database built from the ground up to support business intelligence needs.

Development

SQL is supported along with Java in stored procedures. The developer can write procedures with SQL only, a mix of SQL and Java, or with only Java. Part 1 of the SQLJ standard is fully complied with to allow Java-based, object-oriented application development.

Informix Dynamix Server

Informix Dynamix Server is the database server software provided by Informix. The following sections discuss its manageability, data integration capabilities, performance and scalability, security, business intelligence, and development.

22

Manageability

The IBM Informix Server Administrator is a browser-based database administration tool that integrates database administration and development into one application. The platform-independent ServerStudio JE (Java Edition) eases some complex developer tasks, such as table editing. A new feature called Dynamic Logs reduces hands-on manipulation of disk space for log files.

Data Integration

IDS supports IBM Informix DataBlade modules. Module types such as Spatial data, TimeSeries data, Geodetic data, and C-ISAM allow the user to extend IDS to meet business requirements. IDS also supports replication, which moves copies of data to where it is needed in your business environment.

Performance and Scalability

IDS has a multithreaded architecture for Simultaneous Multiple Processing (SMP) machines. Connections can be concentrated using the IDS tool MaxConnect. MaxConnect is a connection server that increases the number of people who can be connected to the database at the same time. The I-Spy tool is used for data warehouse monitoring, optimization, and tuning.

Security

Standard login/password user security is used in IDS. Various levels of access privileges determine what can be done in the database. These privileges include all the way down to column-level security for users. Roles allow the administrator to lump together privileges for easy security administration. Security auditing is also available to help you determine any object manipulation actions taken by database users.

Business Intelligence

A separate product, Informix MetaCube, provides a "smart" view of your warehouse data via charts and graphs. This tool includes tools to ease the administration and tuning of IDS data warehouses. Another business intelligence tool, Informix Visionary (now owned by Rocket Software), is a GUI development and deployment application to bring analytical data to users.

Development

IDS supports Java with its embedded Java Virtual Machine so that Java code can run inside the database. It also supports stored procedures, SQL functions, and a third-party Bladelet library. The Client SDK is a package of API's available to programmers so that they can write database applications in a language they know. The 4GL tool is a rapid-application development environment used to create server-side batch-processing applications, character-based applications, and advanced business reporting. The 4Js Universal Compiler gives applications a GUI on a Windows and Linux application server.

DB2 UDB

DB2 UDB is the database server software provided by IBM. The following sections discuss its manageability, data integration capabilities, performance and scalability, security, business intelligence, and development.

Manageability

The DB2 Universal Database version 8.1 from IBM is a RDBMS with many features. DB2 offers easy maintenance with its Self-Managing and Resource Tuning (SMART) technology. Management of enterprise-wide databases, both remote and local, is made easy with the Health Center and Health Monitor tools.

Data Integration

Data integration can be accomplished in several ways using DB2. Replication can replicate data sources across DB2 and Informix Dynamix Server platforms. XML, flat files, Web services, and spreadsheets can be easily integrated into DB2.

Performance and Scalability

Scalability in DB2 is accomplished in part with its Connection Concentrator. The Connection Concentrator allows multiple client connections to be multiplexed across a few full-time database connections. Multidimensional clustering reduces the need for indexing and speeds query responses. Global temporary tables have minimal logging with support for indexes.

Security

Security is performed by DB2 in four areas: authentication, authorization, privileges, and integrity. The database authenticates users when they log in, tracks the functionality of the user through authorization, allows object viewing and manipulation via privileges, and integrity keeps the data integrity intact using referential integrity constraints.

22

Business Intelligence

An infrastructure is provided by IBM in DB2 that will help you manage, maintain, and build your data warehouses. The DB2 Warehouse Manager is the tool to help you accomplish this important business goal.

Development

The Personal Developers Edition, and the Developer's Edition of DB2 has an extensive toolkit available with them. The DB2 Development Center is an environment that helps ease the process of building triggers, stored procedures, and user-defined functions. DB2 now supports INSTEAD OF triggers, along with improved performance of standard interfaces such as ODBC, ADO, SLQJ, and DB2 CLI. DB2 continues to support technologies such as the Java 2 platform, JavaBeans, and Microsoft's COM.

SQL Server 2000

SQL Server 2000 is the database server software provided by Microsoft Corporation. The following sections discuss its manageability, data integration capabilities, performance and scalability, security, business intelligence, and development.

Manageability

Enterprise Manager is the main tool used to administer SQL Server 2000 databases. With this tool, you can create databases, create objects within those databases, create users, and set up permissions and security for databases and users. Enterprise Manager can be used to invoke the Query Analyzer tool for development and any number of wizards to make database administration easier.

Data Integration

Sql Server 2000 supports replication using the publisher/subscriber model to distribute data. SQL Server 2000 has a GUI tool that allows the easy imports and exports of data. In addition, DTS will help you consolidate and transform data from another data source at the column level. This is a very powerful tool for data integration.

Performance and Scalability

Distributed Partition views allows the data to be spread across several database servers to distribute the processing load. This is accomplished by shared-clustering technology. The Log Shipping feature of SQL Server allows several backup servers to exist, which are synchronized with the main server by sending log files to the backup servers and rolling the database forward. This will create warm standby servers. The DBCC utility and index creation takes more advantage of SMP hardware in SQL Server 2000.

Security

Sql Server 2000 now installs with a high level of security using Windows 2000 security right out of the box. File and network encryption is supported—SSL and Kerberos among others. SQL Server 2000 has role-based security for the server, database, and applications, along with integrated security auditing by tracking security events and subevents.

Business Intelligence

SQL Server 2000 allows unique clustered indexes to be created on views to improve query performance on complex views. When one of these indexes is created on a view, the results are written to disk and stored in the database in the same manner as tables with clustered indexes. SQL Server 2000 offers Distributed Partitioned Cubes for scaling to Data Warehouse solutions.

Development

Query Analyzer is SQL Server 2000's SQL and stored-procedure development tool, used to develop with SQL Server 2000's Transact SQL. It comes with a debugger so you can trace through stored procedures, create breakpoints, and step through from any point in your code. Server-side tracing and client-side statistics are now available via Query Analyzer for better SQL tuning and optimization.

Open Source Database Servers

Open source database servers are an excellent alternative to commercial database software. Open source database servers typically are free or have a nominal software usage license. The name *open source* implies that the back-end code is "open" and can be modified or customized for any given organization's needs. Open source databases are excellent for learning and for home-based systems, and they are also being used commercially. The open source solution is the most cost effective for small-size businesses. The open source database servers discussed in the following sections are

- MySQL
- PostgreSQL
- SAP DB

MySQL

MySQL (My Ess Que Ell or my sequel) is an open source database server. This database server can run on many platforms, such as Windows NT, Windows XP, Sun Solaris, many distributions of Linux, Mac OS, HP-UX, AIX, and other operating systems.

Because it is open source, you can download it for free from `http://www.mysql.com`. Here are some features of MySQL:

- Multithreaded, so it can use multiple CPU's if they are available.

- Data types include signed/unsigned integers, float, double, char, varchar, text, blob, date, time, datetime, timestamp, year, set, and enum.

- Group functions and left and right outer joins are supported. An EXPLAIN command enables you to see how the optimizer resolved a query.

- A flexible privilege and encrypted password system also allows for host-based verification.

- The MySQL technical reference claims to have databases with 50 million records. Thirty-two indexes are allowed per table and they can be 500KB long, but this can be changed by recompiling.

- Users may connect to a MySQL database using TCP/IP Sockets, Unix Sockets, NT Named Pipes, or ODBC.

Many tools are available for use with MySQL. MyODBC is the downloadable ODBC driver for MySQL that runs on Windows and most versions of Unix. Connector/J is a pure Java driver that converts JDBC calls to the network protocol being used. MyCC is a graphical user interface to MySQL. This tool lets you do many of the tasks associated with database management, such as database creation and deletion, table creation and deletion, running SQL queries, and database diagnostics.

PostgreSQL

PostgreSQL is an open source Object Relational Database Management System (ORDBMS). It is based on a database called POSTGRES developed at the University of California, Berkeley. The POSTGRES database pioneered many object-oriented features now available in commercial database server software. PostgreSQL can run on many operating systems, including but not limited to Windows 2000/NT, Linux, Sun Solaris, HP-UX, and Mac OS X. PostgreSQL has many features, some of which are listed next.

- PostgreSQL supports all SQL99 join types, including inner join, all outer joins (left, right, and full), and the natural join. The optimize can use different join algorithms.

- Views are supported, as are updateable views. An updateable view propagates the changes made to a view to the underlying table.

- Most of the SQL92 and SQL99 data types are available. These are INTEGER, NUMERIC, BOOLEAN, CHAR, VARCHAR, DATE, INTERVAL, and TIMESTAMP. Binary Large Objects (BLOBs) can be stored and retrieved by applications from the database.

- Subqueries, all grouping functions, SELECT DISTINCT, and unions are supported. A full set of built-in functions exists also.

- Transactions are supported, so if a database transaction fails, it will roll back to the original data before the transaction started. PostgreSQL uses Multi-Version Concurrency Control (MVCC) to ensure that database readers don't block database writers and vice versa. This is said to be better than row-level locking. Row-level and table-level locking are also used.

- A backup and recovery tool, several GUI's, and different security models are available to make this a very manageable database system.

- PostgreSQL can serve many programming languages and interfaces. Programming languages such as Perl, Python, C/C++, and so on are choices. Interfaces such as ODBC and JDBC are available for use as well.

As you can see, PostgreSQL is a very powerful database server. You can download this software from many postgreSQL mirror sites. Start by going to `http://www.postgresql.com`.

SAP DB

SAP DB was a commercial database product that was turned over to open source in the year 2000. This RDBMS was originally developed to support mySAP.com products, such as mySAP Supply Chain Management, and mySAP Product Lifecycle Management. It was developed to be a strong OLTP e-business database. Following are some of the features of SAP DB:

- Runs on Windows NT/2000, Linux, Sun Solaris, AIX, HP-UX, and more.

- SAP DB supports the entry level ANSI SQL 92 standard for SQL. SQL Studio and Web SQL are two GUI tools available for running SQL in SAP DB.

- The Database Manager is the tool used for SAP database management. It can be either a command-line tool, or to easily manage more than one SAP database instance, the GUI or Web version of Database Manager is also available.

- SAP DB's Replication Manager is a tool that allows for the loading of external file data into a SAP database, or unloading SAP database data into another database. Replication Manager used SQL as the data load/unload mechanism.

- Database backups can be done while the database is running, a "warm" backup, or after the database has been shut down, known as a "cold" backup.

- ODBC, JDBC, and C/C++ precompilers and others are the programming interfaces to SAP DB. ODBC is the official C API. Most of the external SAP DB tools use ODBC as its interface into the database.

Even though SAP DB is now open source, SAP will still develop and support enhancements to the database with the open source community.

Desktop Databases

Desktop databases reside on a single computer and are typically designated as a single-user environment. However, some desktop databases, such as Microsoft Access, also have networking capabilities. The following desktop database software is discussed next:

- Microsoft Access 2002 (XP)
- FileMaker Pro 6

Microsoft Access 2002 (XP)

Microsoft Access has been around since 1992. Over the years, it has developed into one of the most powerful applications in the Microsoft Office Suite. The latest version, Access 2002, comes with Office XP. It has very powerful functionality for the experienced Access user, yet it is still simple and easy enough for the novice to utilize. A short list of features follows:

- Access 2002 will run on Windows and is now speech enabled. You can issue voice commands and voice dictation. Access 2002 also uses the Access 2000 file format as its default, so backward compatibility is not a problem.

- A new feature is the Data Access Page Designer. This tool lets users design their Data Access Pages more efficiently.

- There is a Compact and Repair function in Access 2002 so that files that have broken forms or reports are recovered after being damaged. When errors occur while converting an older Access database to Access 2002, the errors are put into a table to make problem solving easier.

- Access 2002 has a whole development environment built right into the software. A developer can create forms and reports using drag-and-drop technology and can write programming code using Visual Basic for Applications. XML is supported throughout Access 2002.

- Users can create and modify SQL Server-compatible databases and then deploy them seamlessly without modifications using the included SQL Server 2000 Desktop Engine.

This list of features only scratches the surface of Access 2002. It is full of data access, development, and ease-of-use wizards that will make creating a database simple. You can read more about Microsoft Access 2002 by visiting
`http://www.microsoft.com/office/access/default.asp`.

FileMaker Pro 6

FileMaker Pro 6 is workgroup database software. Built-in templates enable you to quickly design and deploy a customized database solution for your business. It supports image and multimedia importing and data sharing with most other applications via XML. Some features of FileMaker Pro are listed next:

- Data sharing is easy in a multiplatform environment. FileMaker Pro supports Windows XP/2000/NT/98, Mac OS X, and Mac Classic.
- FileMaker Pro has a built-in Web server to allow a single-click Web publishing feature. You can give up to 10 authorized users access to the FileMaker Pro database via your company intranet.
- Excel spreadsheets can be dragged and dropped onto FileMaker Pro to create fully functional databases.
- Use the Layout/Report Assistant to make your forms and reports look like you want. You can customize letters with FileMaker Pro mail-merge capabilities.
- Two way ODBC connections with database servers such as Oracle and SQL Server allow data to be moved back and forth using dynamically calculated SQL queries.
- Record-level security enables you to protect your important data.

Other FileMaker products to go along with the FileMaker Pro database include FileMaker Server, FileMaker Developer, and FileMaker Mobile. Find out more at http://www.filemakerpro.com.

Table 22.1 lists some other desktop database choices and their Web sites.

TABLE 22.1   Desktop Databases

Desktop Database	Company	WWW URL
Paradox	Corel	http://www.corel.com
FoxPro	Microsoft	http://www.microsoft.com

Third-Party Database Administration Software

Many database vendors provide built-in tools and utilities for assisting the DBA in database administration. There is also a great selection of third-party DBA software on the market. Some of these are excellent alternatives, and often better, than software provided by vendors themselves. The third-party DBA software discussed in the following sections includes:

22

- Quest Central
- DBArtisan

Quest Central

Quest Software has combined some of its best database administration software components into a centralized console called Quest Central. It has a consistent interface so the DBA can work on several tasks at once. If the DBA has not finished with a task, but a more important task needs to be done, he or she does not have to start over again with the original task. Quest Central supports Oracle and DB2 database systems. Following is an overview of the components that make up Quest Central:

- Database Administration eases database and object maintenance with a graphical user interface. Database objects can be created, altered, or dropped quickly. DBA scripts can be scheduled and run at desired times, with error-checking capabilities. Database security and permissions is another aspect of database administration where Quest Central excels. The DBA can control security and permissions at both the object level and the user level to ensure the data can be seen, manipulated, or used only by appropriate users.

- Performance Diagnostics can be used in real time by using Quest Software's Spotlight. Database data flows can be seen graphically, which enables you to see what is happening in the database in real time. Any possible bottlenecks can be reported via an audio or visual alarm. Database analysis is made possible by keeping statistics on database performance and storing them in a repository. You can run an analysis on this repository data and the Performance Diagnostics will recommend actions that need to be taken for performance improvements.

- SQL Tuning uses SQLab Vision for nonintrusive collection and expert tuning advice. All the SQL statements are collected and then analyzed. When the slow SQL is identified, it can be rewritten automatically for maximum performance.

- Space Management is used to reorganize and restructure your database. The Space Management module calculates the best strategy for database reorganization and restructuring. Excessive extents, data fragmentation, and other related space problems can be detected and corrected using the Space Management module.

Database administration and management is much easier with all the necessary tools available in one integrated solution. These tools work together seamlessly to provide a quick solution to your management problems.

DBArtisan

DBArtisan by Embarcadero Technologies is a database administration tool designed to help DBA's cut down on the tedious work needed to keep their databases running smoothly. The GUI interface will increase the productivity of seasoned DBA's and novices alike. Following is a list of features included in DBArtisan.

- DBArtisan enables management of Oracle, Sybase, DB2, and SQL Server using a single graphical interface.

- The Security Management portion of DBArtisan enables DBA's to manage roles, users, logins, profiles, and groups. You can automate the creation of user accounts to run when you and/or your database are not so busy. Object security and privileges can be granted or revoked as well.

- Performance management is achieved with a color-coded view of object locking and database processes running on the server. These locks and processes can be sorted in many ways. Diagnostics can be seen for processes, and the capability to kill runaway processes is also available.

- A tuning and performance suite can be created by using the separate Embarcadero Performance Center and Embarcadero SQL Tuner software packages. These can be tightly integrated into DBArtisan to produce a single database administration tool.

- DBArtisan uses a standard tabbed graphical editor for database object creation, deletion, and manipulation. DBArtisan has built-in knowledge of each supported RDBMS's object creation syntax and management rules.

- Programmers can easily write database queries using Embarcadero's Query Builder. This tool automatically generates SQL code while the programmer points and clicks objects and methods to use for the query. The DataGrid allows row-level data editing.

- DBArtisan makes database schema migration easy by providing a wizard to walk you through copying a single table, a whole schema, or even a complete database to another instance.

Embarcadero software offers two optional modules for DBArtisan: the SQL Debugger and the SQL Profiler, both of which help ease SQL and PL/SQL development. For more information on this and other Embarcadero products, visit `http://www.embarcadero.com`.

Third-Party Data-Mining Software

As with third-party DBA software, a nice selection of third-party data mining software is available for developers and end users. The third-party data-mining software discussed in the following sections includes

- Cognos PowerPlay
- Clementine

Cognos PowerPlay

22

Cognos PowerPlay is an Online Analytical Processing (OLAP) tool used by companies all over the world to get the most value possible out of their business data. PowerPlay has a multiple-tier architecture using a single application server. This server, called PowerPlay Enterprise Server (PPES) has three services or clients: Web, Windows client, or the Excel client. The PPES can be installed on several computers and has automatic load balancing. The work on the data is completed by the application portion of the PPES, so only the data the user needs is sent over the network, saving network bandwidth. PPES stores query results in a cache, so when new queries can use the data stored in the cache, the return time is much quicker. Following are some other features of Cognos PowerPlay:

- PowerPlay can use OLAP cubes created by other vendor software such as Microsoft OLAP Services, SAP BW, Hyperion Essbase, and IBM OLAP for DB2, along with its own OLAP cubes.

- PowerPlay can put several sources of data into a single cube.

- Rapid development can be achieved using PowerPlay's drag-and-drop environment. Transformer, PowerPlay's transformation engine, takes advantage of both the star and snowflake schema designs of today's data warehouses.

- PowerPlay uses Secured Sockets so that data on the Web is secure. Access to PowerCubes can be controlled by defining User Classes, whose definitions are stored in an LDAP security component. User Classes can restrict user access to the whole dimension or just part of it.

- Users will have a short learning curve because they will be able to use interfaces they are already familiar with.

- Administration of PowerPlay is platform independent by using a Java Administrator program. The administrator will have full control of auditing, cube creation, monitoring, performance tuning, and logging.

Cognos PowerPlay is a powerful tool for OLAP. To get more information about Cognos, visit www.cognos.com.

Clementine

Clementine is a workbench for data mining. It is used to create predictive models for decision-making improvement. Clementine uses the CRISP-DM (Cross-Industry Standard Process for Data Mining), which makes data mining a business process. Following are some features of Clementine.

- Clementine provides several Clementine Application Templates (CATs) that use the CRISP-DM methodology. Some of the templates available are used for Web analysis and visitor behavior to detect fraud in financial transactions, for customer retention, to analyze crime and offender characteristics, and to target customer acquisition and growth.

- Clementine uses a visual approach to data mining. No code needs to be written while you are trying to solve problems. This technique helps you understand the relationships in your data and helps you get to a solution faster. You can explore multidimensional data with animation, 3D, and panel data visualization.

- Many data-mining techniques are available with Clementine. You can even use plug-in analytics from third-party vendors in the Clementine Partner Plus Program.

- Clementine has native access to Oracle, SQL Server, DB2, and any ODBC-compliant database. Data output can be delimited text, ODBC, SPSS, Microsoft Excel, and SAS 6, 7, and 8.

- The Clementine client runs on Windows 95/98/NT/2000. The Clementine Server runs on Windows NT/2000, Solaris, and HP-UX.

If you want to find out more about Clementine or any other SPSS software, visit `http://www.spss.com`.

Table 22.2 lists some other data-mining software.

TABLE 22.2   Other Data-Mining Software

Mining Software	Company	WWW URL
DBMiner	DBMiner	`http://www.dbminer.com`
KnowledgeSTUDIO	Angoss Knowledge Engineering	`http://www.angoss.com`
DataScope Suite	Cygron	`http://www.cygron.com`
Data Mining Suite	Information Discovery, Inc.	`http://www.datamining.com`

Database Development Software

For those developers not comfortable with using the command-line and vendor-provided development tools, a variety of database development software is available, some of which is freeware, and some requires the purchase of a software license. The third-party database development software discussed in the following sections includes:

- TOAD
- Rapid SQL

TOAD

22

TOAD is a PL/SQL development tool for Oracle database developers and DBAs. This tool makes application support and database management very easy. TOAD has a single environment for both development and testing. Some of the features of TOAD are listed next:

- The Schema Browser allows for quick viewing of Oracle data dictionary objects using a multitabbed browser. Details of each object can be displayed by clicking that object.

- TOAD comes with powerful editors that allow the user to edit more than one file of more than one type at the same time. SQL, PL/SQL, HTML, and Java files can be used in the editor. The SQL Editor also has bookmarks, hot keys, pop-up selectors for database object names, and version control.

- The TOAD SQL Modeler lets you create queries by allowing you to drag and drop tables and state your query criteria; it will generate the SQL code automatically. You will be able to test the query and see the results.

- The PL/SQL Debugger module is integrated into the Procedure Editor. Developers can step through the code line by line and watch it as it is run on the server. Variable values can be "watched," and those variable values can even be changed while the code is running.

- The DBA Module is integrated into TOAD's interface. This module has database creation wizards, as well as the capability to manage database objects via the Schema Browser. Import and export wizards and a GUI interface to Oracle's SQL*Loader utility are also included. Other DBA tasks such as space management, schema comparison, security, and batch-job scheduling can also be accomplished.

TOAD comes in three configurations: Xpert Edition, Professional Edition, and the Standard Edition. To read more about TOAD, visit `http://www.quest.com`.

Rapid SQL

Rapid SQL is a graphical development environment for writing SQL code on Oracle, SQL Server, DB2, and Sybase database servers. It also has HTML and Java programming capabilities built in. Following are the features of Rapid SQL:

- Rapid SQL has Visual SQL creation and Visual data editing. The Embarcadero Query Builder is a query-by-example tool that facilitates drag-and-drop SQL. When you drag tables to the screen and input your query criteria, the Query Builder writes the SQL code in the background, ensuring a syntax-correct SQL statement. The Embarcadero Data Grid allows data manipulation from within the integrated development environment (IDE).

- Several features of Rapid SQL facilitate high productivity while writing server-side code. Users can have multiple windows open to work on more than one thing at once. More than one database can be connected to at one time. The IDE provides syntax highlighting for Oracle, SQL Server, DB2, Sybase, Java, and HTML coding. Error location is easy with the automatic split screen.

- Rapid SQL provides features for Web development and syntax highlighting for both Java and HTML development. It has a built-in Web browser that is Java enabled for your testing purposes. Rapid SQL can easily be integrated with any Java compiler, including SUN.

- Other features of Rapid SQL include easy integration with either PVCS or Microsoft Source Safe version control systems, powerful scripting, and graphical object management via database object editors and wizards. The Embarcadero SQL Debugger and SQL Profiler are optional modules available from Embarcadero.

Rapid SQL is a great tool for server-side database development. For more information, visit `http://www.embarcadero.com`. Table 22.3 lists more database development software.

TABLE 22.3   Database Development Software

Development Software	Company	WWW URL
Visual Basic	Microsoft Corp.	`http://www.microsoft.com`
Oracle 9i Development Suite	Oracle Corp.	`http://www.oracle.com`
SQL Station	Computer Associates	`http://www3.ca.com`
SQL Navigator	Quest Software	`http://www.quest.com`

Summary

In this hour, you read an overview of the major RDBMS database vendors. To decide which one to use, visit the vendor Web site for more information. Three open source database systems were overviewed as well. After open source databases, you read about two popular desktop databases, and Web sites for others were listed in Table 22.1. The functionality of two third-party database administration tools was the next topic. Data mining is a complicated topic with complicated tools, but you learned about the general functions of two data-mining packages. Finally, you looked at some database development tools and a list of Web sites.

Workshop

The following workshop is composed of quiz questions and practical exercises. The quiz questions are designed to test your overall understanding of the current material. The practical exercises are intended to afford you the opportunity to apply the concepts discussed during the current hour, as well as build on the knowledge acquired in previous hours of study. Please take time to complete this workshop before continuing. You may refer to the answers at the end of the hour.

Quiz

1. Name three of the five major commercial database systems discussed.
2. What does OLAP stand for?

Exercise

1. Download and install the MySQL GUI SQL client.

Answers to Quiz

1. The five major commercial database systems discussed are Oracle 9i, SQL Server 2000, IBM DB2, Sybase ASE, and Informix Dynamix Server.
2. Online Analytical Processing.

PART VI

Future of Databases

Hour

HOUR 23

Previewing Emerging Database Trends

In the world of computers, things evolve at an astounding rate. Just a few years ago, hard drives of more than a gigabyte were unheard of in PCs. Over the years, databases also have evolved. In the 1950s we had flat files; then in the 1960s we had the hierarchical model, which was improved on by the network database model in the 1970s. Currently, most of the database work uses the relational database model. That is not to say that there are not other technologies just over the horizon. Database technologies such as object-relational and pure object-oriented databases are in use and gaining popularity. There is more and more reliance on data and the information that data provides in today's world, so new and improved technology will continue to be sought.

With database technology growing as it is, the technology that helps support these databases also will grow and improve. Who would have thought a programming language would be integrated into databases alongside the standard SQL of the time? Now Java is integrated into many database packages. Databases have to interact with users on the Web in a manageable fashion.

This means there is a need for more database management than ever before, which has brought about the creation of businesses that will host databases for a customer, or even support and manage a database remotely. In this hour, you will learn about the following topics relating to emerging database trends:

- Mass storage to keep the vast amounts of data generated now
- Object-oriented database concepts
- The integration of Java in databases
- An overview of database migrations
- Database hosting and remote database administration
- Embedded, mobile, and handheld databases

Modern Database Technologies

Databases are used in many places you might not think a database could be used. How are all those phone numbers in your cell phone stored and retrieved? The doctor who has your records in his PDA must be using a database. Databases have had other technologies integrated into them that used to serve only a single purpose, such as a programming language or programming paradigm. You will learn about several of these database technologies in the sections that follow.

Integration of Object-Oriented Concepts

The idea of object-oriented programming languages has been in use since the mid 1960s. The object-oriented database came about many years later in the 1990s. To help you better understand an object-oriented database, this section will begin with a basic overview of object orientation. You will then learn who is using these types of databases.

Object-Oriented Concepts

Before you can begin to fully understand object-oriented databases, you should understand three concepts:

- Data abstraction
- Encapsulation
- Inheritance

Abstract data used in an OODB is data that represents something in its most basic form. An example of abstract data is a person. There are certain characteristics that all people have, such as first name, last name, and an age. By creating data types using the combined parts that make up a person, you have created an abstract data type. These data types can be used to create objects. A person object would hold all the essential information of a person, a first name, a last name, and an age. Figure 23.1 uses a person to show an example of an abstract data type.

 NEW TERM *Abstract Data* represents a thing of significance, but in its most basic or fundamental form.

NEW TERM The combination of data and the methods used to access that data is the definition of an *object*.

23

FIGURE 23.1

Example of an abstract data type.

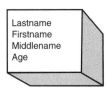

Lastname
Firstname
Middlename
Age

The capability to interact with the data of the object by using methods that are also part of the object is *encapsulation*. These methods are the object's way of allowing its data to be manipulated. A *method* is programming code written to serve as access to the objects data. Suppose that a *person* object was created with the data Sally, Smith, 40; then Sally got married. A method would be available to change Sally's last name to her new last name. Other methods would be included that would allow the addition, changing, or retrieval of the other data within the object. See Figure 23.2 to get a better understanding of objects and encapsulation.

NEW TERM In an Object Oriented Database a *Method* is programming code that is written to access the data in an object.

FIGURE 23.2

Encapsulation in the person object.

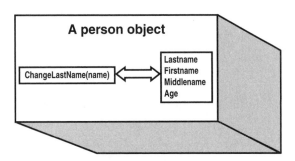

A person object

ChangeLastName(name)

Lastname
Firstname
Middlename
Age

In object orientation, inheritance is the capability to create objects that have the methods and data of a more abstract object, in addition to new methods and data. For instance, object orientation gives you the capability to create an employee object from the person object. The newly created employee object will inherit the methods and data of the person object. So, if your employee object will have an employee number, a title, and a salary, it will inherit first name, last name, and age. Figure 23.3 illustrates this concept.

FIGURE 23.3
Inheritance from person object to employee object.

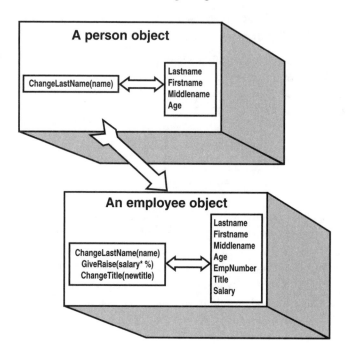

Object-Oriented Databases

An object-oriented database is a merging of the capabilities of databases such as persistent data, the capability to back up and recover data, and the capability to easily query and manipulate that data with the concepts of an object-oriented programming language such as data abstraction, encapsulation, and inheritance. Table 23.1 lists some companies that are using object-oriented databases and shows what purpose those databases serve.

TABLE 23.1   Sample Implementations of Object-Oriented Databases

Toyota	A dealership kiosk for customers to view multimedia about their cars
J. P. Morgan	Modeling financial instruments such as derivatives and bonds
Citibank	Modeling financial instruments such as derivatives and bonds
Chase Manhattan	Modeling financial instruments such as derivatives and bonds

Java Integration with Databases

Over the previous few years, the Java language has come out on top as the language used to extend the functionality of major database software. Vendors such as Oracle, Microsoft, Sybase, and IBM have incorporated Java into their software. This section covers

- An overview of the Java programming language
- Database extensibility using Java

Java Language Overview

Java is a programming language that was invented by James Goslin, Henry McGilton, and many others at Sun Microsystems in 1994. Java is an object-oriented language. It is very portable, meaning the code that a program consists of can be used on any platform. For example, a simple program that figures out how old a person is by figuring the difference of that person's birthday and the current date can be run on Windows 2000, Solaris, Linux, and iMac without changing the code. This is done by using the Java Virtual Machine (VM).

 Portability is the ability of a program to be used on a variety of platforms with little or no adjustments to that code.

The VM is a program that is written for each platform a Java program can run on that will interpret the Java program. The Java program has to be compiled only one time on the platform it will run on, which changes it to bytecodes, which is what the VM will interpret as the program runs.

A Java program is written with the Java API. The Java API is a collection of program objects such as graphical user interface (GUI) windows, buttons, text boxes, and the like that the programmer can use to create the program. When this program is finished, it is compiled on the platform (Solaris, Windows, iMac) that it will run on, which changes it to bytecodes. When the program is run, the VM will interpret the bytecodes while the program is running. If you wanted to run the same program on an iMac, you would only have to compile that program on the iMac, and it would run. Remember, you must have a VM installed on the platform you want to run a Java program on.

New Term *Java Virtual Machine* interprets Java program code so that it will run on a given platform.

Java Embedded in Databases

More and more database vendors are embedding the Java Virtual Machine into their server software to aid in database extensibility. These Java extensions can be implemented in several ways:

- Using a DLL (dynamic link library)
- Using a shared library
- Using Embedded Java classes

A Java-enabled database adds new capabilities to the database.

- *Java stored procedures*—Stored procedures run on the server side. These stored procedures can have Java embedded in them or be written entirely in Java (depending on vendor). An advantage of Java stored procedures is the power a programming language can add to traditional SQL data processing.

- *User-defined functions*—Some databases allow SQL to perform processing of data on the server and return the result of that processing. This can also be done with some Java-enabled databases.

The use of Java in the database can save network traffic because the processing that typically is done on the client can be done on the server and only the results return over the network. The stored procedures and user-defined functions written in Java are portable across many platforms, so the code has to be written only once.

NEW TERM   *Server Side* generally refers to procedures that are accomplished on the server machine rather than a client machine.

Embedded, Handheld, and Mobile Databases

This section covers three types of databases together because often they are spoken of in the same breath. In some cases, you can't have one without the other. You will learn about the following databases and how they are associated.

- Embedded databases
- Handheld databases
- Mobile databases

Embedded Databases

The simplest definition of an embedded database is any database whose programming code is mixed in with the program code of the application that uses the embedded database. Many applications on a standard home computer have applications which use embedded databases. A user of an application that uses an embedded database cannot directly access or manipulate the database.

Another definition of embedded database has to do with hardware devices. An embedded database can be the data management portion of an embedded system.

NEW TERM   An *embedded system* is a small operating system that is programmed to complete a small number of specialized tasks that reside on a chip in a device such as a cellular phone.

The very nature of the embedded database does not allow any administration-type functions to occur. An embedded database must be very stable. The following are some requirements an embedded database must have:

- The capability to fix itself when an error occurs
- The capability to work without administration
- Must be reliable and robust

The Embedded Database in Use

Embedded databases are not marketed toward the end user like large relational database systems are, such as Oracle 9i or Microsoft SQL Server 2000. One target market of the embedded database is software developers. When a commercial software package needs to have a database to operate, but the design or intent does not allow a large RDBMS such as Oracle, an embedded database is the answer. Table 23.2 lists some applications that use embedded database technology.

TABLE 23.2   Applications Using Embedded Databases

Company	Product
Intuit	Quicken 2003
Exchequer Software	Midrange accounting systems

Embedded databases also play a large role in the growing market for "intelligent devices." Embedded databases are showing up in all types of devices from cell phones to kitchen appliances. When you look up a phone number in your cell phone, you have used an embedded database. The following are some devices that use an embedded database:

- *Cell phones*—Cell phones have become very sophisticated in the last few years. Cell phones can store many names and numbers in addition to other data, such as Internet access information and email addresses.
- *Internet appliances*—Internet Service Providers (ISPs) use Internet appliances to ease administration of their systems. An Internet appliance can have an embedded database in it to track and sort through the thousands of emails processed every day for its customers.
- *Smart cards*—Smart cards are credit card sized cards with memory and a processor embedded on them. These cards can serve multiple purposes, such as credit and

debit functions, employee information, and mass transit ticketing information. These cards need an embedded database on board to deal with this information.

- *Personal Digital Assistants (PDAs)*—Handheld devices can have date books and other features that help you keep track of your appointments and meetings.

- *Medical devices*—Many medical devices have embedded databases, such as dialysis machines, ventilators, and pacemakers. Embedded databases should be self-reliant and robust in these devices for sure.

Handheld Databases

A neat tool is available to the consumer, called a Personal Digital Assistant, or PDA. There are many brands of PDAs to choose from, each having its own special features. PDAs run on an operating system designed for small computing platforms. The random access memory (RAM) is used for permanent storage. Because handheld PDAs run off a battery, their runtime is limited, as is the size of their screen. Table 23.3 lists some PDA manufacturers and the operating system they use. Later in this section, you will see a list of databases for each operating system.

TABLE 23.3   PDA's and their Operating Systems

PDA	Operating System
Palm	Palm OS
Handspring	Palm OS
Sony	Palm OS
Compaq	Microsoft Pocket PC 2002
Hewlett-Packard	Microsoft Pocket PC 2002
Toshiba	Microsoft Pocket PC 2002

As you can see from Table 23.3, two handheld operating systems cover several manufacturers' PDAs. The Palm OS has some built-in applications that use databases that are basically flat file databases. Several third-party database applications are available to the users of Palm OS-powered PDAs. Many specialized database applications have data all ready for use. The following list describes database applications that you can build your own database with.

- *ThinkDB*—ThinkDB is a useful database tool you can use to synchronize to various database server software by using .csv files. It is a good way to take your corporate data on the road. Small applications called TinyBytes can be created to help you organize the data. (For the Palm OS)

- *FileMaker Mobile*—This product lets you synchronize between your PDA and a FileMaker Pro 5 or 6 database. You are able to edit the data on the PDA, and when it is time to synchronize, the data is updated in the FileMaker Pro database. (For the Palm OS and Pocket PC)

- *HanDbase*—This handy database application gives the user the capability to create forms and synchronize with other database applications; the top–of–the–line version has ODBC driver capability. (For the Palm OS and Pocket PC)

A plethora of database products exists on the market for the Palm OS and Pocket PC. Most are databases designed for a specific purpose, such as a travel and expense database or a sales database. You can find one on the Web to fit your needs or use one of the previously listed products to build your own.

Mobile Databases

Mobile databases are necessary when a database user needs the information a database holds but cannot regularly access that data. An example of this is a traveling salesman. This person might have his laptop computer and a small printer with him when he makes sales calls. The information he needs to make the sale must be available to him and the information he gets from the customer must be saved for input into the main database.

Most mobile databases are just small footprint models of the databases they eventually connect to. The mobile version holds only the data needed for the user in a particular situation. At some point, the mobile database must synchronize with the main database so that any changes that have been made are reproduced in both. Figure 23.4 illustrates the use of mobile databases.

FIGURE 23.4
Mobile database usage.

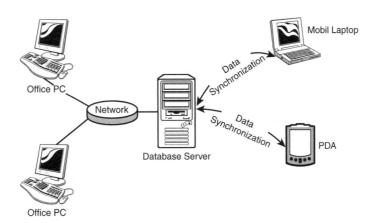

Mobile databases are necessary—and very popular in the business world. Just about every major database vendor has its own version of a mobile database system for use with its database server software. Table 23.4 lists some of the vendors who have mobile database solutions on the market today.

TABLE 23.4   Mobile Databases

Company	Product
Oracle	Oracle 9i Lite
Microsoft	SQL Server CE
Sybase	SQL Anywhere Studio
IBM	DB2 Everyplace

Data Storage and Migration

The modern database needs to utilize the latest technology to perform at its best and still be manageable. Recent advances in storage technology allow the size of most databases to be a non-factor in their administration. When old technology is phased out in corporate America, data and database migrations will be performed to utilize the newest in database technology. In this section the following topics are discussed:

- Massive data storage technologies
- Database migrations

Massive Data Storage

As databases become more intrinsic to everyday business, they can grow very large. Companies save years of data in data warehouses and use that data to forecast future trends in their businesses. As technology progresses, so does the area of electronic storage. Many types of mass storage devices and techniques can help solve the data storage problems. In this section, the different types and uses of mass storage are discussed.

Storage Area Networks

A storage area network, or SAN, is a computer or group of computers that reside on a special high-speed "network within a network," whose sole purpose is to provide many storage devices to a local area network (LAN) or a wide area network (WAN). On these LANs and WANs can be an array of different computers and servers that use the storage of the SAN. Figure 23.5 illustrates a simple SAN.

A SAN can be used for more than providing storage space for databases. It can be used to store database backups or used as disk space for any number of operating systems, file servers, applications, or even for file archiving and retrieval. A SAN is very scalable, which means the growth can be relatively painless to the IT manager.

FIGURE 23.5

A simple storage area network (SAN).

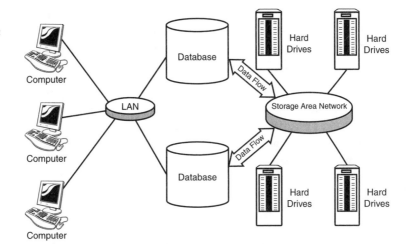

Directly Attached Storage

Most people who use computers are familiar with directly attached storage (DAS). When you buy a PC, it usually comes with a hard drive, a CD-ROM, a floppy drive, and maybe even a DVD drive. These storage devices are directly connected to the computer that uses them. This is a technology that has been around for quite some time and is still in use on most networks today. A good example of DAS in action is a file server on a network. The files accessed by users are stored on a file server computer's hard drive. The user's computer usually has a folder mapped to a portion of the file server's storage area, as shown in Figure 23.6.

FIGURE 23.6

A file server using directly attached storage (DAS).

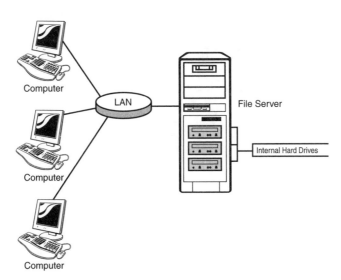

NEW TERM A *file server* is a computer that allows access to its file system from other computers on the network. It is often used to supplement space requirements of PCs. It can be used to set up a "shared" directory or directories for multi-user file sharing and collaboration.

The implementation of a DAS system on the network is inexpensive, but access speed and resource limitations can become a stumbling block when growth needs to occur. The access speed can be a bottleneck because the files are on a computer running an operating system such as Window NT or Novell, and when access to a file is needed, the operating system must be called on to do the work. The storage is limited partly because of the physical restraints of the computer hardware. You can have only so many hard drives on a box.

Network Attached Storage (NAS)

By consolidating the storage on a network, speed and scalability are greatly increased. A self-contained device that is easily attached to a network that contains storage media is called *network attached storage* (NAS). This device, sometimes called an appliance, has the appropriate software and hardware built in, including the storage media, a small, efficient operating system, and network connectivity hardware required to easily connect to any network. Figure 23.7 shows a NAS appliance in a heterogeneous computing environment.

FIGURE 23.7
A NAS appliance in a heterogeneous environment.

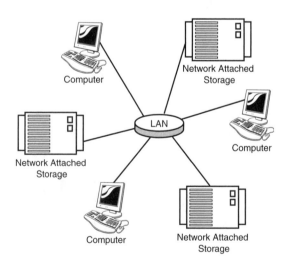

A NAS device is not really the best choice for holding database files because of the nature of its file-level interface. This device is optimized for serving shared files, or even for storing backups of database files.

NEW TERM A *file-level interface* is a device that serves well when users are accessing shared files. SAN and DAS access files use a block-level interface, which means that much smaller portions of the files can be accessed at any given time, which is the way database files are designed to be accessed.

Data Migrations

When a company has a need to move its data from one system to another or from one database to another, that is called a *data migration*. This section on data migrations is not a guide to that process. You will, however, be exposed to the tasks and tools needed for a successful data migration. In this section you will learn the following:

- Reasons for data migrations
- Some basic steps for data migration
- A list of available migration tools
- Companies that specialize in data migrations

Why Migrate?

Businesses today need to have fast access to their vital data to stay competitive. They also need to keep costs down as much as possible. One way to accomplish both is to put forth money and effort into modernizing the very heart of their business—their database. The following list shows some common reasons companies might want or need to migrate their current data system to a modern relational or object-oriented database:

- Data still resides on a mainframe.
- Current database technology is no longer supported.
- The company changed from one database vendor to another.
- The business is merging one or more databases into one.

If care is taken during the planning stages of a database migration, minimal downtime and no loss of existing data should occur.

NEW TERM *Data Migration* is the process of moving data from one system to another.

Basic Database Migration Steps

The most important part of a database migration is the planning stage. The better planned a migration is, the greater the likelihood of success. The following is a list of the basic steps that need to be taken for a successful database migration. These could vary depending on the scenario of the migration. For example, a great difference would exist between moving data from a mainframe using data in flat files to a server running an RDBMS and migrating from one RDBMS to another.

1. An analysis of the target and source systems should be accomplished. This analysis entails determining the best type of RDBMS to migrate to and what data needs to be transferred. These decisions are made based on the type of data to be migrated, the usage of that data, and the types of applications that access the data.

2. After the structure of the existing legacy data is known and understood, the design of the new database should begin. The design process will include any considerations such as porting existing legacy source code to the new database. The method of data transfer should also be considered during design. This can be a long, tedious process, but when it is done correctly, a robust system is likely to be born.

3. Methods are devised to pull the desired data out of the legacy system. These methods can vary depending on the target and source systems. This step may also include any data "cleaning" that might need to be done prior to loading it into the new system. Cleaning could also be a separate step.

4. Import the data using the methods identified during the design step. This step should include the analysis of the data after the import is complete. Ensure that the integrity of the data is intact and business rules have been adhered to. Any database procedures or code that needs to be ported to the new system also will occur during this step.

5. Extensive functional testing should be completed before any database goes into production. This includes any applications or middleware that accesses the data.

These basic steps are just that—basic! Plenty of time and effort should be spent on the migration so that the job gets done correctly.

Available Migration Tools

Several tools are designed to ease the burden of a data migration. Some of these tools are provided by the database vendors to help with a migration from a competing database to their database software. Table 23.5 lists some companies and their database migration tools.

TABLE 23.5 Database Migration Tools

Company	Product	Web URL
Net Migrations	XenoBridge Suite	www.netmigrations.com
Ispirer Systems	Chyfo 2.9.6	www.ispirer.com
RealSoftStudio	SQLPorter	www.realsoftstudio.com
Applied Database Technology	DataMAPPER 3.6	www.abdtech.com

Migration Services

Many consulting companies specialize in database migrations. Some are specialists on certain database platforms, and some will do migrations from any platform. There are several reasons why a company might want to employ a hired service rather than tackle that database migration on its own.

- The company might not have migration experts on staff.
- The more experienced service will be able to complete the migration in a reasonable time frame.
- Most migration services will support their work for a limited time.
- Internal resources are not exhausted during the migration.

Database Technology and Business

Two trends are emerging in how businesses handle the administration of their databases:

- Database hosting
- Remote database administration

These are services that businesses provide to other businesses. For example, a business provides support to handle another business's database administration needs. The following sections discuss these two trends.

Database Hosting

The software and hardware needed to operate a large enterprise database can be very expensive. With the hardware and software comes the need for maintenance and upgrades. For the small-to-medium size company that deals with large amounts of data, the solution could be to use another company's computers and software for their data.

A company that hosts databases usually has a data center with all the hardware and software required to run enterprise class databases. For a fee, these companies will "host," or let another company use their equipment. Depending on the amount of data and what the customer needs, a hosted database could reside on the same server as other databases. If required, a database hosting company could offer a dedicated server. Of course, this would cost more.

NEW TERM — *Database Hosting* is a service provided to customers where an organization will 'rent' it's software and hardware space to another organization so that they may store their data.

Many times, a hosting company will pair Web site hosting with database hosting. This allows the user of the hosting services to put its data on the Web. Figure 23.8 shows a basic database hosting setup.

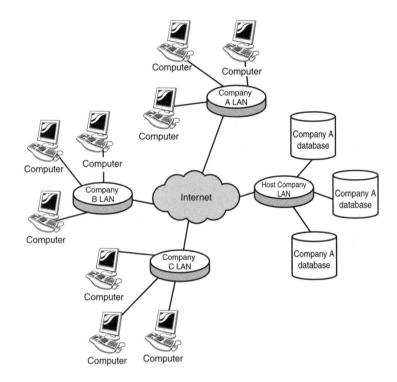

FIGURE 23.8

A database hosting setup.

Remote Database Administration

Database administration is an important task that has to be done to maintain today's corporate databases. Many tasks are involved in database administration, such as

- Proactively monitoring databases to ensure uptime
- Designing and implementing a backup and recovery plan
- Installing database software
- Ensuring that the database is running proficiently
- Protecting the data

Most of the preceding tasks are done by a database administrator (DBA). A DBA can wear many hats today. Larger companies can afford to hire a full-time DBA, but smaller companies might not be able to do so, even though they have the same size database to maintain. A possible solution to this problem is remote database administration (RDBA). An RDBA is a DBA who is not an employee of the database's company, but is contracted to maintain the data from a remote location. The RDBA can connect to and maintain any database, anywhere in the world, where permission is granted to access that database. Following are some reasons why your company might consider using an RDBA:

- Eliminate DBA training costs
- No employee benefit costs
- Can be done on a part-time basis
- Relieve some workload from current DBA
- Save money on office space and equipment
- Cannot afford a full-time DBA

The use of an RDBA can be a big cost-saving move, but it is not for every company. If you need to have a full-time DBA onsite or the DBA has to be present at meetings, an RDBA might not be the answer.

NEW TERM *Remote Database Administration* is the administration of a database from a remote or off-site location.

Companies that offer RDBA services vary in the services they offer, but the end goal is the same. They will take care of your databases to the level agreed upon. This level of agreement is called a Service Level Agreement. With this, you are guaranteed the service you are paying for—no more, no less. Table 23.6 lists some companies that offer RDBA services.

TABLE 23.6 RDBA Service Providers

Company	Web URL
Perpetual Technologies Inc.	www.perptech.com
DBAZone Inc.	www.dbazone.com
Xtivia Technologies Inc.	www.virtual-dba.com
TUSC	www.tusc.com

Summary

In this hour you learned the concepts of object orientation, such as data abstraction, encapsulation, and inheritance and how they relate to object-oriented databases. A simple overview of the Java programming language was presented, along with an overview of what a Java-embedded database is. Embedded, handheld, and mobile databases were discussed, and you learned how this technology can be used in the business world. The different technologies used to store the massive amounts of data in today's databases was discussed, along with a simple step-by-step overview of data migration. You also learned what remote database administration and database hosting are, and how they may be beneficial.

Workshop

The following workshop is composed of quiz questions and practical exercises. The quiz questions are designed to test your overall understanding of the current material. The practical exercises are intended to afford you the opportunity to apply the concepts discussed during the current hour, as well as build on the knowledge acquired in previous hours of study. Please take time to complete this workshop before continuing. You may refer to the answers at the end of this hour.

Quiz

1. How are Java programs and procedures able to run on any platform?
2. Why are mobile databases necessary in today's business world?
3. Why would a company choose RDBA over hiring a DBA?
4. What is the most important step in a database migration?

Exercises

1. Write down the steps to migrate a database at your work to another platform.

Answers to Quiz

1. A Java program is able to run on any platform where there is a Virtual Machine. The Java code is compiled only once into bytecodes on the platform it will run on. From then on, the VM will interpret those bytecodes for the platform.
2. Businesses rely on their data in today's world. That data must be available at all times. When a user can't get to the database, a subset of that data can be made available through mobile databases.
3. A small–to-medium size company might not be able to afford a full-time DBA to maintain its data. A larger company might want to relieve some of the workload of its full- time DBAs by utilizing a RDBA.
4. The planning stage is the most important step. A well-planned database migration will run more smoothly than a poorly planned migration.

Hour **24**

Where Do I Go from Here?

Now that you have been introduced to the database world and you understand what databases are and how they function, it is time to go one step further. In this hour, you will discover what you can do to further your understanding of databases and pursue a career in database technologies.

In this final hour, you will learn how to set up a career path, choose training options, obtain certifications, and keep your database skills up to date.

The objectives of this hour are

- How to choose a database vendor and a career path with that vendor's product.
- Learn about the training options that are available.
- How to stay current in your technical skills.
- How to get hands-on experience with your new skills.
- Obtaining certifications and using them for your advantage.

Choosing a Database Vendor

The first step in getting started on a career path in database technologies is to choose a database software package to learn thoroughly. A variety of database software is available in today's market—Microsoft, Oracle, and DB2 to name a few. It is very difficult to learn more than one or two database systems in sufficient detail. Most professionals choose one system and learn it inside and out. This becomes the system that they use daily.

When researching which database management system is right for you, the Internet can play an important role. Internet searches are easy to perform and can be efficient. You can gather and learn a lot of information in a short amount of time.

A great Web site that covers databases and database careers is `http://databases.about.com/mbody.htm`. This site contains numerous articles about database technologies and pursuing careers in database technology. These articles are well written and worth reading.

Choosing a Career Path

You can choose from a variety of paths when selecting a career in database technologies. If you plan to be a database administrator, the ultimate position in database technologies, you must plan your training courses so that they provide the instruction required to pass the relevant certification examinations. You can start your database career as a database designer or developer and then use these positions as stepping-stones to achieve the position of database administrator. Many database administrators have risen through the ranks in this manner. In fact, most database administrators have experience as a database designer or developer. It is not uncommon for database administrators to have experience in system administration. Frequently, when the database administrator leaves the company, the system administrator takes over the position.

Careers in Database Technology

When you plan a career in database technologies, a variety of choices are available. Some of the common database career paths include

- *Database developer*—Develops database applications using GUI design and GUI report tools.
- *Database designer*—Designs logical and physical databases using design tools. These database design tools are also called CASE tools. (CASE stand for Computer Aided System Engineering.)

- *Database administrator (DBA)*—Performs database maintenance and monitoring. Examples include database optimization and tuning; creation, implementation, and verification of database backups; creation and maintenance of database security procedures; installation of patches and upgrades to the database; and management of database licenses. The DBA also collaborates with project managers and developers during requirements definition.

Training

Depending on the amount of time and money you are willing to spend, you can learn about database technology in various ways. First, for any database technology specialty you choose, visit the company's Web site and review their training recommendations. Several vendors have a recommended curriculum outlined on their Web sites. Also on these Web sites, you will find other useful information, such as instructor-led courses, college courses, or self-study books.

24

Instructor-Led Courses

Instructor-led courses are very intensive and costly, but they definitely have strong benefits. Students can interact with the instructors and other students in the class to make the most of the material being presented.

Most instructor-led classes involve hands-on training. This provides the student with valuable experience in an assisted environment. If the student encounters an error or needs clarification on a point, the instructor is available to help.

Another benefit of instructor-led courses is that many instructors are employed in the database field. They bring knowledge of the database system and industry experience to the classroom. There is no substitute for experience.

One of the drawbacks regarding instructor-led training is that the lectures are fast paced. If a student is completely new to the information technologies field, it may take some time to adjust to the class. There is a chance that some new students may fall behind.

Online Courses

Online courses cost less than instructor-led classes, but they require motivation on the part of the student. People often lose interest in online training. They get tired of clicking the mouse button and reading through pages of text. When choosing an online course, always pick one that is interactive. The interactive course should consist of a number of quizzes and simulations to retain the student's interest. Most online training courses also provide some type of interaction with the instructor. This instructor interaction might be via online chat, message boards, and/or traditional email.

Computer-Based Training

Computer-based training (CBT) courses are taught via downloaded software or CD-ROM. CBT courses are one of the best ways to get up to speed if you are completely new to the information technology field. These courses are self-paced and the students have an opportunity to take the course over again if the concepts are not clear. Before taking an instructor-led course, it is a good idea to complete some computer-based training courses that cover the subject matter. The computer-based training will help you to get more out of the instructor-led classes.

 CBT or Computer Based Training is software that is designed to instruct the user in a course of study.

Self–Study Courses

Self-study courses come in the form of a kit. Usually, there are several study books or reference books with a CD-ROM for the software being taught. Self-study kits are mostly for people who are well disciplined and are willing to devote a lot of time studying the material provided in the kits. We all know that studying about the databases is not the only thing we are working on. Most people already have a full-time job, and they are learning databases either to start a second career or to add new skills to their current ones. A variety of self-paced courses are available on the market today. These courses can be easily found online. Check www.amazon.com and www.bookpool.com for self-study materials. On Amazon.com, you can find some used courses. Buying used can save you a substantial amount of money.

Boot Camps

Boot camps are highly intensive training programs. They usually last from one to three weeks and are geared for students to pass certification exams. Boot camps are quite expensive but include everything needed to pass the certification exams. The tuition for these boot camps is usually several thousand dollars, depending on the certification being pursued. The program cost typically includes room, board, lectures, study material, practice exams, and exam vouchers. Boot camps are the perfect solution for people who already have knowledge about the software and want to concentrate on passing the certification exam. During boot camp, classes are long and labor intensive. Classes during the boot camp tend to last 12 hours and meals are usually served during the class. After lectures the students devote a lot of time to hands-on exercises and practice exams.

Following are some of the Web sites to get more information about the boot camps:

www.asap-computer.com

www.ccprep.com

www.drake.intl.on.ca

www.bootcamp2000.com

www.mcseacademy.com

www.learnquick.com

www.ntschool.com

www.trainingcamp.net

www.wavetech.com

Certifications

Certification is the hot thing in the information technology field. These days, when businesses hire people, they look for certification(s) in related fields. In the database field, a
variety of certifications are available from a variety of database vendors. Certifications
exist for database developer, database designer, content manager, and database
administrator.

By getting a professional certificate, you validate your skills and demonstrate proficiency
with the database product. It gives the employer confidence in the employee.
Certification programs are designed to validate your skills and demonstrate your proficiency with the software product. Certifications will help you excel in your position by
giving you and your employer confidence that your skills have withstood certification
testing. Certification can also help place you on a faster career track.

Some of the most popular database certifications are described in the following sections:

Microsoft Certified Database Administrator (MCDBA)

This certification is designed to show your skills with Microsoft SQL Server. To be certified, you must pass three core exams and an elective.

Core Exam I: SQL Server Administration   One of these two exams will qualify you
for this section, depending on the software version. Both exams cover database administration and troubleshooting skills.

- Exam 70-028, covering SQL Server 7.0
- Exam 70-228, covering SQL Server 2000

Core Exam II: SQL Server Design   One of these two exams will qualify you for this
section, depending on the software version. Both exams in this section deal with successfully designing and implementing the SQL Server.

- Exam 70-029, covering SQL Server 7.0
- Exam 70-229, covering SQL Server 2000

24

Core Exam III: Networking Systems   Only one exam qualifies for this section and is common for both software versions.

- Exam 70-215, Installing, Configuring, and Administering Microsoft Windows 2000 Server

Microsoft plans to offer Exam 70-275, Installing, Configuring, and Administering Microsoft .NET Enterprise Server. After this exam is released, this exam will also qualify you for this section.

Elective Exam   For this section, a number of exams are offered on a variety of topics. For example, application development techniques, data warehousing, and network design fundamentals qualify for this requirement.

Some of these exams can also be counted for other Microsoft certifications such as Microsoft Certified Systems Engineer (MCSE), Microsoft Certified System Administrator (MCSA), and Microsoft Certified Solution Developer (MCSD). By carefully planning the order of the exams, you can save time and money by applying the exams to multiple certifications.

For more information about the Microsoft certifications, go to the following Web site:

```
http://www.microsoft.com/traincert/default.asp
```

Oracle Certified Professional (OCP)

If you visit Oracle's Web site, Oracle describes their certification as a three-step process.

Step 1. Choose an Oracle certification path. Oracle offers a variety of certification paths.

Step 2. When pursuing a career in Oracle technology, you need to read the Oracle Certification Program Candidate Agreement.

Step 3. Prepare for the exam. There are a variety of ways to prepare for any of Oracle's certifications.

Oracle recommends taking instructor-led courses in combination with technology-based training, which is the same as computer-based training.

In addition to instructor-led training, Oracle offers technology-based training, online courses, seminars, and self-study kits. Any of these courses will enable you to pass the certification exams.

Oracle offers the following certifications paths:

Database Administrator

- Oracle 8i Track

- Oracle 9i Track
- Upgrade to Oracle 9i Exam

Oracle Application Developer

- Oracle Forms Developer, Release 6.o and 6i Track
- Oracle Certified Solutions Developer Track
- Oracle Certified Enterprise Developer Track

For more information about the Oracle certifications, visit the following Web site:

`http://www.oracle.com/education/certification/`

IBM DB2

To qualify as an IBM Certified Solutions Expert for DB2, Database Administration for UNIX, Windows, and OS/2 certification, candidates must pass the following:

- Test 509 Fundamentals
- Test 510 Database Administration

Test 509, Fundamentals Objectives　This exam covers DB2 database fundamental topics in the following areas:

- Installation, Planning, Security, and Instances
- Creating and Accessing DB2 Databases
- Basic SQL Usage
- Database Objects and Database Concurrency

Test 510, Database Administration Objectives　This exam covers DB2 Database Administration topics in the following areas:

- DB2 Universal Database Server Management
- Data Placement
- Database Access
- Monitoring DB2 Universal Database Activity
- DB2 Utilities
- Database Recovery, Maintenance, and Problem Determination

For more information about the IBM DB2 certifications, see the following Web site:

`http://www-3.ibm.com/software/data/db2/`

24

Test Preparation Software

Self Test Software, Inc. and Trascenders.com offer sample exams and preparation guides that can help you prepare for any of the preceding certification exams. These exams are structured like the corresponding certification exams and are great for last-minute preparation. Self Test Software, Inc. also has a test preparation tool called Flash Card. This tool is similar to the flash cards students make in high school and college.

For more information about exam questions, go to the following Web sites:

```
http://www.selftestsoftware.com/dept.asp?dept%5Fid=600&
```

```
http://www.readmedoc.com/promo/transcender.asp
```

Hands-on Experience

It is very hard to find a good job if you lack industry experience. One of the best ways to gain experience is to volunteer your services to a local church or nonprofit organization. You will get experience and help the community at the same time.

Internships are another good way to get this experience. A lot of businesses offer internship positions in their organizations, but these positions do not always pay. Some of the internship positions can turn into full-time paid positions, however. The reason businesses offer internships is because it gives businesses an opportunity to evaluate the intern. If the intern meets the needs of the business, and the position filled by the intern is beneficial to the business, the intern might be offered a full-time position. Internships offer businesses a cheap labor supply and, at the same time, allow interns to pick up experience necessary to get a full-time paid position.

Not everybody is lucky enough to find a volunteer position or an internship. Another option is to set up a computer lab at home. Personal computers are now relatively inexpensive. Two or three personal computers can make a great personal computer lab. Connect these computers into a network with network cards, cables, and a hub. Large computer labs at schools and computer institutes have similar setups, just on a larger scale. When setting up a computer lab at home, one of the personal computers can be configured as a server and the other two as clients.

When setting up a personal lab, it would be wise to replicate a real-world network configuration. Install the database software on a machine designated as a server. This mimics the way that it is done in the real world; database servers are used solely for the database management system software. Other daily-use software should not be installed on the server. Client machines, on the other hand, can sport all sorts of other software.

See Figure 24.1 for a sample home computer lab:

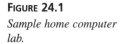

Figure 24.1

Sample home computer lab.

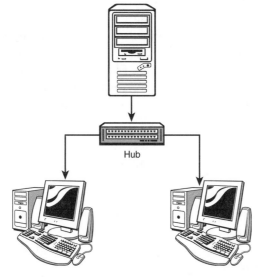

24

Staying Current with Technology

After you reach the status of database professional, the learning never stops. New database software versions, patches, upgrades, modifications, and so on are released frequently. As a database professional, you are expected to keep up with new technologies and industry standards.

Publications

Publications are a great way to keep up with current technology issues. Free technology magazines are offered online. However, the publishers of these magazines expect you to fill out a survey in exchange for the publication. After you complete the survey, you are offered a free monthly periodical.

Following are some of the links to follow for free information technology magazines:

```
http://otn.oracle.com
```

```
http://www.omeda.com/ziff/ewk/ewk.cgi?&t=whback&p=hpnav2
```

```
http://www.intelligententerprise.com/
```

Book a Month

Allocate a small amount in your budget to buy one new book each month or every other month. You will develop a good reference library and stay current on the new technologies.

Learning New Technology

The demand for professionals in database technology is high, and the competition for jobs is intense. Individuals, experienced or new to the profession, need to know what skills make them attractive job candidates. Employers look closely at candidates who have solid foundations of technology skills. As the demand for database administrators increases, it is important to remain current with technology trends.

It is becoming increasingly important for database administrators to have skills other than database administration. The best way to learn what skills compliment a certain database technology is to search job postings.

Web Technology Experience

More and more businesses are taking their applications to the Web. Employees who have Web skills in combination with database design skills are in demand for this certain market. Having experience with one of the application servers greatly enhances your career in database technologies.

System Administration Experience

Consider the small companies with limited budgets that require the database administrator to double as the system administrator. In companies like that, having both skills puts a candidate in a good position for a higher salary.

Application Developer Experience

If you want to become a database application developer, having programming language skills will greatly increase your success rate when searching for a job. Hot languages to know these days include Java, C, C++, and Microsoft's .NET.

Setting Your Career Agenda

When considering a career in database technology, it is important to have a plan. Specify goals with dates, and try hard to achieve those goals on time. You will be able to tell if you are on track or straying away, and when you are ready to seek employment—you will know! See Figure 24.2 for a sample learning plan.

FIGURE 24.2
Sample learning plan for database technology careers.

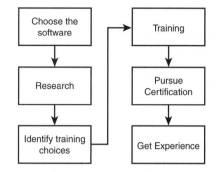

Summary

Now that you have learned about databases and the technology involved, you might be interested in pursuing a related career. A variety of specializations are available in the database technology profession. After a specific area is chosen, a software vendor should be researched for information, training requirements, and training recommendations. A variety of training options exist. Careful planning and selecting the right methods should help you meet these training requirements. After the training has been completed, it is time to pick up hands-on experience. Remember to look to local churches and nonprofit organizations for volunteer opportunities. After you have experience, and possibly a position, stay current with technology. This is a very critical part of any field. Numerous sources exist that can help you stay current. When you are in the information technology field, learning never stops!

Workshop

The following workshop is composed of quiz questions and practical exercises. The quiz questions are designed to test your overall understanding of the current material. The practical exercises are intended to afford you the opportunity to apply the concepts discussed during the current hour, as well as build on the knowledge acquired in previous hours of study. Please take time to complete this workshop before continuing. You can refer to the answers at the end of the hour.

Quiz

1. List three common database-related careers.

2. Name three common database application development languages.

3. Why is it so important to stay current with technology?

Exercises

1. Visit the following database vendor Web sites and identify their certification requirements.

   - Oracle Corporation

   - Microsoft Corporation

   - IBM Corporation

2. Go to the About.com Web site and study their database career guide.

3. Go to the following Web site and register for the free "e week" magazine.

   `http://www.omeda.com/ziff/ewk/ewk.cgi?&t=whback&p=hpnav2`

Answers to Quiz

1. List three common database related careers.

   Database developer

   Database designer

   Database administrator

2. Name three common database application development languages.

   Java

   C

   C++

3. Why is it so important to stay current with technology?

   Database technology is always changing. If you do not stay current, your knowledge can grow stale, and your value to the database market can decrease.

PART VII
Appendices

Appendix

APPENDIX A

SQL Command Quick Reference

SQL Statements

ALTER TABLE

```
ALTER TABLE TABLE_NAME
[MODIFY | ADD | DROP]
 [COLUMN COLUMN_NAME][DATATYPE|NULL NOT NULL] [RESTRICT|CASCADE]
[ADD | DROP] CONSTRAINT CONSTRAINT_NAME]
```

Description: Alters a table's columns.

COMMIT

```
COMMIT [ TRANSACTION ]
```

Description: Saves a transaction to the database.

CREATE DOMAIN

```
CREATE DOMAIN DOMAIN_NAME AS DATA_TYPE [ NULL | NOT NULL]
```

Description: Creates a domain—an object that is associated with a data type and constraints.

CREATE INDEX

```
CREATE INDEX INDEX_NAME
ON TABLE_NAME (COLUMN_NAME)
```

Description: Creates an index on a table.

CREATE ROLE

```
CREATE ROLE ROLE NAME
[ WITH ADMIN [CURRENT_USER | CURRENT_ROLE]]
```

Description: Creates a database role to which system and object privileges can be granted.

CREATE TABLE

```
CREATE TABLE TABLE_NAME
( COLUMN1  DATA_TYPE  [NULL|NOT NULL],
 COLUMN2  DATA_TYPE  [NULL|NOT NULL]É)
```

Description: Creates a database table.

CREATE TABLE AS

```
CREATE TABLE TABLE_NAME AS
SELECT COLUMN1, COLUMN2,...
FROM TABLE_NAME
[ WHERE CONDITIONS ]
[ GROUP BY COLUMN1, COLUMN2,...]
[ HAVING CONDITIONS ]
```

Description: Creates a database table based on another table.

CREATE TYPE

```
CREATE TYPE typename AS OBJECT
( COLUMN1  DATA_TYPE  [NULL|NOT NULL],
 COLUMN2  DATA_TYPE  [NULL|NOT NULL]É)
```

Description: Creates a user-defined type that can be used to define columns in a table.

CREATE VIEW

```
CREATE VIEW AS
SELECT COLUMN1, COLUMN2,...
FROM TABLE_NAME
[ WHERE CONDITIONS ]
[ GROUP BY COLUMN1, COLUMN2,... ]
[ HAVING CONDITIONS ]
```

Description: Creates a view of a table.

DELETE

```
DELETE
FROM TABLE_NAME
[ WHERE CONDITIONS ]
```

Description: Deletes rows of data from a table.

DROP INDEX

```
DROP INDEX INDEX_NAME
```

Description: Drops an index on a table.

DROP TABLE

```
DROP TABLE TABLE_NAME
```

Description: Drops a table from the database.

DROP VIEW

```
DROP VIEW VIEW_NAME
```

Description: Drops a view of a table.

GRANT

```
GRANT PRIVILEGE1, PRIVILEGE2, ... TO USER_NAME
```

Description: Grants privileges to a user.

INSERT

```
INSERT INTO TABLE_NAME [ (COLUMN1, COLUMN2,...]
VALUES ('VALUE1','VALUE2',...)
```

Description: Inserts new rows of data into a table.

A

INSERT...SELECT

```
INSERT INTO TABLE_NAME
SELECT COLUMN1, COLUMN2
FROM TABLE_NAME
[ WHERE CONDITIONS ]
```

Description: Inserts new rows of data into a table based on data in another table.

REVOKE

```
REVOKE PRIVILEGE1, PRIVILEGE2, ... FROM USER_NAME
```

Description: Revokes privileges from a user.

ROLLBACK

```
ROLLBACK [ TO SAVEPOINT_NAME ]
```

Description: Undoes a database transaction.

SAVEPOINT

```
SAVEPOINT SAVEPOINT_NAME
```

Description: Creates transaction SAVEPOINTs in which to ROLLBACK if necessary.

SELECT

```
SELECT [ DISTINCT ] COLUMN1, COLUMN2,...
FROM TABLE1, TABLE2,...
[ WHERE CONDITIONS ]
[ GROUP BY COLUMN1, COLUMN2,...]
[ HAVING CONDITIONS ]
[ ORDER BY COLUMN1, COLUMN2,...]
```

Description: Returns data from one or more database tables; used to create queries.

UPDATE

```
UPDATE TABLE_NAME
SET COLUMN1 = 'VALUE1',
  COLUMN2 = 'VALUE2',...
[ WHERE CONDITIONS ]
```

Description: Updates existing data in a table.

SQL Clauses

SELECT

```
SELECT *

SELECT COLUMN1, COLUMN2,...

SELECT DISTINCT (COLUMN1)

SELECT COUNT(*)
```

Description: Defines columns to display as part of query output.

FROM

```
FROM TABLE1, TABLE2, TABLE3,...
```

Description: Defines tables from which to retrieve data.

WHERE

```
WHERE COLUMN1 = 'VALUE1'
 AND COLUMN2 = 'VALUE2'
...

WHERE COLUMN1 = 'VALUE1'
  OR COLUMN2 = 'VALUE2'
...
WHERE COLUMN IN ('VALUE1' [, 'VALUE2'] )
```

Description: Defines conditions (criteria) placed on a query for data to be returned.

GROUP BY

```
GROUP BY GROUP_COLUMN1, GROUP_COLUMN2,...
```

Description: A form of a sorting operation; used to divide output into logical groups.

HAVING

```
HAVING GROUP_COLUMN1 = 'VALUE1'
  AND GROUP_COLUMN2 = 'VALUE2'
...
```

Description: Similar to the WHERE clause; used to place conditions on the GROUP BY clause.

A

ORDER BY

```
ORDER BY COLUMN1, COLUMN2,...

ORDER BY 1,2,...
```

Description: Used to sort a query's results.

APPENDIX B

Glossary

alias   An alternative name for a database object, such as a column or table. Aliases are also called synonyms.

ANSI (American National Standards Institute)   ANSI is an organization that provides standards for various industries, such as that of the computer and relational databases.

atomic value   A value that occurs only one time per row in a table.

attribute   The smallest structure in an RDBMS. The data stored represents a characteristic of the subject of the table. An attribute is also known as a field.

Boolean value   A value consisting of one of the following values: TRUE, FALSE, or NULL. Boolean values are typically used as switches and are common in database programs.

Boyce-Codd NORMAL FORM   This form is in effect when an entity is in THIRD NORMAL FORM and when every attribute or combination of attributes (a determinant) on which another attribute is functionally dependent is a candidate key (that is, unique).

BPR (business process reengineering)   The process of revising existing business processes and data model features to improve the daily operations of a business through the use of the current information system.

business function   A process or related block of work that a business needs to accomplish in the course of meeting its business goals. Functions can be studied and manipulated to support different and better ways to accomplish these tasks.

business modeling   Capturing the needs of a business from a business perspective.

business process   The daily activities that take place in a commercial venture.

business process reengineering   The task of redesigning an existing system to improve business processes and methods for storing and accessing the data.

business requirement   A mandate for how the business should operate in order to function on a daily basis.

business rule   A rule that places restrictions and limitations on a database, based on how the company uses the data.

business system life cycle   The seven stages that make up the development of a business system. The stages are strategy, analysis, design, build, documentation, transition, and production. The business system life cycle is also known as the development life cycle.

canned transaction   A transaction that is embedded into a user interface, designed to perform a specific task, and cannot be modified from its intended purpose.

cardinality   The multiplicity of possible relationships between entities, such as one-to-one, one-to-many, and many-to-many. For instance, an instance in one entity may have multiple matching instances in a second entity.

Cartesian product   The result set of a multitable query with no join operation, matching every row in the first table with every row in the second table. The Cartesian product shows all possible combinations of data between tables and should be avoided in most cases.

CASE (Computer Aided Systems Engineering)   A combination of software tools used to assist developers in developing and maintaining systems for the end user.

catalog   The database objects to which a user has access.

change control   A mechanism for achieving a smooth transition between software versions; it is essential to avoid disrupting the work of users.

client/server   This environment involves a main computer, called a server, and one or more personal computers (clients) that are networked to the server.

cold backup   A process in which the database is shut down and all the physical files associated with the database are copied using operating system utilities.

column   Also known as a field, it is a subdivision of a table. A column is assigned a specific data type.

composite or concatenated key   The combination of two or more column values used to define a key in a table.

constraint   Rules and or restrictions to control data integrity.

cursor   A pointer to a row in a table. Cursors are created automatically by the RDBMS when SQL commands are issued to access data.

data   A collection of information.

data dictionary   Also called system catalog. Stores metadata about the database, such as users, objects, space allocation and consumption, and privileges.

data integrity   The assurance of accurate data in the database.

data integrity   The maintenance of accurate, valid, and consistent data; this is a major concern for the design of any database.

data migration   See migration.

data modeling   The process of visually representing data for a business and then eventually converting the business model into a data model.

data redundancy   See redundant data.

data type   The particular type of data that is stored. Common data types are number, varchar2, and date.

data warehouse   A database that is designated as read-only. Modification to data occurs during offline hours.

database   A database is a collection of files or tables owned by a database management system.

dataflow   A named flow of data among datastores, functions, and any external entities.

DBA (database administrator)   A person who manages the database. The DBA is responsible for installing database updates, database patches, assisting with development of schemas, and maintaining good database performance (among other things).

B

DBMS (Database Management System)   A software product that allows the storage and access of data.

denormalization   The process of taking a normalized database and modifying table structures to allow controlled redundancy for increased database performance.

DFD (data flow diagram)   The DFD shows processes and data flows like the process modeler, but it also assigns an ID number to each process.

distributed database   A database that exists on several computers throughout a network. Distributed databases offer performance advantages.

domain   A domain is a set of business data validation rules, data range limits, and data type and data format standards that will be applied to attributes of common types.

domain tables   Tables that are used to enumerate acceptable values for attributes in other tables.

DSS (Decision Support System)   Databases that hold data destined to be processed.

entities   Classes of things of importance about which data must be stored or manipulated in the course of business processes. Entities are the nouns of your information system. Entities represent one occurrence of an object. An entity may have only one value for any attribute at any one time. See subtype entity and supertype entity.

equi join   The type of join operation that merges data from two tables based on equality of compared key values.

ERD (Entity Relationship Diagram)   A tool used in the analysis phase of development to model the initial design of your data structures in an unconstrained, logical environment.

ERD process   The ERD process models logical data structures during the analysis phase of system development.

FHD (functional hierarchy diagram)   Best for displaying the process hierarchy. An FHD can show processes in various levels of decomposition (parent and child processes) depending on the point of interest at the time.

field   See column.

firewall   A combination of hardware and software intended to keep hackers out of your network while letting in those who are allowed access.

flat-file database   A database composed of readable text files. It stores records as lines in a file with columns that are fixed length or separated by some delimiter.

Foreign Key   The combination of one or more column values in a table that reference a primary key in another table. In other words, a child key that references a parent key.

functions   Blocks of code within the database; also known as methods.

GUI (graphical user interface)   A presentable, visual display that allows the use of the keyboard and the mouse. An example is a user input form.

hierarchical database   The structure of a hierarchical database uses a single table as the root of an inverted tree. The other tables act as branches going down from the root table.

history tables   Tables that are used to track changes to other tables.

hot backup   Backup that occurs while the database is operational.

index   An index is an object in a relational database that is used to increase performance of data retrieval. An index can also be used to enforce uniqueness of values.

inner join   A join that tests for equality between key values in two tables. See equi join.

ISO (International Standards Organization)   An organization that works in conjunction with ANSI to provide standards for various industries, such as the SQL3 (SQL-99) standard for relational databases.

JDBC   Java's database programming interface. Allows seamless connectivity to different types of databases.

join   A method of combining two or more tables, and in some cases a table with itself, to retrieve necessary data.

join table   A table that resolves a relationship between two other tables, which would otherwise have a single many-to-many relationship, into two one-to-many relationships

key   In the relational database, a key is a column that contains unique values. No duplicates can be present in a key column. See also primary key, foreign key.

legacy database   A database that is currently in use by a company.

locks   A mechanism used to restrict user access to a row of data while that same row is being modified by another user, to maintain consistency.

log tables   Tables that are used to record events such as updates, program exceptions, or various user activities.

logical backup   Data is exported from the database into export files.

B

logical database   Related data that is stored in one or more schemas.

logical modeling   Gathering business requirements and converting those requirements into a model.

mainframe   A large, central server that can be accessed directly or over a network with "dumb terminals" (a monitor and keyboard).

metadata   Data about other data.

metadata tables   Tables that are used to record information about other information, such as descriptions of other tables and table columns or notes on the database design.

migration   The process of moving data from one database management system to another, usually to meet the requirements of a new application environment.

mission objective   An objective that lists the tasks that will be performed against the data in a database.

mission statement   A summation of the overall purpose of a proposed database system.

multimedia database   A database designed to efficiently store and manipulate large objects such as movies, music, text, and video. Multimedia databases differ from object and object-relational databases in that they are optimized to handle the demands of multimedia files.

multitier environment   A computing environment in which functionality is divided among layers of computers. Layers are separated to provide security, performance, and efficiency.

network   A connection between computers to exchange information or data.

network database   A database structured as an inverted tree. Several inverted trees can share branches and still be considered in the same database structure. Tables in a network database are related by one table as an owner and the other table(s) as members.

NORMAL FORM   A degree of normalization, such as FIRST NORMAL FORM, SECOND NORMAL FORM, and THIRD NORMAL FORM. The THIRD NORMAL FORM is typically the highest degree of normalization applied in real-world production environments. However, additional NORMAL FORMS exist, such as Boyce-Codd, FOURTH, and FIFTH —these forms are used more in theory, but not realistically practiced.

normalization   The process of reducing the redundancy of data in a relational database.

Not NULL   Not NULL is a form of constraint on a column in a table. If a column is labeled as Not NULL, the column must contain data.

NULL   A form of constraint on a column in a table. If a column is labeled as NULL, the column may or may not contain data.

object   Used to represent or access data in an RDBMS; also known as an element. Common types of objects are tables and indexes. An object in an object-oriented database is a unit of storage. Objects are organized and created in object-oriented programming languages and then mapped to the object-oriented database.

object-oriented database (OO)   The OO database design is based on object-oriented analysis and design. An OO database combines database capabilities with an OO programming language, such as Java or C++. Object orientation views programming and database elements as objects with properties that can be distributed to or inherited from other objects.

object-relational database (OR)   An object-relational database supports not only the RDBMS features but also object-oriented features such as inheritance and encapsulation.

ODBC (Open Database Connectivity)   A driver that allows the connection of a client to a remote relational database.

ODL (Object Definition Language)   Used to define object storage in an object-oriented database.

OLAP (Online Analytical Processing)   OLAP databases are designed for a high volume of transactions that do not modify the data (select queries).

OLTP (Online Transaction Processing)   OLTP databases are designed for a high volume of transactions that actually modify the data (insert, update, delete queries).

OML (Object Manipulation Language)   Used to modify the state of object data inside the object database.

optionality   The optionality of a relationship is either "must be" or "may be." Optionality is used to specify whether a relationship between two or more entities is optional or required.

outer join   An equi join that shows all data from the first table even if a matching key value does not exist in the second table.

packages   Objects that logically arrange procedures and functions into groups.

physical database   A physical database consists of the data files.

physical modeling   Physical modeling involves the actual design of a database according to the requirements that were established during logical modeling.

primary key   The combination of one or more column values in a table that make a row of data unique within the table.

procedure   An object that allows an operation to be performed against one or more database tables.

process control tables   Tables used to set up parameters and manage events for internal or external processes that may be managed by the database.

programmer analyst   Examines the database application system design and determines necessary outputs. Outputs include reports, screens, and output files.

privilege   A privilege can be a system-level or object-level permission to perform a specific action in the database.

query   A database request, written in SQL, for data that meets given criteria.

query language   A high-level language that is used to update, retrieve, insert, or otherwise modify data stored within a database.

RAID (Redundant Arrays of Inexpensive Disks)   The use of multiple storage devices to stripe data to increase performance and to store redundant data in case of hardware failure.

RDBMS (Relational Database Management System)   A program used to store and retrieve data that is organized into tables.

record   A set of fields in a table. It is also known as a row.

record type   A predetermined set of fields within a file.

redundant data   The same data that is stored in more than one location in the database.

referential integrity   Referential integrity guarantees that values of one column will depend on the values from another column. Enforcement is through integrity constraints.

relationship   A two-directional connection between two entities. In some cases, an entity will have a relationship with itself. This is called a recursive relationship.

relational database   A database model in which data is stored in tables or relations.

requirements analysis   The process of analyzing the needs of a business and gathering system requirements from the end user, which will eventually become the building blocks for the new database.

requirements gathering   The process of conducting meetings and/or interviews with customers, end users, and other individuals in the company to establish the requirements for the proposed system.

role   A privilege or a set of privileges that may be granted to users of a database. Roles provide security by restricting what actions users may perform in a database.

row   A primary key value and columnar data associated with a particular instance of a table.

schema   An owner of objects in a relational database.

security table   A security table stores user data such as name, phone number, systems assigned to, and so forth.

self join   A join that merges data from a table with data in the same table, based on columns in a table that are related to one another.

server   A computer on a network that supplies a certain service, such as a database, to other computers on the network.

SQL (Structured Query Language)   The standard language of relational databases.

staging tables   Tables that are used as a temporary storage location when batch-loading data in order to insulate production tables from unexpected events that may occur during loading.

subset table   Subset tables contain columns that describe specific versions of the subject that is in the main table. Columns that would represent the same characteristics in the subset table as in the main table should be only in the main table.

subtype entity   A subtype entity is an entity that has common attributes and relationships. A subtype entity may have lower levels.

supertype entity   A supertype entity is an entity that has a subtype entity.

synonyms   Alternative names for database objects. Synonyms are also called aliases.

system analyst   Examines a database and the requirements of software applications and designs suitable queries to interface the database and the application.

table   A grouping of columns of data that pertains to a single, particular class of people, things, events, or ideas in an enterprise, about which information needs to be stored or calculations made.

TCP/IP   The standard data communication protocol for the Web.

transaction   A process in which the database is sent a command, work is performed on or with the data, and results (if any) are returned.

B

trigger   A trigger is a stored procedure that is associated with a specific table and will automatically fire or execute when a specified event occurs, such as a delete, an update, or an insert.

tuple   A record. See record.

validation table   Validation tables store data used to validate values that end users enter into a data table for data integrity. The data in the validation table rarely changes.

view   A view is a virtual table that takes no physical storage space in the database. A view is accessed as if it were a table.

INDEX

How can we make this index more useful? Email us at indexes@samspublishing.com

C

isolation properties, OLTP (Online Transaction Processing), 314

ISP (Internet Service Provider), Web component, 24

Ispirer Systems Web site, 388

IWS (Industry Warehouse Studio), 356

J

Java, 241

database application connections, 345

EJBs (Enterprise Java Beans), Sybase ASE, 356

embedding, 379-380

OODBs (object-oriented databases), 78-79

overview, 379

Java Database Connectivity (JDBC). *See* JDBC

Java Forms, 328

Java objects, schema organization, 142

Java Runtime Environment, 328

JDBC (Java Database Connectivity), 100

components, 241-242

database application connections, 345-348

driver, 345

Type 1 JDBC Drivers, 242

Type 2 JDBC Drivers, 242

Type 3 JDBC Drivers, 242

Type 4 JDBC Drivers, 242

URLs, database user account information, 346

join tables, 177-178

joins, 282

relational databases, 74

relational tables, 157

tables, 99, 131-132, 298-299

jukeboxes, 326

K-L

key systems, 200

keys

artificial, 108-109

candidate, 108

compound, 112-113

foreign, 109-112, 139

Natural, 109

partitions, 130

primary, 73, 108-110, 139

primary keys, IOT (Index Organized Tables), 128

relational databases, 93-94

KnowledgeSTUDIO, 368

languages. *See also* DDL (data definition language); SQL (Structured Query Language)

CFML (ColdFusion Markup Language), 328

data-definition, 159

DCL (Data Control Language), 250

DDL (data dictionary language), 176

DML (Data Manipulation Language), 98, 249

DELETE command, 278-279

INSERT command, 276-277

UPDATE command, 277-278

M

How can we make this index more useful? Email us at indexes@samspublishing.com

W-Z

Your Guide
to Computer
Technology

www.informit.com